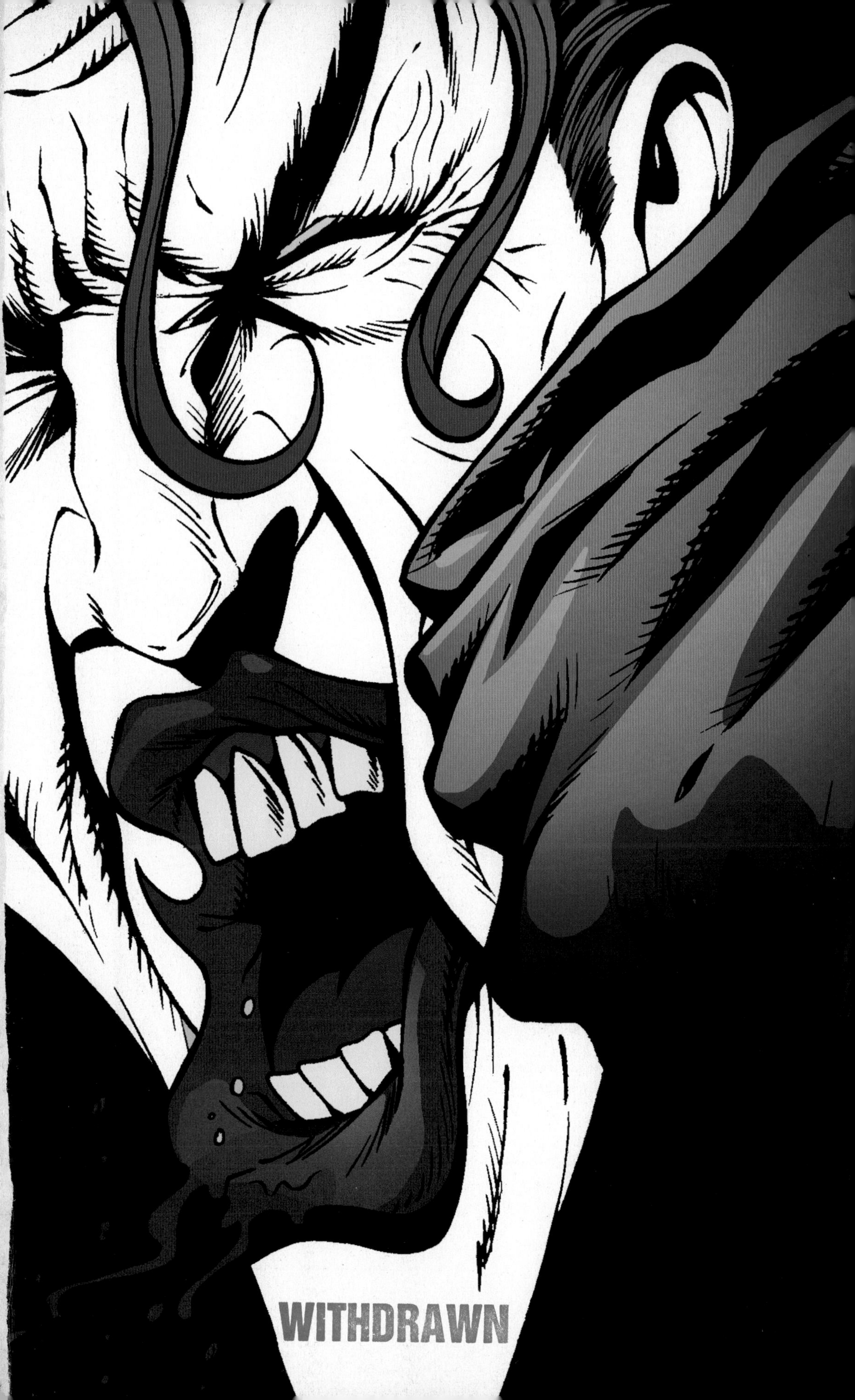

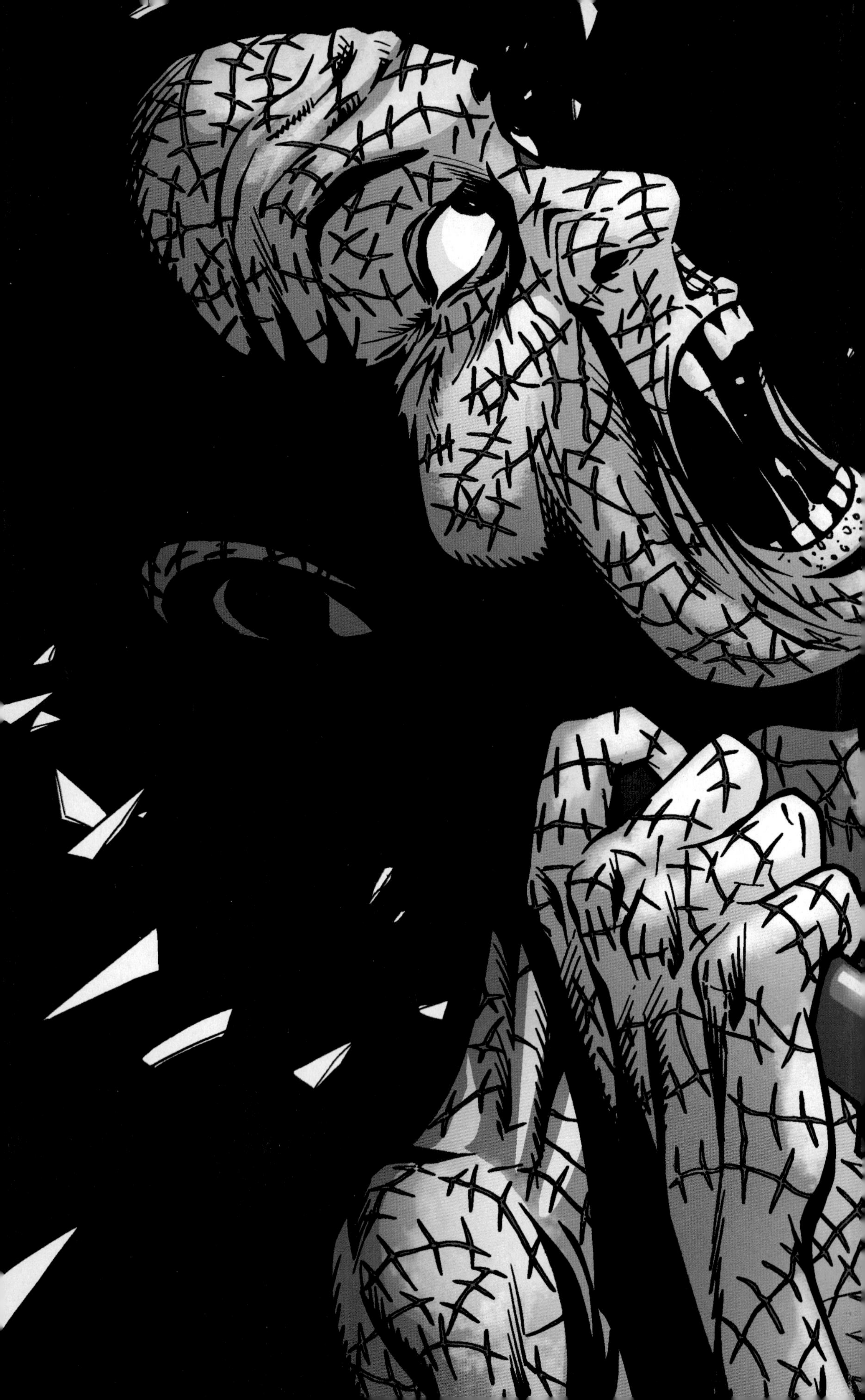

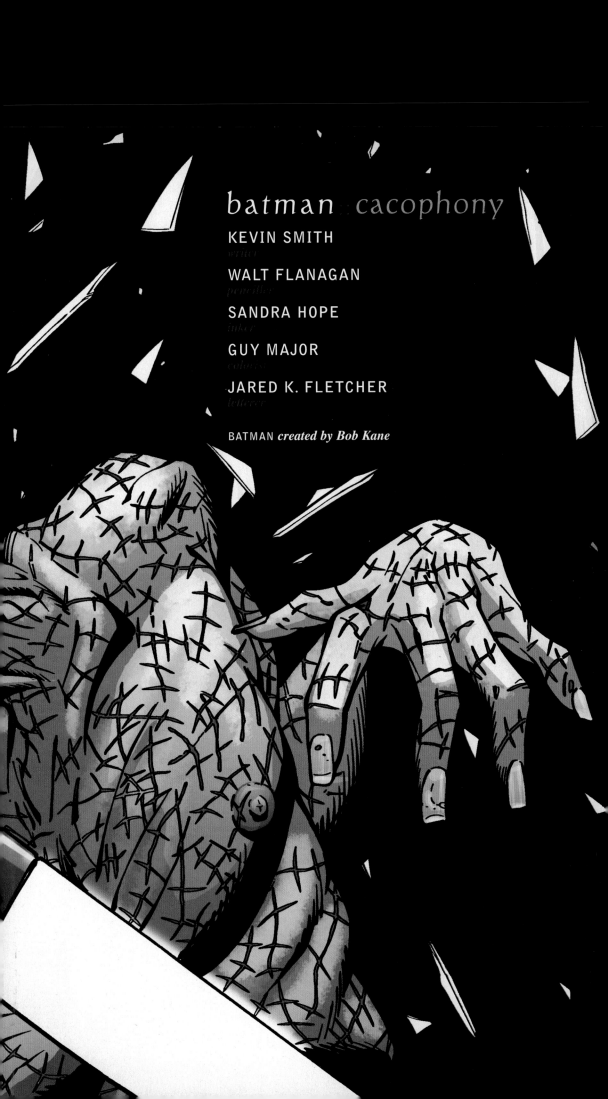

batman: cacophony

KEVIN SMITH
writer

WALT FLANAGAN
penciller

SANDRA HOPE
inker

GUY MAJOR
colorist

JARED K. FLETCHER
letterer

BATMAN *created by Bob Kane*

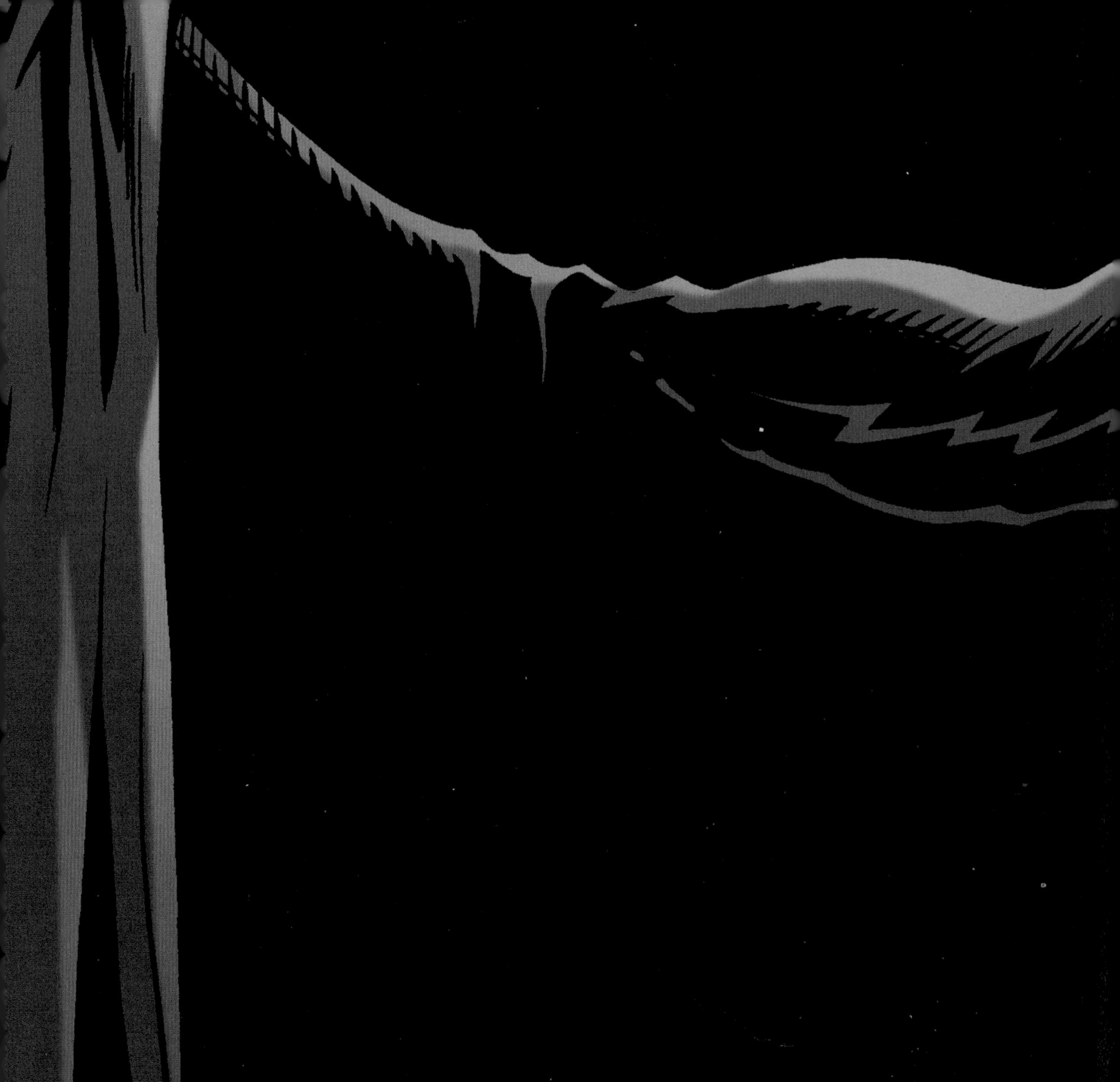

DAN DIDIO SVP-EXECUTIVE EDITOR & EDITOR-ORIGINAL SERIES
GEORG BREWER VP-DESIGN & DC DIRECT CREATIVE
BOB HARRAS GROUP EDITOR-COLLECTED EDITIONS
SEAN MACKIEWICZ EDITOR
ROBBIN BROSTERMAN DESIGN DIRECTOR-BOOKS

DC COMICS
PAUL LEVITZ PRESIDENT & PUBLISHER
RICHARD BRUNING SVP-CREATIVE DIRECTOR
PATRICK CALDON EVP-FINANCE & OPERATIONS
AMY GENKINS SVP-BUSINESS & LEGAL AFFAIRS
JIM LEE EDITORIAL DIRECTOR-WILDSTORM
GREGORY NOVECK SVP-CREATIVE AFFAIRS
STEVE ROTTERDAM SVP-SALES & MARKETING
CHERYL RUBIN SVP-BRAND MANAGEMENT

Cover by Adam Kubert
Publication design by Robbie Biederman

BATMAN: CACOPHONY

DC Comics, 1700 Broadway, New York, NY 10019.
A Warner Bros. Entertainment Company
First Printing. Printed by RR Donnelley, Roanoake, VA, USA. 8/19/09
HC ISBN: 978-1-4012-2418-9
SC ISBN: 978-1-4012-2419-6

KEVIN SMITH

o address the elephant in the room, yes —
Walt got the job because he's my friend.
And, yes — it's unseemly and unprofessional to
trade in such naked nepotism; so much so that a
base-coach from the *other* team insinuated that I
bullied DC editorial into giving my guy the job.

I mean, sure — that's *one* way to look at it. Or
you can view it through *this* prism: without Walt,
not only would "Cacophony" not exist, I'd have
likely never read any comics beyond *Sad Sack* or
Hot Stuff the L'il Devil.

Walt Flanagan was my comics guru. Circa 1989,
we worked together at the Highlands Recreation
Center for a year, during which time he'd loan
me copies of THE DARK KNIGHT RETURNS,
WATCHMEN and *Mage.*

It was an age of wonders. We'd spend weekends
going to Fred Greenberg's NY comic book shows
at the Penn Hotel, cherry picking the wall books
and discount boxes 'til dusk — at which point, we
two suburbanite lads would scamper back home
to Monmouth County, where nobody's ever been
mugged. When there wasn't a weekend show to
hit, we'd drive from one end of Jersey to the
other with a phone book, tracking down hole-in-
the-wall hobby shops, hoping to find still-racked,
first printings of THE KILLING JOKE
(re: phonebook — mind you, this is in the pre-
internet, pre-GPS, nearly-crustacean era).

Walt Flanagan always liked to draw. He had a
penchant for drawing Metal-influenced zombies.

During those many hours on toll roads, we'd talk
about the story arcs and specific issues we loved,
and — like all comic fans — how we would've
improved plot points or dialogue with our fan-

boy attention to detail and love of continuity.
And after all that unwitting training, a decade or
so later, I was actually writing for those very DC
characters I'd rhapsodized about with Walt while
trekking up and down the state, looking for new
wall books at old rack prices.

No slouch himself, Walt had teamed up with his
cinematic and real world best-y, Bryan Johnson,
to create both *Karney* and *War of the Undead* for
IDW. The most involvement I had with either
mini was an intro I did for the *Karney* trade.

So there we were: two comics-lovin' dudes from
the Jersey 'burbs who both fulfilled dreams of
making funny books.

But we'd never done it *together* (y'know, a comic
book; not "whoopee").

And that's what I was thinking when I saw the
"Dark Knight" billboard.

Oh, I was always a Batman fan: from a childhood
of afternoons spent watching Adam West
"Batman" reruns when school let out, to
Tim Burton's groundbreaking film in '89, to
everything Marshall Rogers and Frank Miller
had ever done that featured the cowled crusader.
But the teaser trailers for Nolan's flick? The
billboards? It reignited my Bat-thusiasm. I fell
in love all over again.

Confession time: I haven't read weekly new
books in over five years. I fell behind in my
reading, then fell even further behind, then
stopped reading altogether. Walt would keep me
updated as to what was happening in the various
plotlines of the many titles I used to regularly
read. I'd long since lost the desire to write

comics — largely because I'd become *persona non grata* in the comics community, due to my incessant lateness. But looking up at that billboard? I became very interested in Batman again. And the more I stared at the billboard, the more I "saw" Walt's name.

Here was one of my closest friends in the world — the guy responsible for my four-color enthusiasm — drawing comics. Here was me, wanting to write some comics. And neither of us were getting any younger.

So I called Dan DiDio, who I'd met many years prior, and asked him if I could write a Batman mini and have my longtime friend draw it. Dan understood immediately that my passion for the project was being fueled by the desire to bring my comics interest full circle: create a miniseries *with* my comics-brother-from-another-mother handling the art chores.

And man, was it fun for us — not to mention a dream come true.

Fun and educational, actually. I banged out the first two scripts in a week, but it wasn't until issue one streeted that I did a second draft — all thanks to a CACOPHONY review in which a critic pointed out that some of the dialogue I'd given Batman didn't sound natural in the least when spoken aloud. I gave it a test run and the blogger was absolutely correct: I'd gotten too showy with the word balloons. So I re-drafted all the dialogue for the next two issues, scraping away the excess verbiage, and boiling each sentiment down to the same Bat-time (same Bat-channel).

On the art front, Walt would draw a rough of the page. If necessary, I'd ask for tweaks, then he'd take it to full pencils. And over the course of three issues, both of us got better at creating a comic book. The writing improved from issue one to issue three, and the art followed suit (indeed, peep out the "Fountainhead" reading sequences in issue one and three; they look like they were drawn by two different artists entirely).

So for those who'd snark about me getting my friend a job: you've got it all wrong. Scrape away everything else, and you'll see that *I'M* the friend who benefited from nepotism; because if it weren't for Walt Flanagan, I wouldn't have this gig. Walt is Batman himself — and me? I've always been nothing more than a fat-and-flabby, immature, over-eager Robin.

But to be fair, once we got the approval from Dan and DC, I started thinking about how I'd written Batman into a bit of my GREEN ARROW run, yet said in many an interview, "I don't wanna write a Batman story ever; it's fun to use him as a supporting player instead." What a stupid thing to say. Why limit yourself when it came to the single most interesting superhero ever created? Why not try to write the best Batman story you could?

No – that's *not* CACOPHONY.

By series' end, I realized it wasn't the best Batman story I could write; nor was it Walt's finest hour. By the time we were finished, I saw CACOPHONY for what it was: a dress rehearsal for the best Batman story I could write/ Walt could draw. It was a warm-up. Quentin Tarantino (yeah, I'm dropping names) once told me that he wanted to do another martial arts flick after the *Kill Bill* films because by the time those flicks were done, he'd learned how to do it. His logic was "Now I've got all this expertise in the field. Why not put it to use immediately?"

So the three issues of CACOPHONY gave birth to a twelve-issue maxi-series that Walt and I are working on now, for release this fall. Entitled BATMAN: THE WIDENING GYRE, it is, for sure, the *best* Batman story either of us can do.

Meantime, 'til that hits the stands? Please enjoy the *second*-best Batman story me and Walt could tell.

Kevin Smith
6/22/09

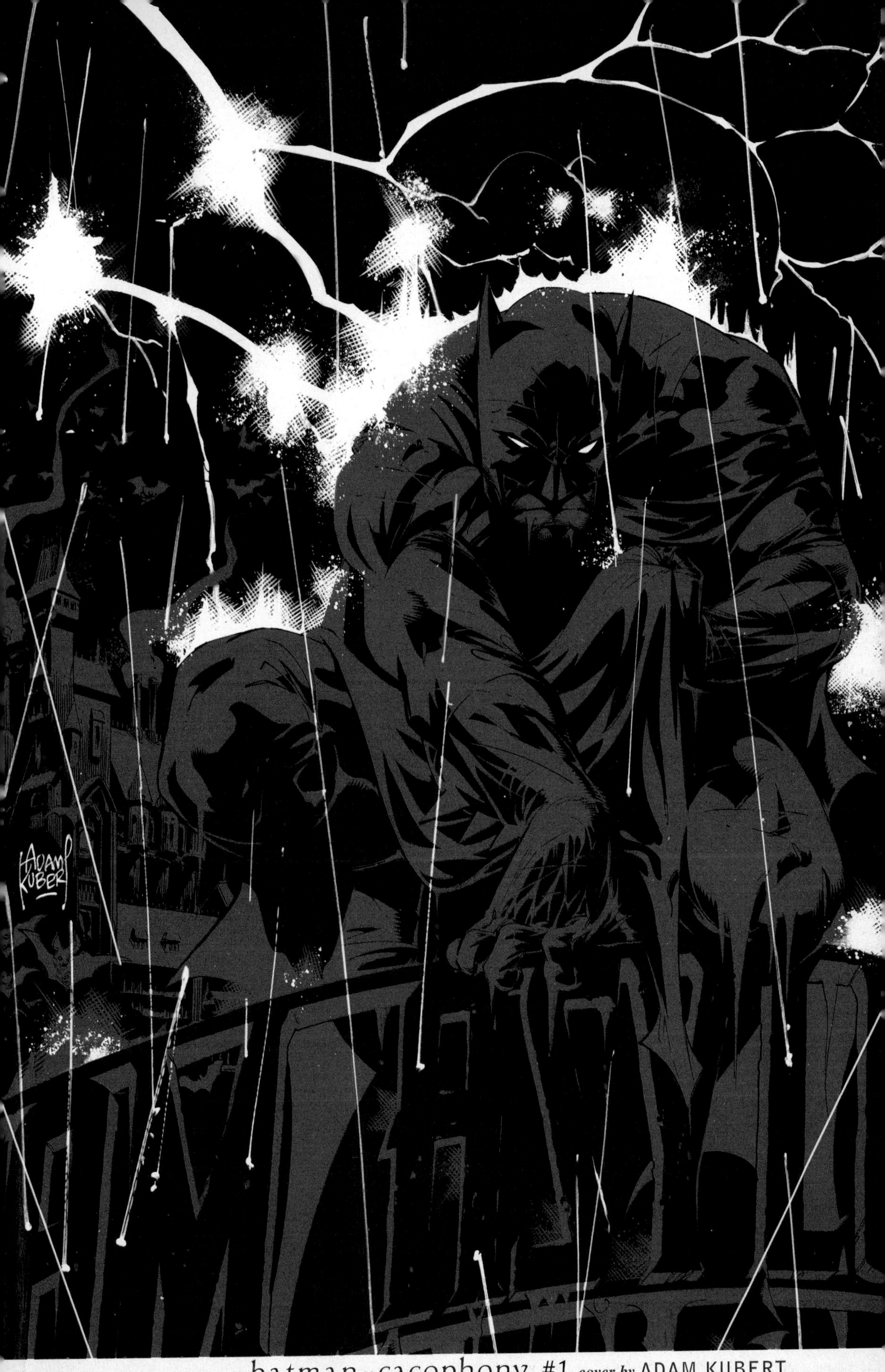
ADAM KUBERT

batman :: cacophony #1 *cover by* ADAM KUBERT

part one BRING THE NOISE

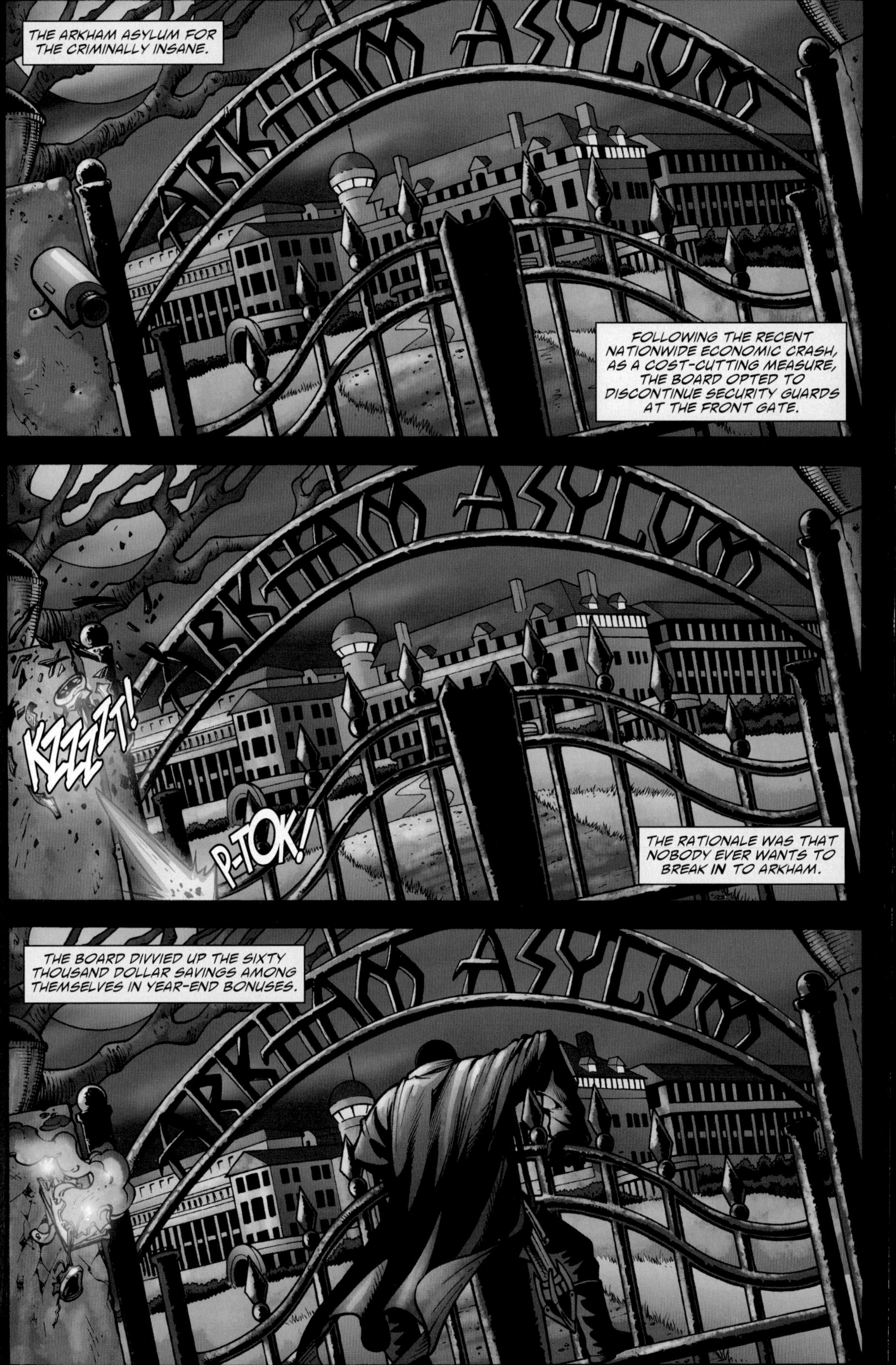

THE ARKHAM ASYLUM FOR THE CRIMINALLY INSANE.
ARKHAM ASYLUM
FOLLOWING THE RECENT NATIONWIDE ECONOMIC CRASH, AS A COST-CUTTING MEASURE, THE BOARD OPTED TO DISCONTINUE SECURITY GUARDS AT THE FRONT GATE.
ARKHAM ASYLUM
KZZZZZT!
P-TOK!
THE RATIONALE WAS THAT NOBODY EVER WANTS TO BREAK IN TO ARKHAM.
ARKHAM ASYLUM
THE BOARD DIVVIED UP THE SIXTY THOUSAND DOLLAR SAVINGS AMONG THEMSELVES IN YEAR-END BONUSES.

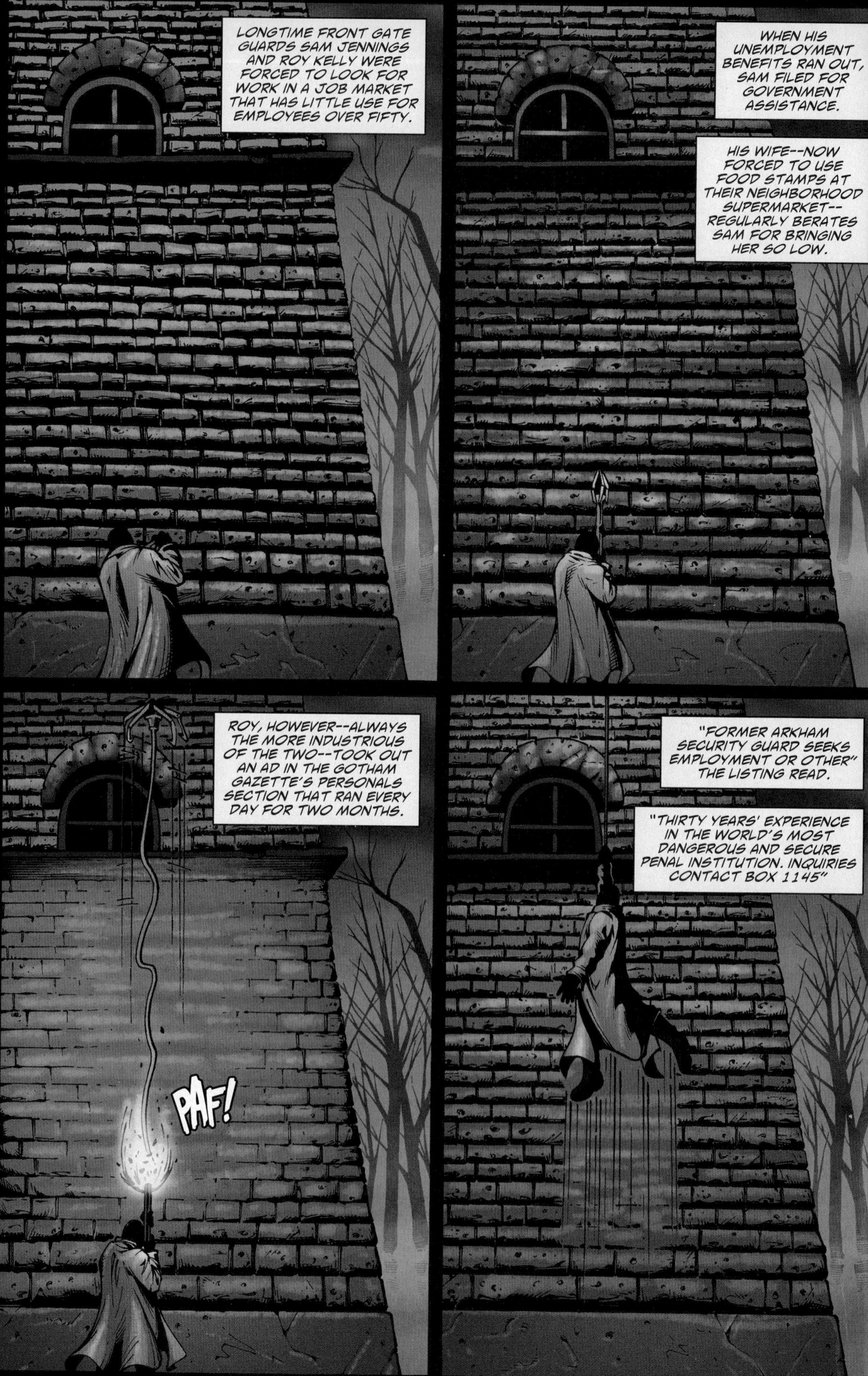
LONGTIME FRONT GATE GUARDS SAM JENNINGS AND ROY KELLY WERE FORCED TO LOOK FOR WORK IN A JOB MARKET THAT HAS LITTLE USE FOR EMPLOYEES OVER FIFTY.
WHEN HIS UNEMPLOYMENT BENEFITS RAN OUT, SAM FILED FOR GOVERNMENT ASSISTANCE.
HIS WIFE--NOW FORCED TO USE FOOD STAMPS AT THEIR NEIGHBORHOOD SUPERMARKET--REGULARLY BERATES SAM FOR BRINGING HER SO LOW.
ROY, HOWEVER--ALWAYS THE MORE INDUSTRIOUS OF THE TWO--TOOK OUT AN AD IN THE GOTHAM GAZETTE'S PERSONALS SECTION THAT RAN EVERY DAY FOR TWO MONTHS.
PAF!
"FORMER ARKHAM SECURITY GUARD SEEKS EMPLOYMENT OR OTHER" THE LISTING READ.
"THIRTY YEARS' EXPERIENCE IN THE WORLD'S MOST DANGEROUS AND SECURE PENAL INSTITUTION. INQUIRIES CONTACT BOX 1145"

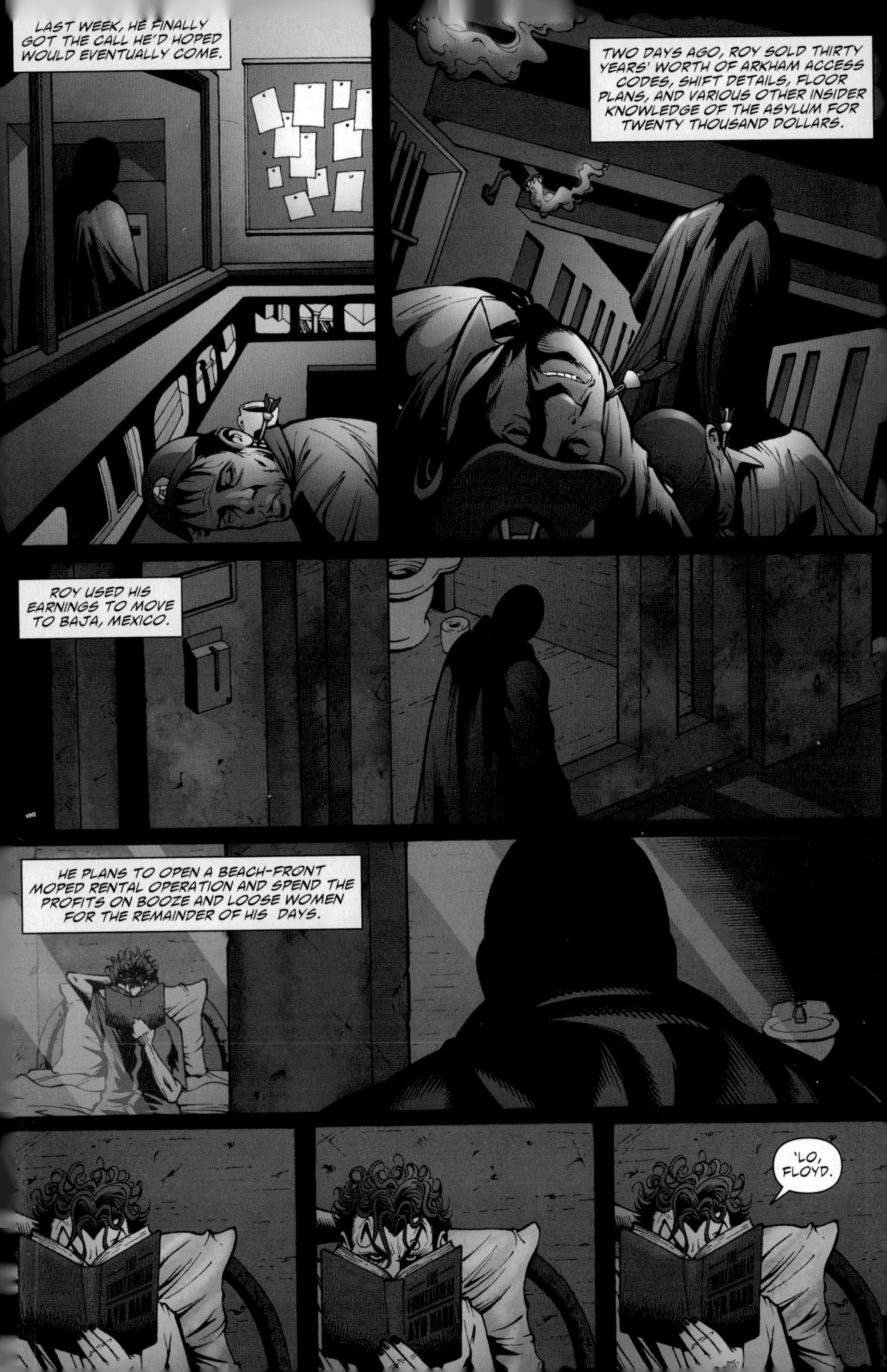
LAST WEEK, HE FINALLY GOT THE CALL HE'D HOPED WOULD EVENTUALLY COME.
TWO DAYS AGO, ROY SOLD THIRTY YEARS' WORTH OF ARKHAM ACCESS CODES, SHIFT DETAILS, FLOOR PLANS, AND VARIOUS OTHER INSIDER KNOWLEDGE OF THE ASYLUM FOR TWENTY THOUSAND DOLLARS.
ROY USED HIS EARNINGS TO MOVE TO BAJA, MEXICO.
HE PLANS TO OPEN A BEACH-FRONT MOPED RENTAL OPERATION AND SPEND THE PROFITS ON BOOZE AND LOOSE WOMEN FOR THE REMAINDER OF HIS DAYS.
'LO, FLOYD.

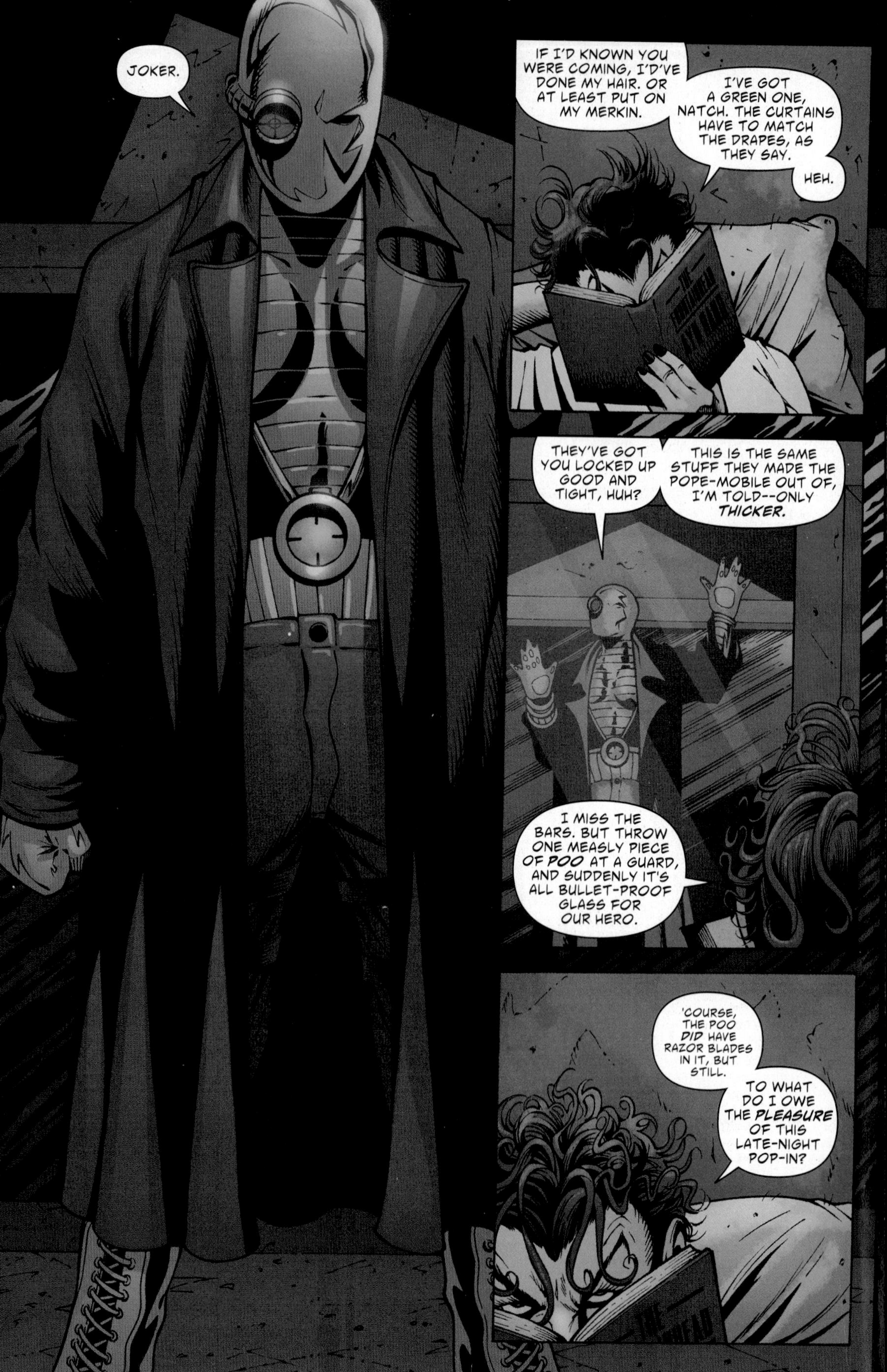
JOKER.
IF I'D KNOWN YOU WERE COMING, I'D'VE DONE MY HAIR. OR AT LEAST PUT ON MY MERKIN.
I'VE GOT A GREEN ONE, NATCH. THE CURTAINS HAVE TO MATCH THE DRAPES, AS THEY SAY.
HEH.
THEY'VE GOT YOU LOCKED UP GOOD AND TIGHT, HUH?
THIS IS THE SAME STUFF THEY MADE THE POPE-MOBILE OUT OF, I'M TOLD--ONLY *THICKER.*
I MISS THE BARS. BUT THROW ONE MEASLY PIECE OF *POO* AT A GUARD, AND SUDDENLY IT'S ALL BULLET-PROOF GLASS FOR OUR HERO.
'COURSE, THE POO *DID* HAVE RAZOR BLADES IN IT, BUT STILL.
TO WHAT DO I OWE THE *PLEASURE* OF THIS LATE-NIGHT POP-IN?

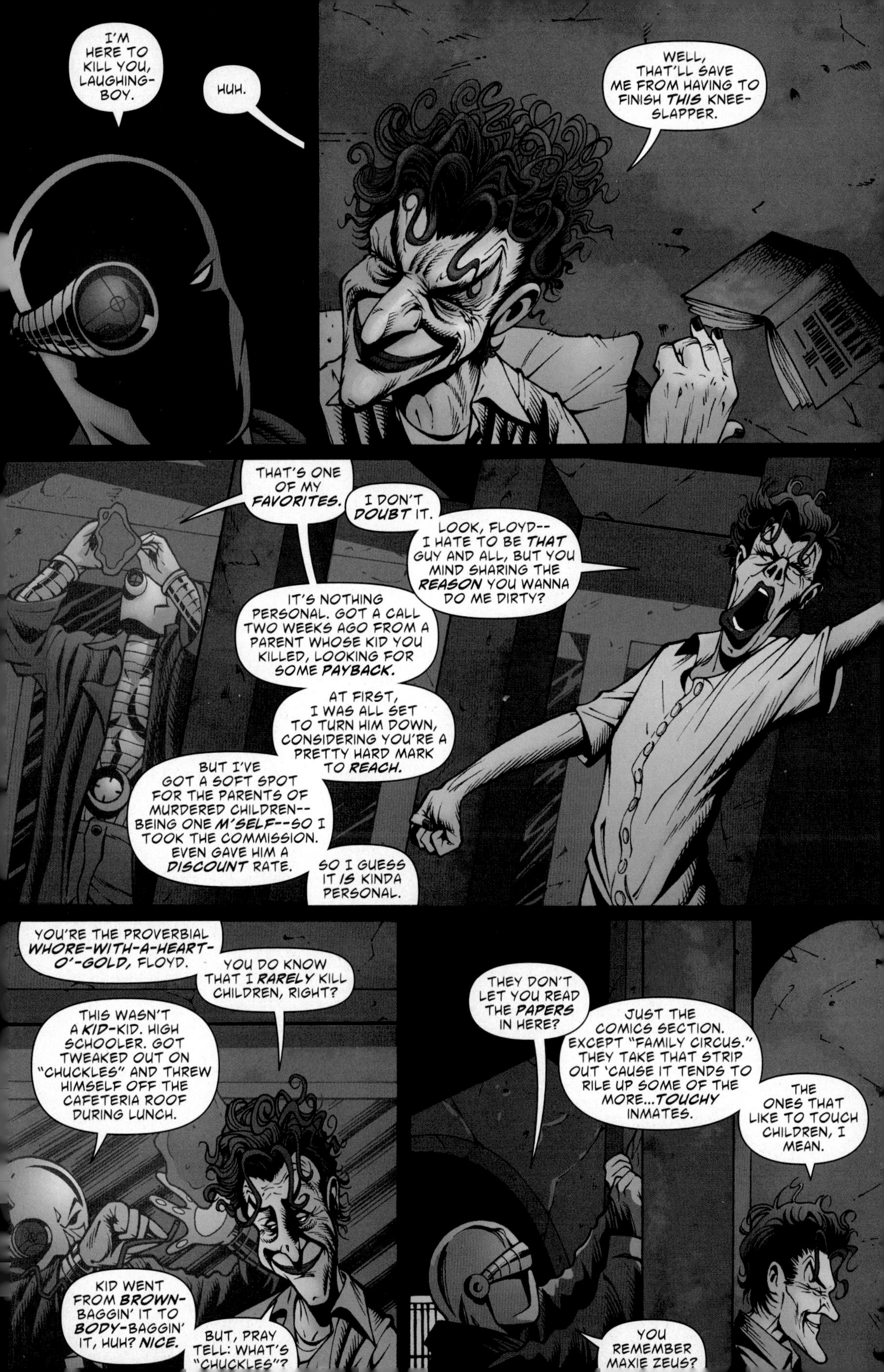
I'M HERE TO KILL YOU, LAUGHING-BOY.
HUH.
WELL, THAT'LL SAVE ME FROM HAVING TO FINISH *THIS* KNEE-SLAPPER.
THAT'S ONE OF MY *FAVORITES.*
I DON'T *DOUBT* IT.
LOOK, FLOYD-- I HATE TO BE *THAT* GUY AND ALL, BUT YOU MIND SHARING THE *REASON* YOU WANNA DO ME DIRTY?
IT'S NOTHING PERSONAL. GOT A CALL TWO WEEKS AGO FROM A PARENT WHOSE KID YOU KILLED, LOOKING FOR SOME *PAYBACK.*
AT FIRST, I WAS ALL SET TO TURN HIM DOWN, CONSIDERING YOU'RE A PRETTY HARD MARK TO *REACH.*
BUT I'VE GOT A SOFT SPOT FOR THE PARENTS OF MURDERED CHILDREN-- BEING ONE *M'SELF*--SO I TOOK THE COMMISSION. EVEN GAVE HIM A *DISCOUNT* RATE.
SO I GUESS IT *IS* KINDA PERSONAL.
YOU'RE THE PROVERBIAL *WHORE-WITH-A-HEART-O'-GOLD,* FLOYD.
YOU DO KNOW THAT I *RARELY* KILL CHILDREN, RIGHT?
THIS WASN'T A *KID*-KID. HIGH SCHOOLER. GOT TWEAKED OUT ON "CHUCKLES" AND THREW HIMSELF OFF THE CAFETERIA ROOF DURING LUNCH.
KID WENT FROM *BROWN*-BAGGIN' IT TO *BODY*-BAGGIN' IT, HUH? *NICE.*
BUT, PRAY TELL: WHAT'S "CHUCKLES"?
THEY DON'T LET YOU READ THE *PAPERS* IN HERE?
JUST THE COMICS SECTION. EXCEPT "FAMILY CIRCUS." THEY TAKE THAT STRIP OUT 'CAUSE IT TENDS TO RILE UP SOME OF THE MORE...*TOUCHY* INMATES.
THE ONES THAT LIKE TO TOUCH CHILDREN, I MEAN.
YOU REMEMBER MAXIE ZEUS?

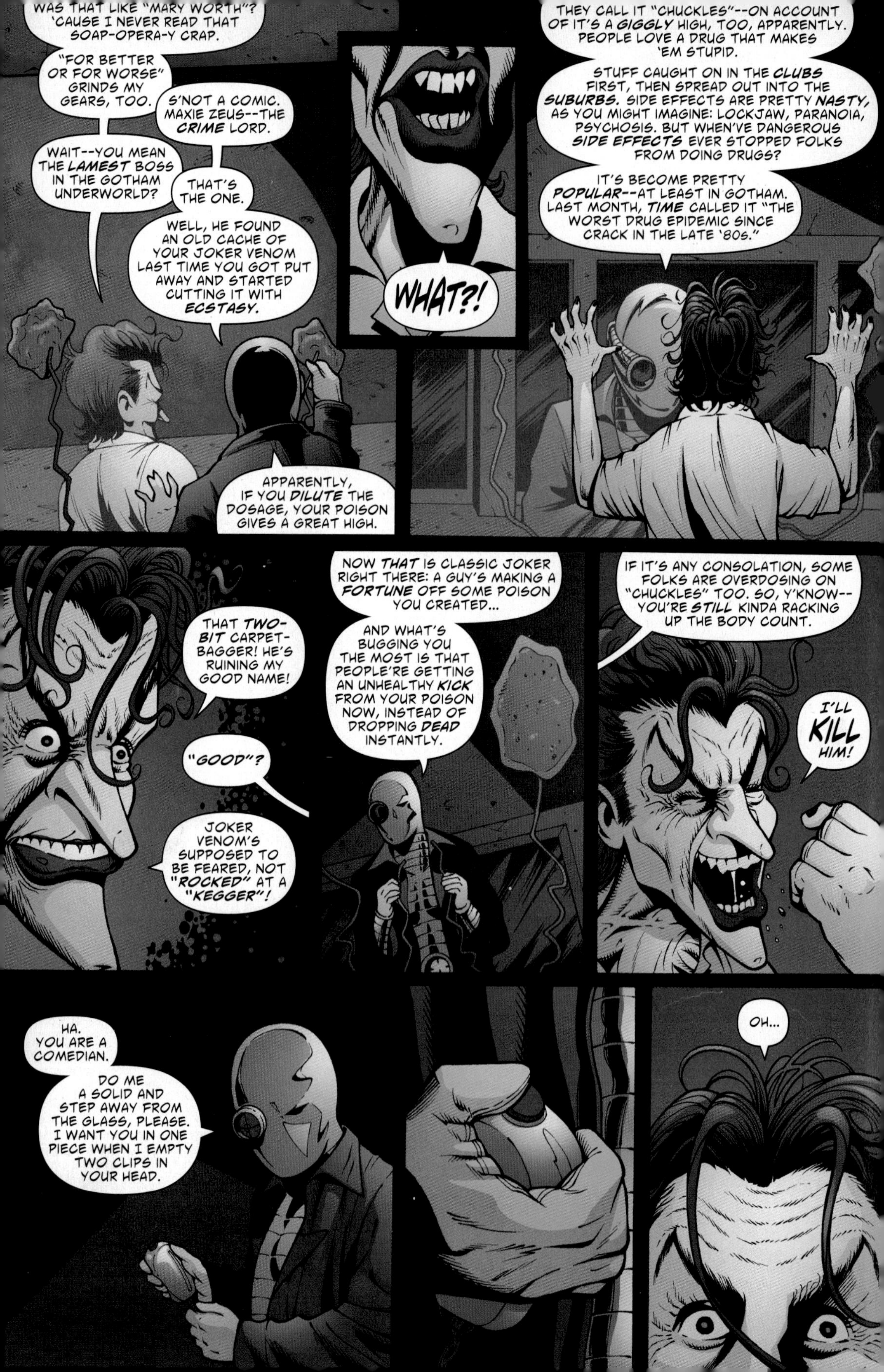
WAS THAT LIKE "MARY WORTH"? 'CAUSE I NEVER READ THAT SOAP-OPERA-Y CRAP.
"FOR BETTER OR FOR WORSE" GRINDS MY GEARS, TOO.
S'NOT A COMIC. MAXIE ZEUS--THE CRIME LORD.
WAIT--YOU MEAN THE LAMEST BOSS IN THE GOTHAM UNDERWORLD?
THAT'S THE ONE.
WELL, HE FOUND AN OLD CACHE OF YOUR JOKER VENOM LAST TIME YOU GOT PUT AWAY AND STARTED CUTTING IT WITH ECSTASY.
APPARENTLY, IF YOU DILUTE THE DOSAGE, YOUR POISON GIVES A GREAT HIGH.
WHAT?!
THEY CALL IT "CHUCKLES"--ON ACCOUNT OF IT'S A GIGGLY HIGH, TOO, APPARENTLY. PEOPLE LOVE A DRUG THAT MAKES 'EM STUPID.
STUFF CAUGHT ON IN THE CLUBS FIRST, THEN SPREAD OUT INTO THE SUBURBS. SIDE EFFECTS ARE PRETTY NASTY, AS YOU MIGHT IMAGINE: LOCKJAW, PARANOIA, PSYCHOSIS. BUT WHEN'VE DANGEROUS SIDE EFFECTS EVER STOPPED FOLKS FROM DOING DRUGS?
IT'S BECOME PRETTY POPULAR--AT LEAST IN GOTHAM. LAST MONTH, TIME CALLED IT "THE WORST DRUG EPIDEMIC SINCE CRACK IN THE LATE '80s."
THAT TWO-BIT CARPET-BAGGER! HE'S RUINING MY GOOD NAME!
"GOOD"?
JOKER VENOM'S SUPPOSED TO BE FEARED, NOT "ROCKED" AT A "KEGGER"!
NOW THAT IS CLASSIC JOKER RIGHT THERE: A GUY'S MAKING A FORTUNE OFF SOME POISON YOU CREATED...
AND WHAT'S BUGGING YOU THE MOST IS THAT PEOPLE'RE GETTING AN UNHEALTHY KICK FROM YOUR POISON NOW, INSTEAD OF DROPPING DEAD INSTANTLY.
IF IT'S ANY CONSOLATION, SOME FOLKS ARE OVERDOSING ON "CHUCKLES" TOO. SO, Y'KNOW--YOU'RE STILL KINDA RACKING UP THE BODY COUNT.
I'LL KILL HIM!
HA. YOU ARE A COMEDIAN.
DO ME A SOLID AND STEP AWAY FROM THE GLASS, PLEASE. I WANT YOU IN ONE PIECE WHEN I EMPTY TWO CLIPS IN YOUR HEAD.
OH...

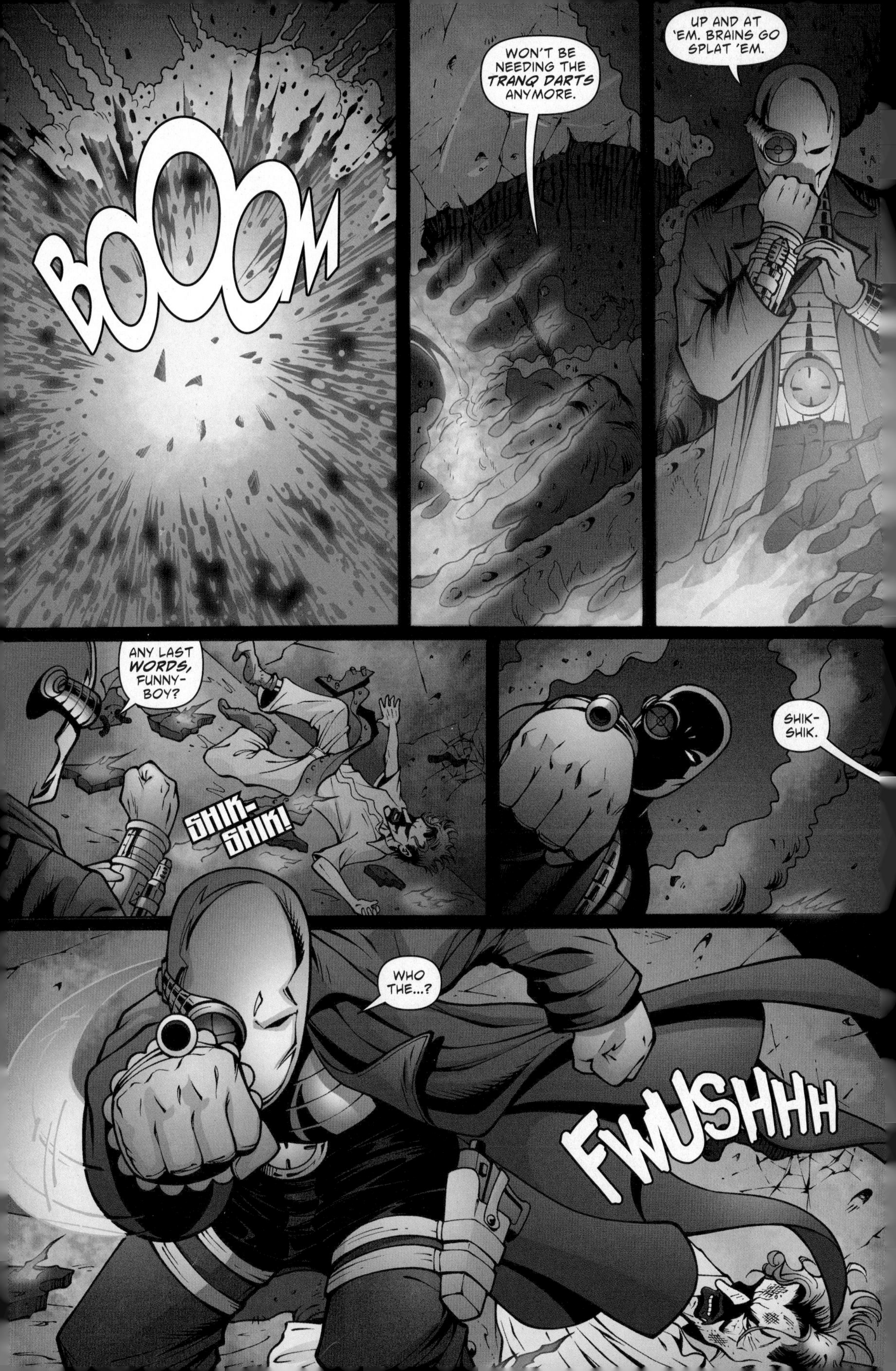
BOOOM
WON'T BE NEEDING THE TRANQ DARTS ANYMORE.
UP AND AT 'EM. BRAINS GO SPLAT 'EM.
ANY LAST WORDS, FUNNY-BOY?
SHIK-SHIK!
SHIK-SHIK.
WHO THE...?
FWUSHHH

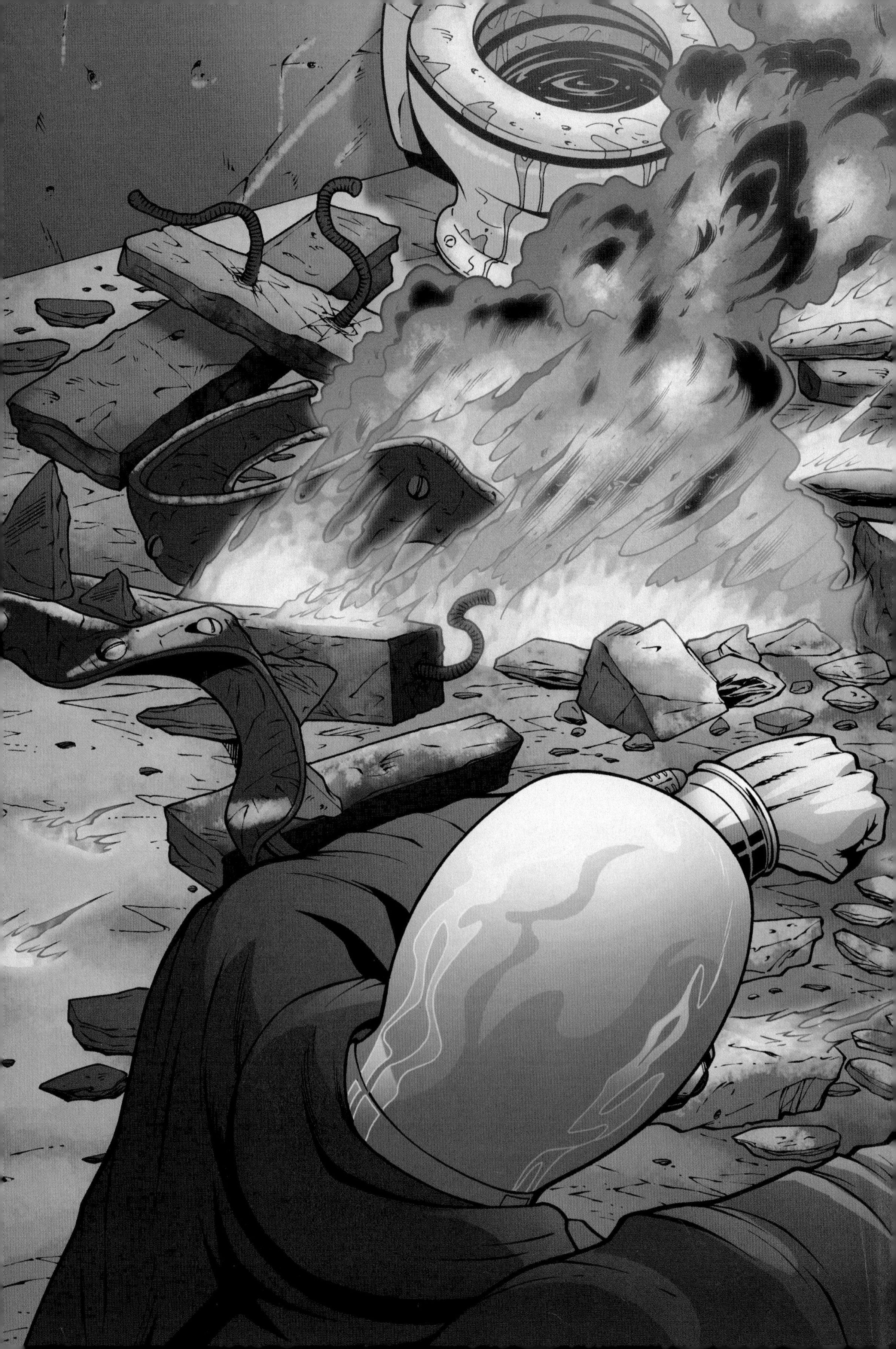

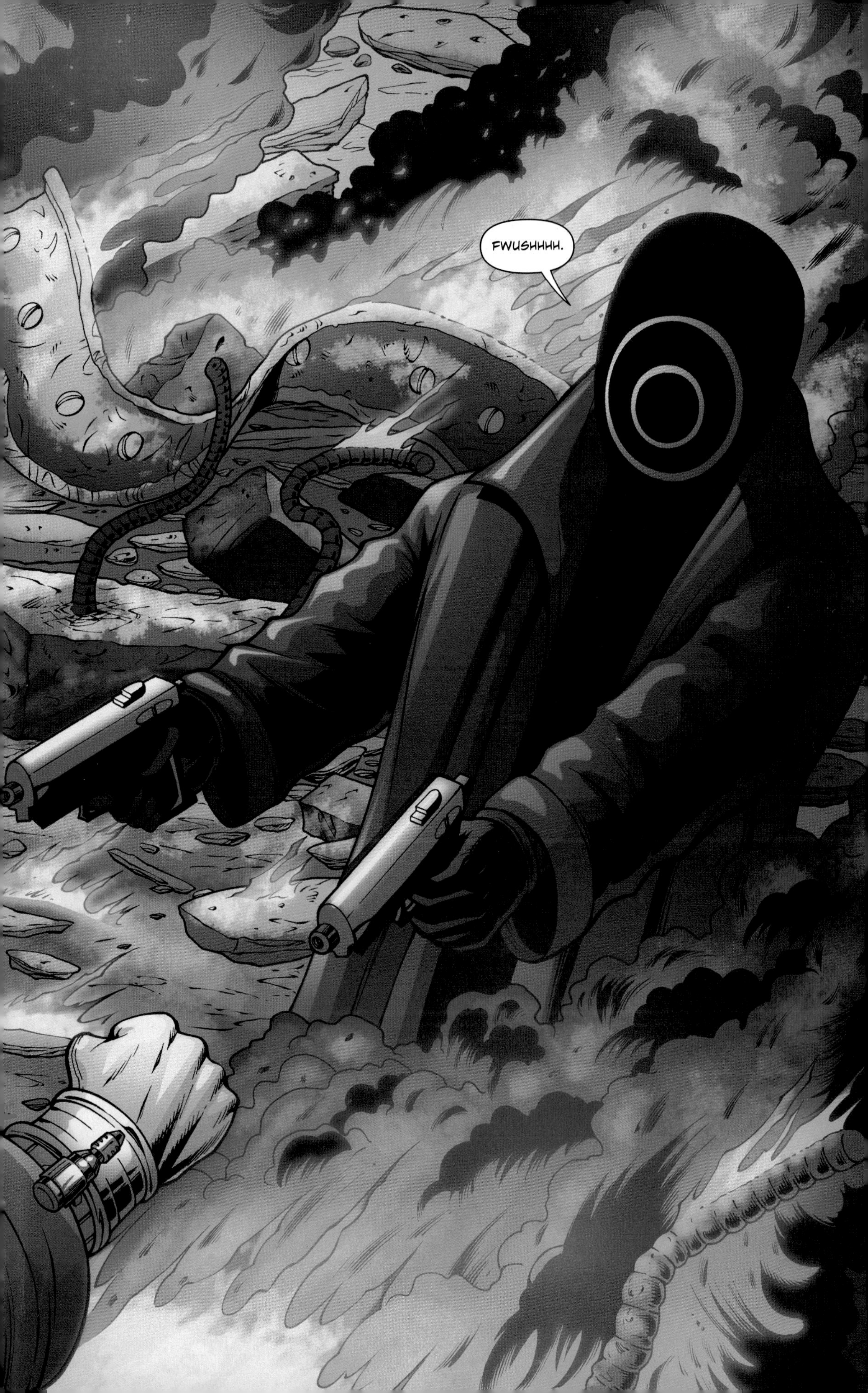
FWUSHHHH.

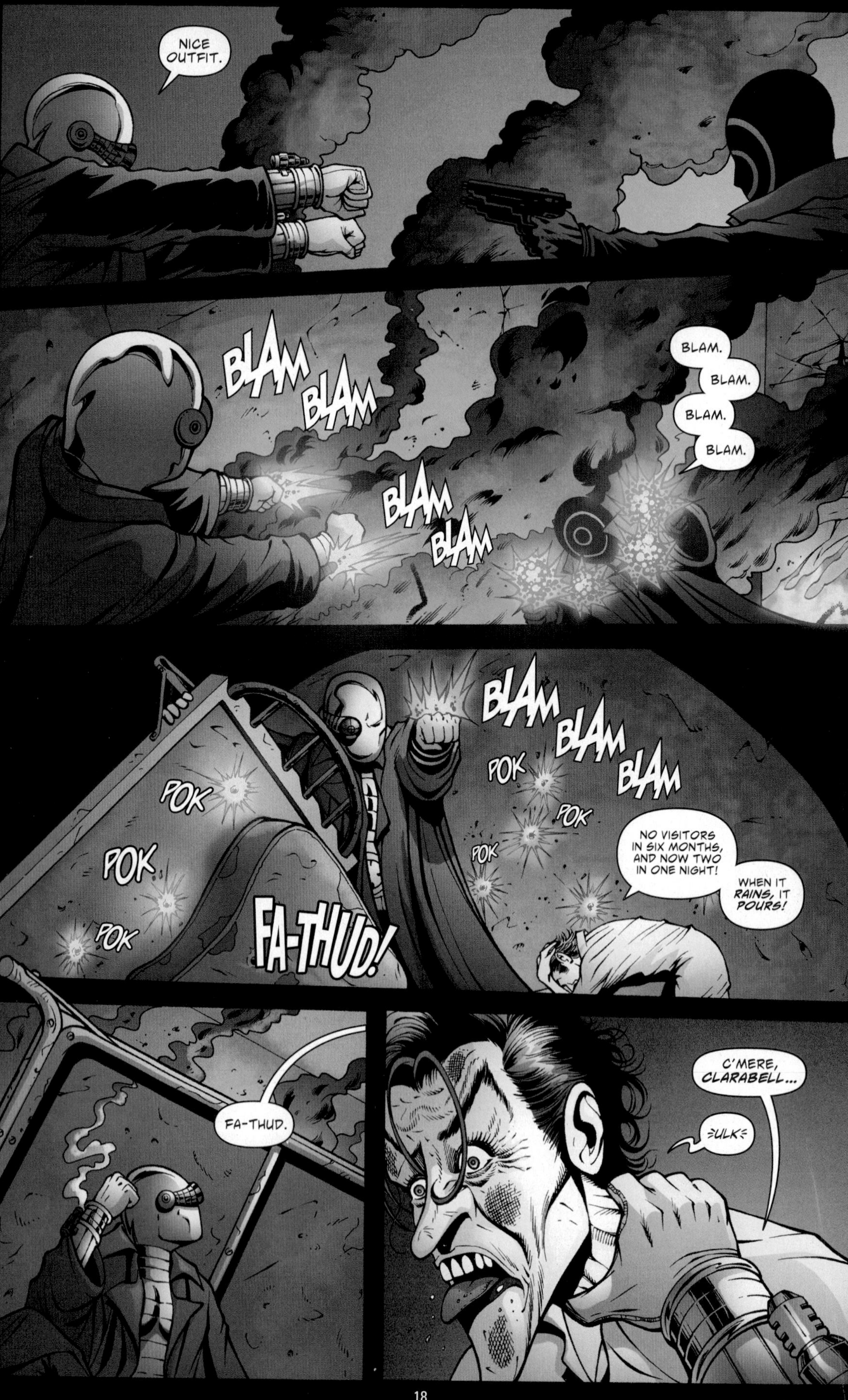
NICE OUTFIT.
BLAM
BLAM
BLAM.
BLAM.
BLAM.
BLAM.
BLAM
BLAM
BLAM
BLAM
BLAM
POK
POK
POK
POK
POK
POK
NO VISITORS IN SIX MONTHS, AND NOW TWO IN ONE NIGHT!
WHEN IT RAINS, IT POURS!
FA-THUD!
FA-THUD.
C'MERE, CLARABELL...
ULK

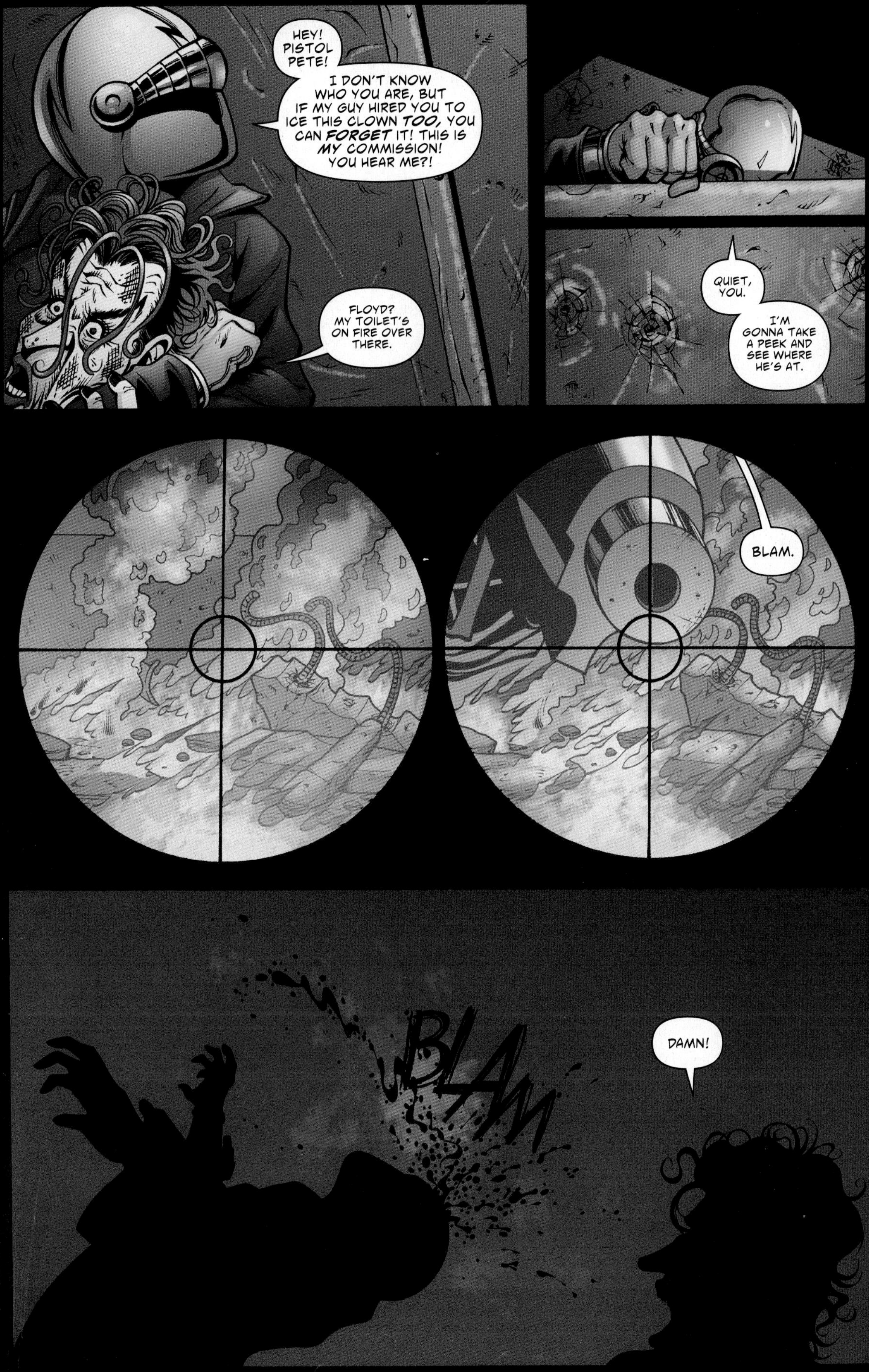
HEY! PISTOL PETE!
I DON'T KNOW WHO YOU ARE, BUT IF MY GUY HIRED YOU TO ICE THIS CLOWN TOO, YOU CAN FORGET IT! THIS IS MY COMMISSION! YOU HEAR ME?!
FLOYD? MY TOILET'S ON FIRE OVER THERE.
QUIET, YOU.
I'M GONNA TAKE A PEEK AND SEE WHERE HE'S AT.
BLAM.
BLAM
DAMN!

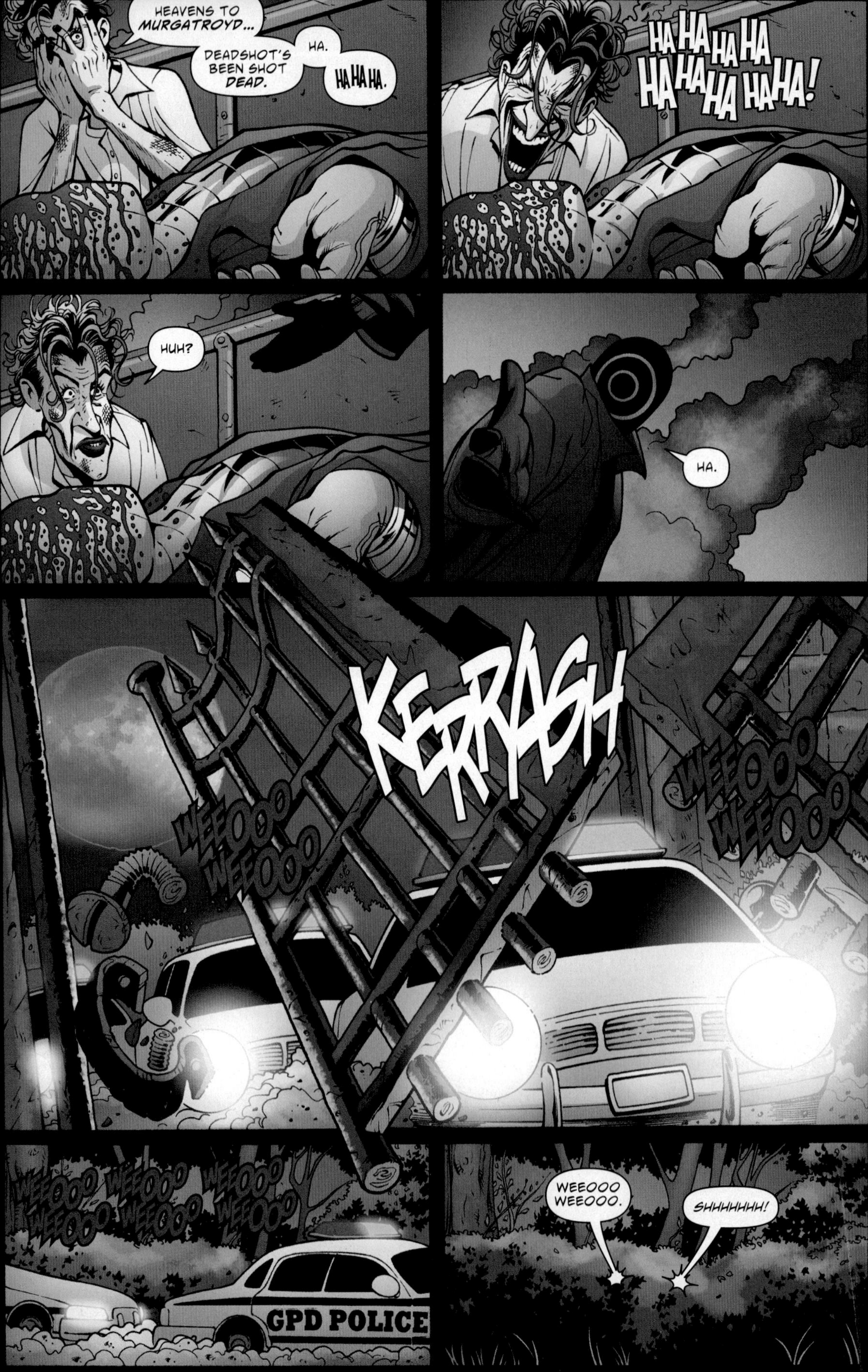
HEAVENS TO MURGATROYD...
DEADSHOT'S BEEN SHOT DEAD.
HA.
HA HA HA.
HA HA HA HA HA HA HA HA HA!
HUH?
HA.
KERRASH
WEEOOO WEEOOO
WEEOOO WEEOOO
WEEOOO WEEOOO WEEOOO
WEEOOO WEEOOO WEEOOO
GPD POLICE
WEEOOO WEEOOO.
SHHHHHHH!

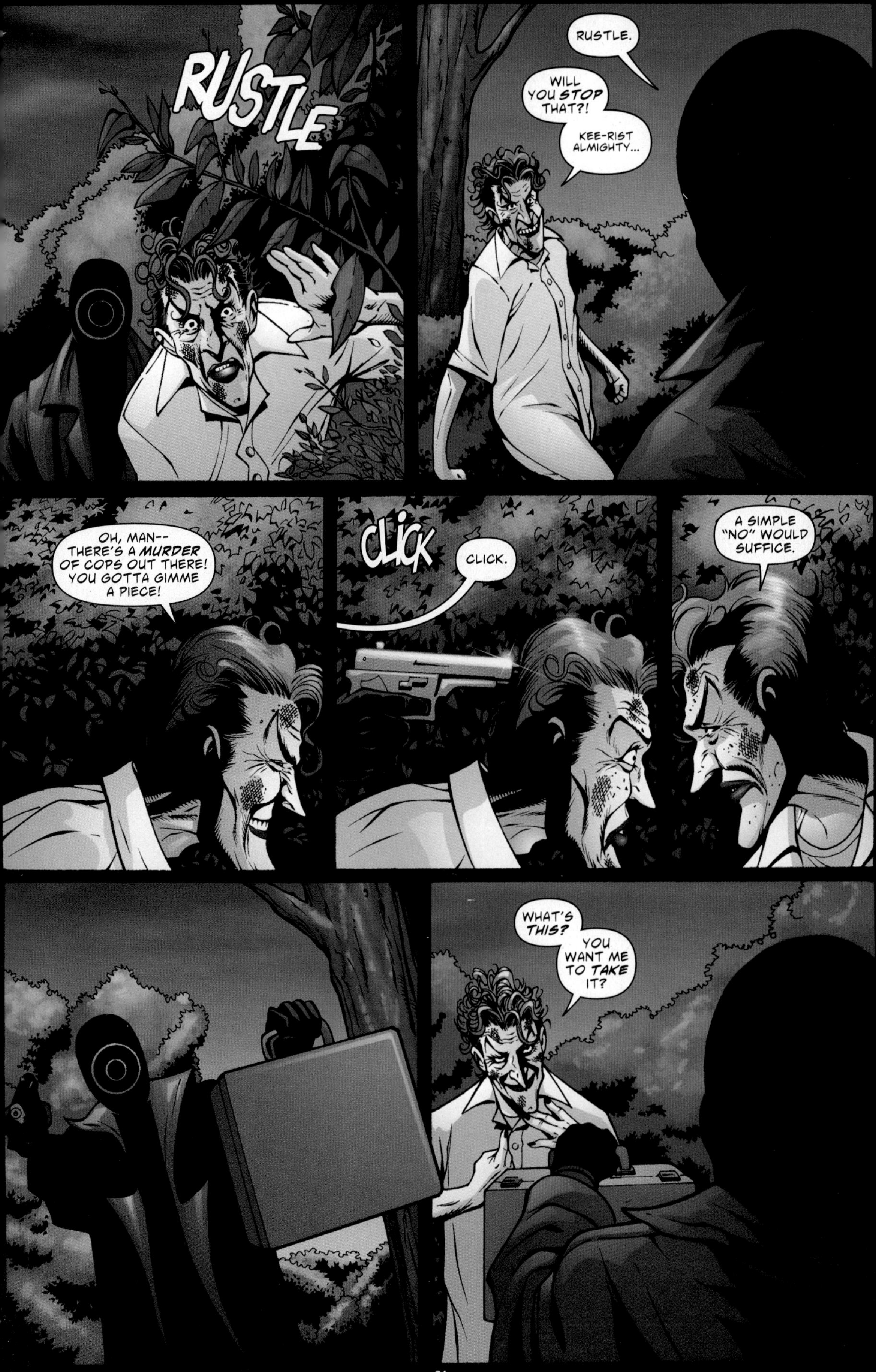
RUSTLE
RUSTLE.
WILL YOU STOP THAT?!
KEE-RIST ALMIGHTY...
OH, MAN-- THERE'S A MURDER OF COPS OUT THERE! YOU GOTTA GIMME A PIECE!
CLICK
CLICK.
A SIMPLE "NO" WOULD SUFFICE.
WHAT'S THIS?
YOU WANT ME TO TAKE IT?

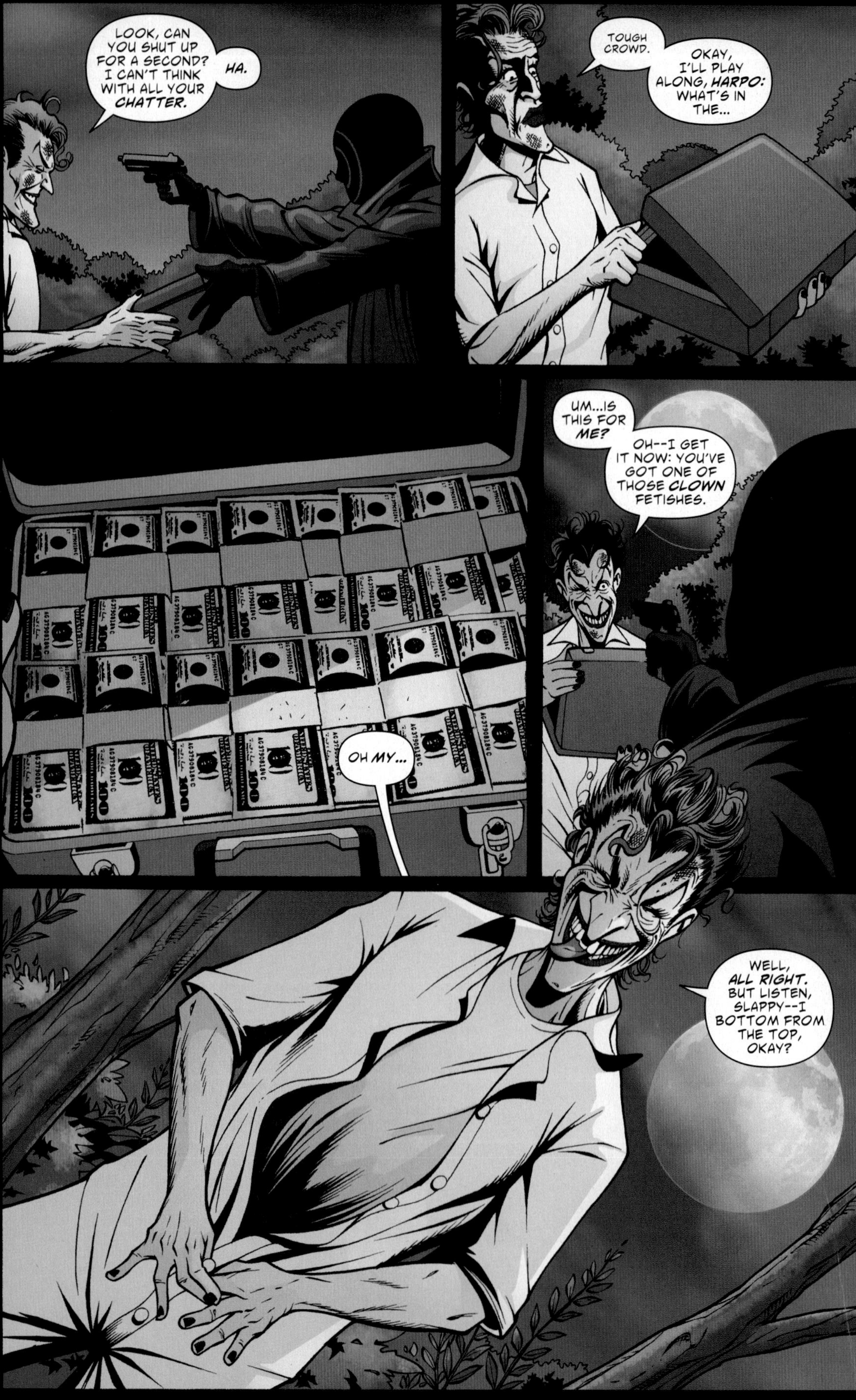
LOOK, CAN YOU SHUT UP FOR A SECOND? I CAN'T THINK WITH ALL YOUR CHATTER.
HA.
TOUGH CROWD.
OKAY, I'LL PLAY ALONG, HARPO: WHAT'S IN THE...
OH MY...
UM...IS THIS FOR ME?
OH--I GET IT NOW: YOU'VE GOT ONE OF THOSE CLOWN FETISHES.
WELL, ALL RIGHT. BUT LISTEN, SLAPPY--I BOTTOM FROM THE TOP, OKAY?

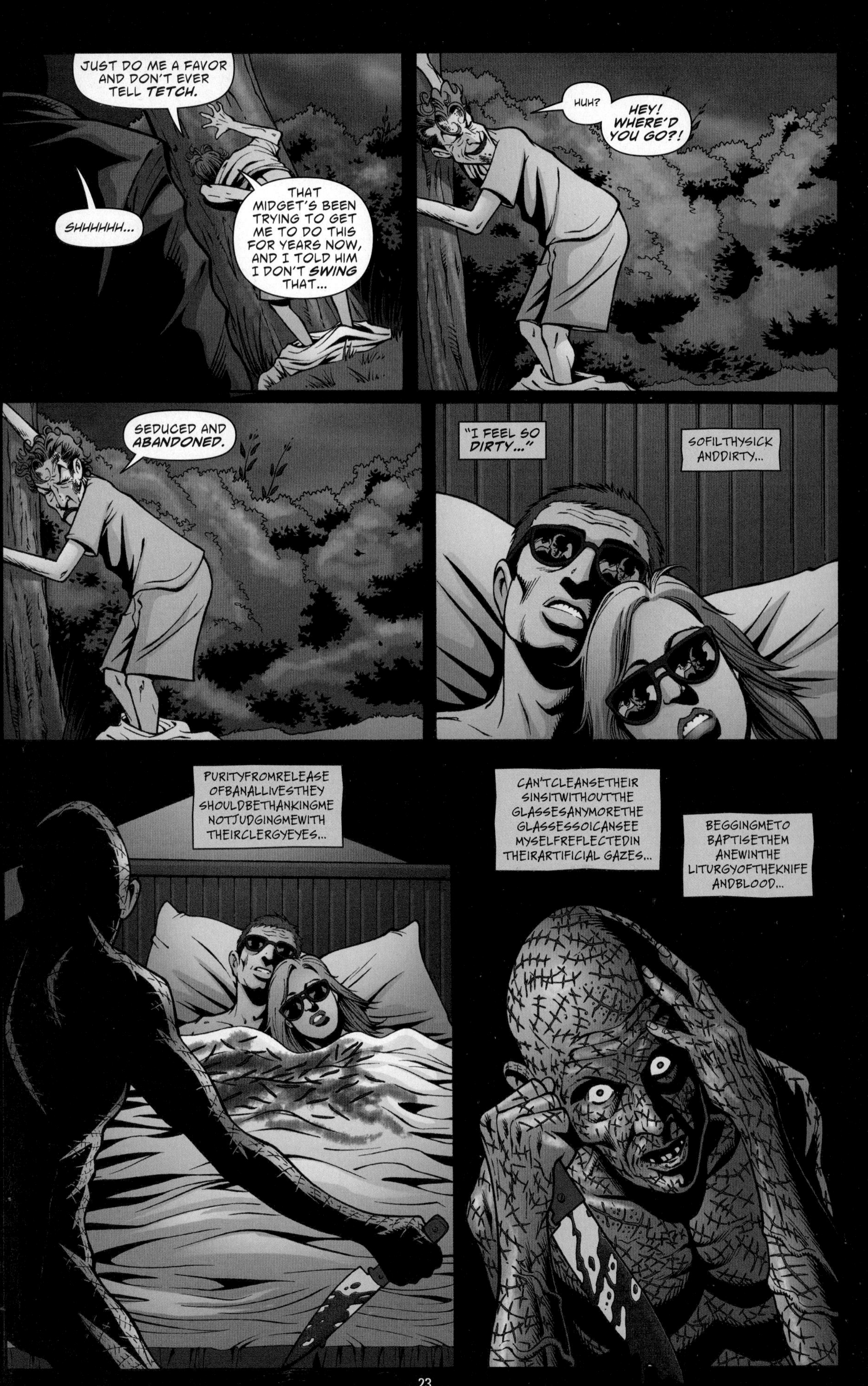

JUST DO ME A FAVOR AND DON'T EVER TELL TETCH.
SHHHHHH...
THAT MIDGET'S BEEN TRYING TO GET ME TO DO THIS FOR YEARS NOW, AND I TOLD HIM I DON'T SWING THAT...
HUH?
HEY! WHERE'D YOU GO?!
SEDUCED AND ABANDONED.
"I FEEL SO DIRTY..."
SOFILTHYSICK ANDDIRTY...
PURITYFROMRELEASE OFBANALLIVESTHEY SHOULDBETHANKINGME NOTJUDGINGMEWITH THEIRCLERGYEYES...
CAN'TCLEANSETHEIR SINSITWITHOUTTHE GLASSESANYMORETHE GLASSESSOICANSEE MYSELFREFLECTEDIN THEIRARTIFICIAL GAZES...
BEGGINGMETO BAPTISETHEM ANEWINTHE LITURGYOFTHEKNIFE ANDBLOOD...

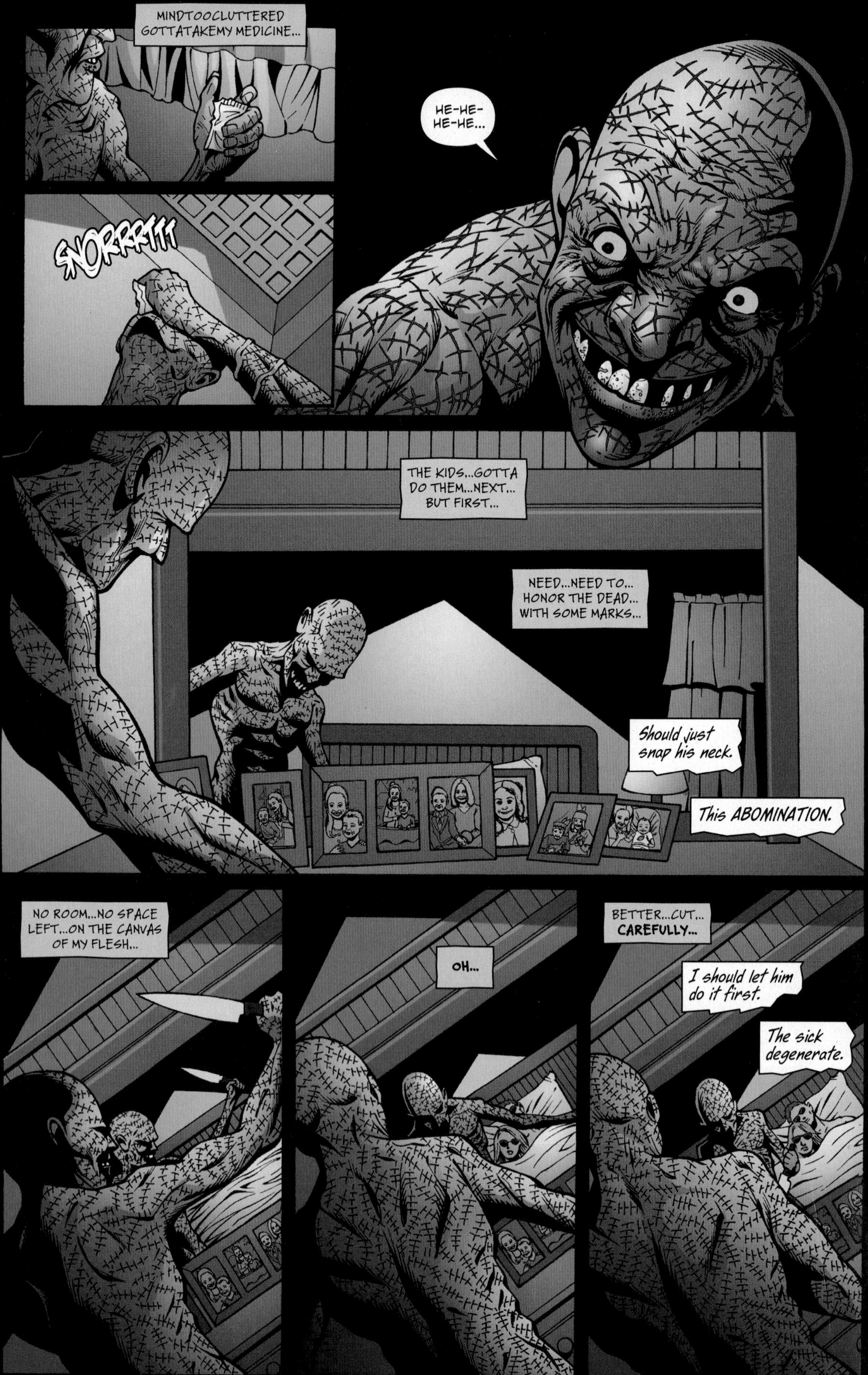
MINDTOOCLUTTERED
GOTTATAKEMY MEDICINE...
HE-HE-
HE-HE...
SNORRRTTT
THE KIDS...GOTTA
DO THEM...NEXT...
BUT FIRST...
NEED...NEED TO...
HONOR THE DEAD...
WITH SOME MARKS...
Should just
snap his neck.
This ABOMINATION.
NO ROOM...NO SPACE
LEFT...ON THE CANVAS
OF MY FLESH...
OH...
BETTER...CUT...
CAREFULLY...
I should let him
do it first.
The sick
degenerate.

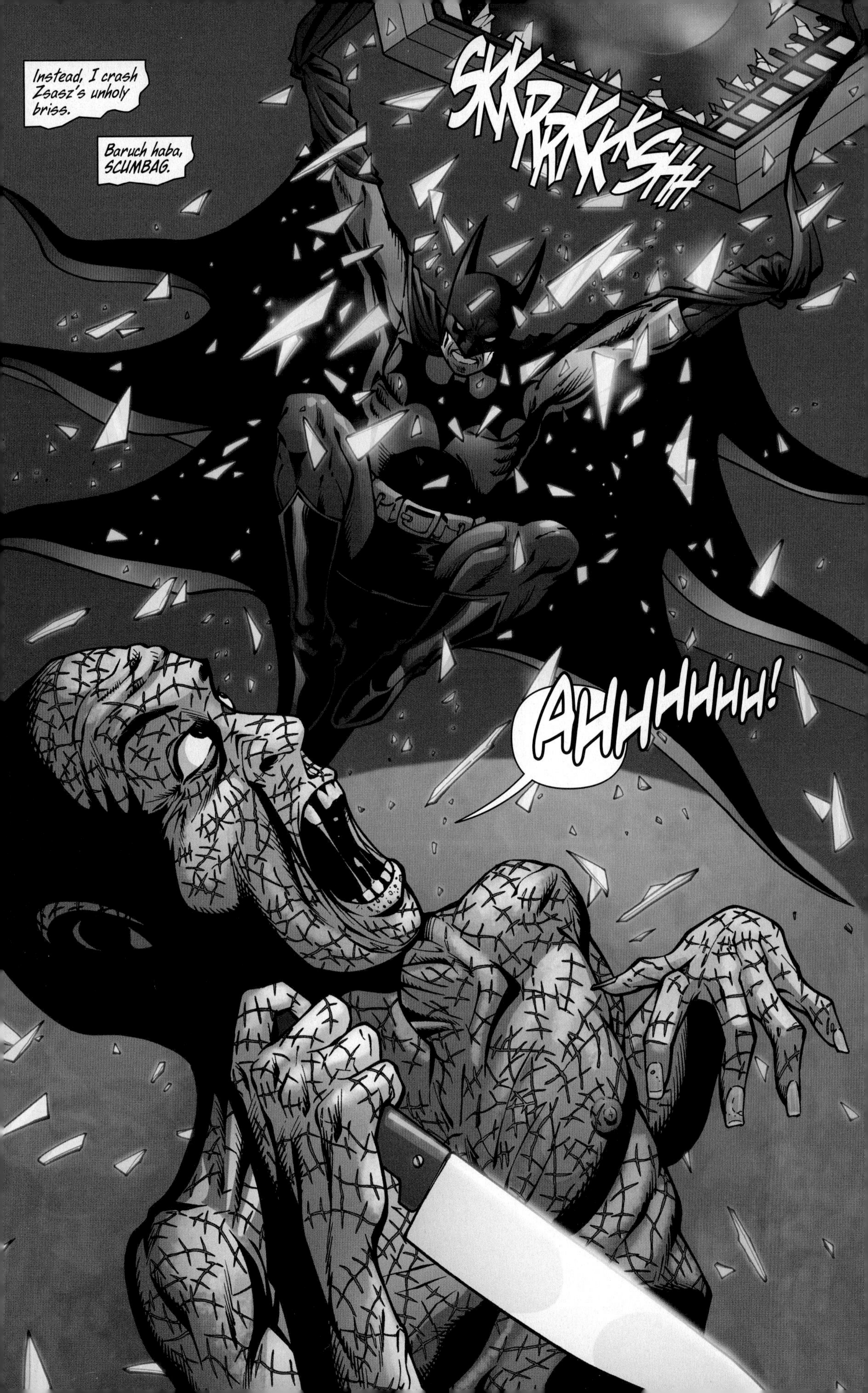
Instead, I crash Zsasz's unholy briss.
Baruch haba, SCUMBAG.
SKKRKKKSHH
AHHHHHH!

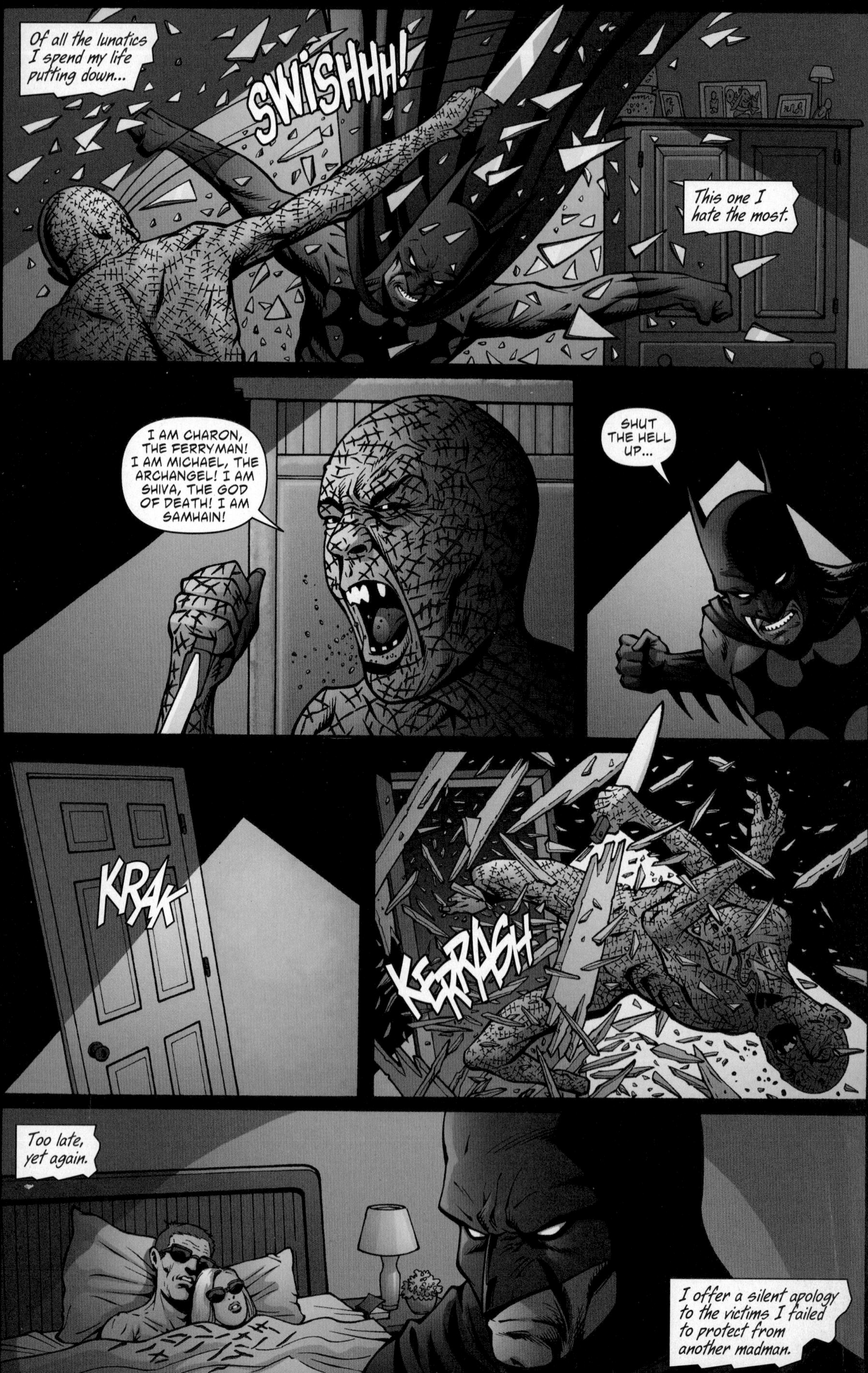
Of all the lunatics I spend my life putting down...
SWISHHH!
This one I hate the most.
I AM CHARON, THE FERRYMAN! I AM MICHAEL, THE ARCHANGEL! I AM SHIVA, THE GOD OF DEATH! I AM SAMHAIN!
SHUT THE HELL UP...
KRAK
KERRASH
Too late, yet again.
I offer a silent apology to the victims I failed to protect from another madman.

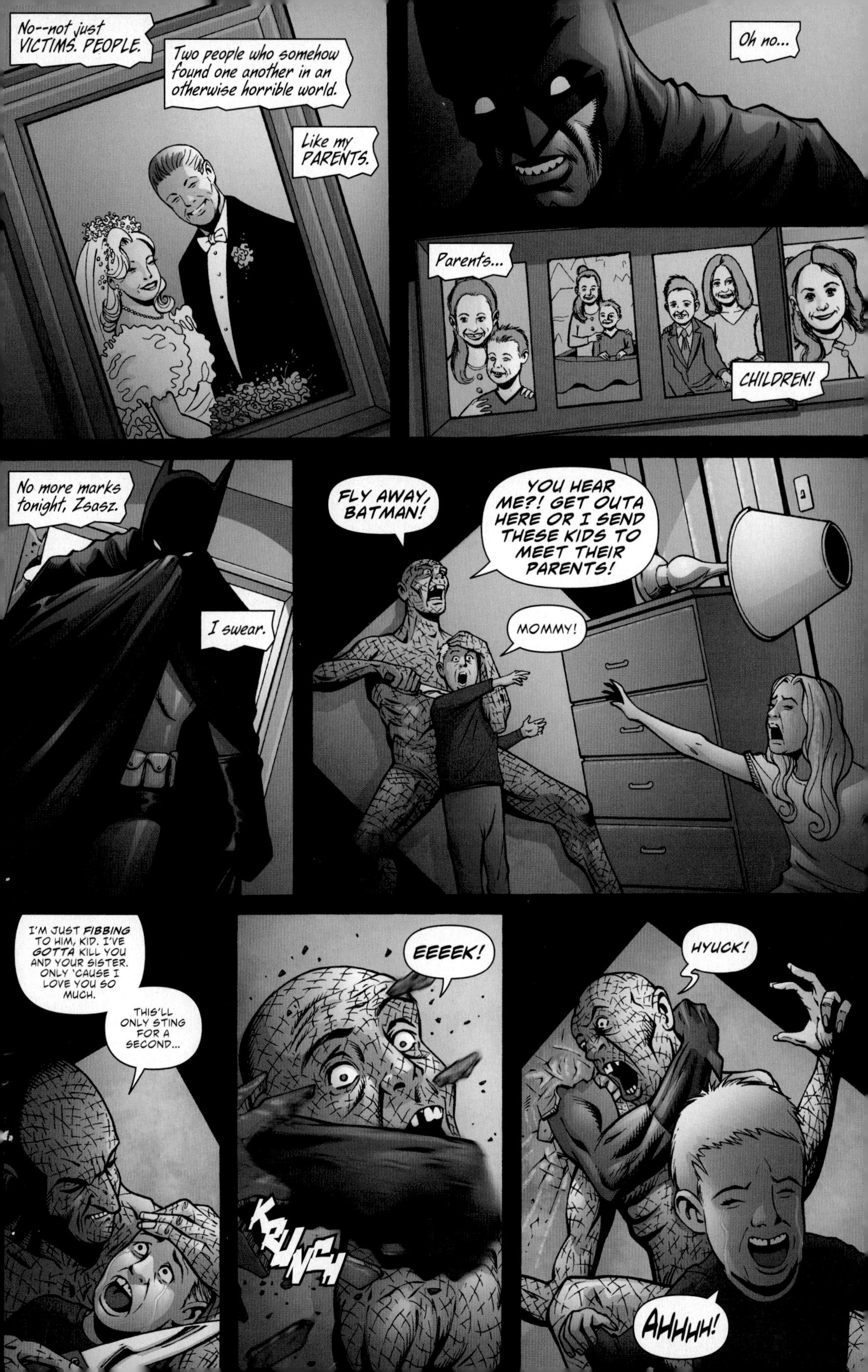
No--not just VICTIMS. PEOPLE.
Two people who somehow found one another in an otherwise horrible world.
Like my PARENTS.
Oh no...
Parents...
CHILDREN!
No more marks tonight, Zsasz.
I swear.
FLY AWAY, BATMAN!
YOU HEAR ME?! GET OUTA HERE OR I SEND THESE KIDS TO MEET THEIR PARENTS!
MOMMY!
I'M JUST FIBBING TO HIM, KID. I'VE GOTTA KILL YOU AND YOUR SISTER. ONLY 'CAUSE I LOVE YOU SO MUCH.
THIS'LL ONLY STING FOR A SECOND...
EEEEK!
KRUNCH
HYUCK!
AHHHH!

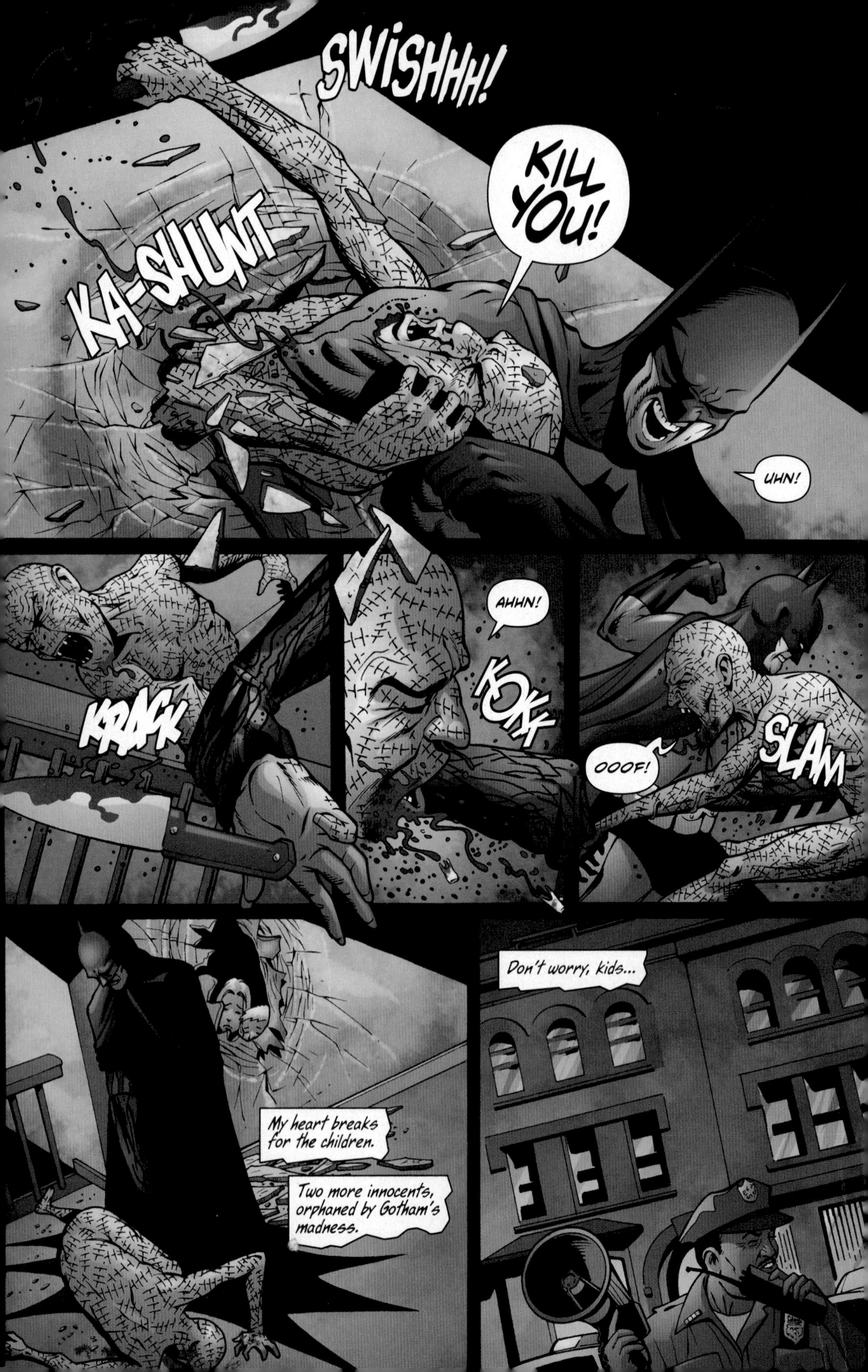
SWISHHH!
KILL YOU!
KA-SHUNT
UHN!
KRACK
AHHN!
KOKK
OOOF!
SLAM
My heart breaks for the children.
Two more innocents, orphaned by Gotham's madness.
Don't worry, kids...

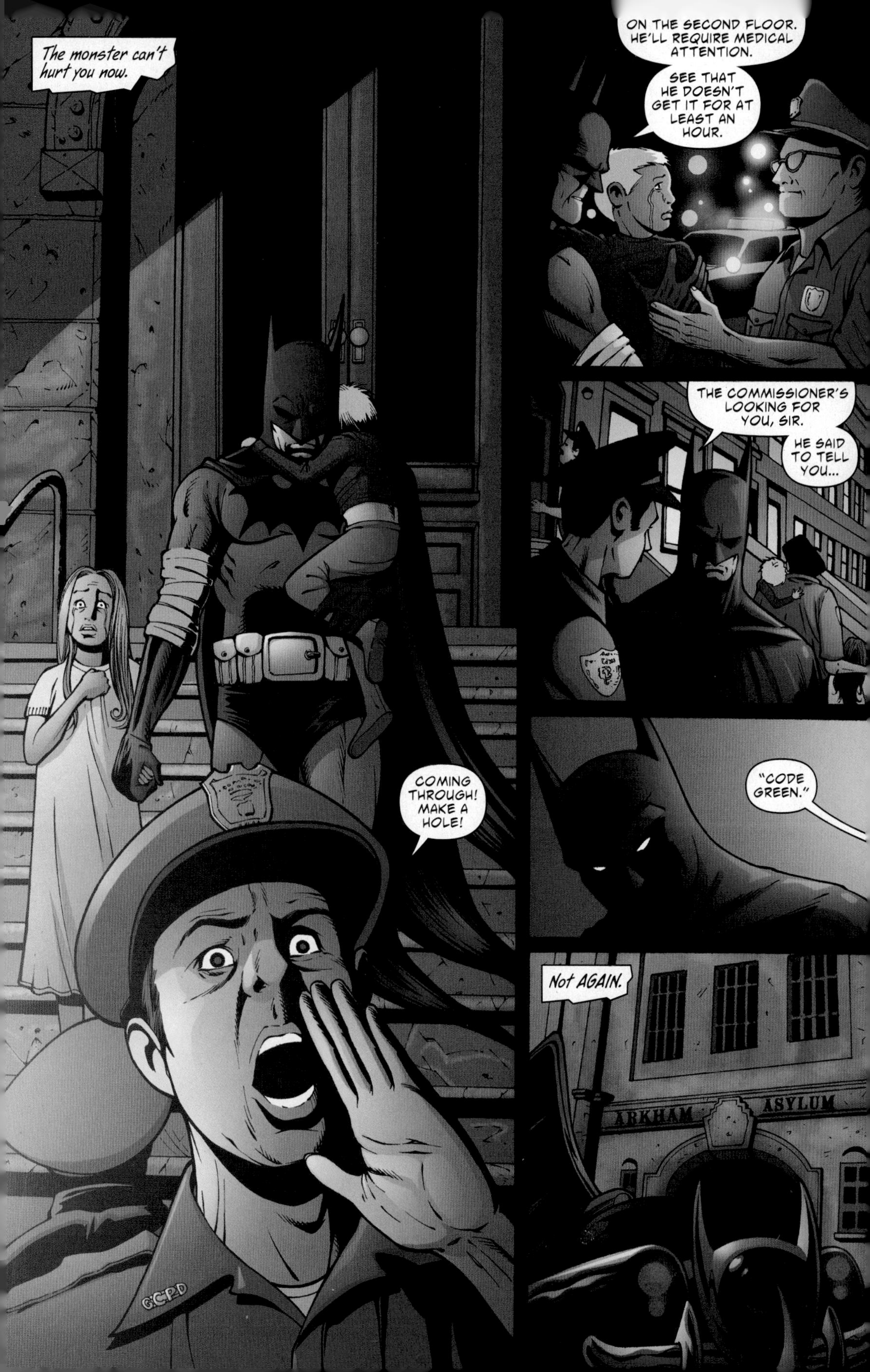
The monster can't hurt you now.
COMING THROUGH! MAKE A HOLE!
ON THE SECOND FLOOR. HE'LL REQUIRE MEDICAL ATTENTION.
SEE THAT HE DOESN'T GET IT FOR AT LEAST AN HOUR.
THE COMMISSIONER'S LOOKING FOR YOU, SIR.
HE SAID TO TELL YOU...
"CODE GREEN."
Not AGAIN.
ARKHAM ASYLUM
GCPD

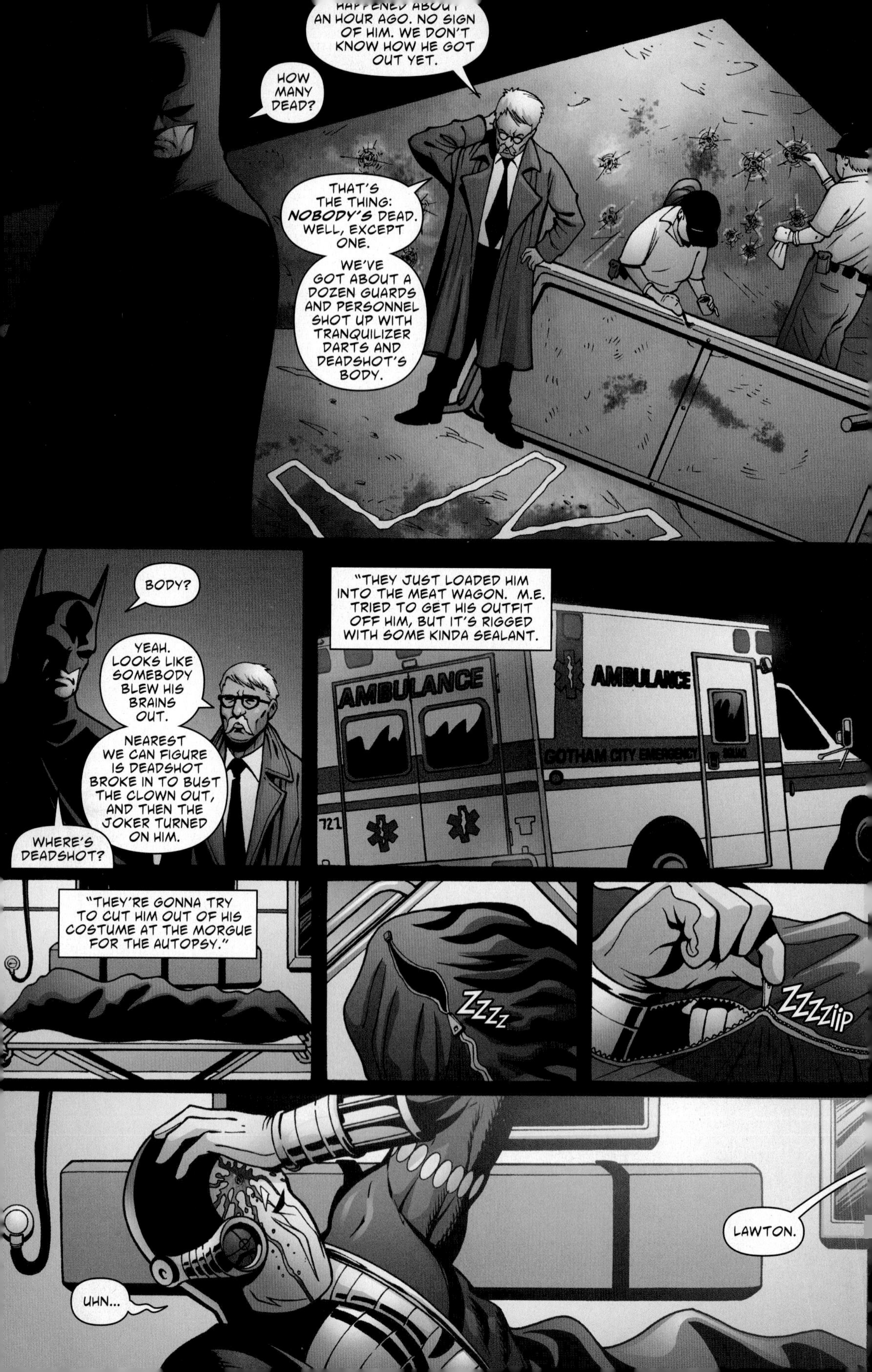
HAPPENED ABOUT AN HOUR AGO. NO SIGN OF HIM. WE DON'T KNOW HOW HE GOT OUT YET.
HOW MANY DEAD?
THAT'S THE THING: NOBODY'S DEAD. WELL, EXCEPT ONE.
WE'VE GOT ABOUT A DOZEN GUARDS AND PERSONNEL SHOT UP WITH TRANQUILIZER DARTS AND DEADSHOT'S BODY.
BODY?
YEAH. LOOKS LIKE SOMEBODY BLEW HIS BRAINS OUT.
NEAREST WE CAN FIGURE IS DEADSHOT BROKE IN TO BUST THE CLOWN OUT, AND THEN THE JOKER TURNED ON HIM.
WHERE'S DEADSHOT?
"THEY JUST LOADED HIM INTO THE MEAT WAGON. M.E. TRIED TO GET HIS OUTFIT OFF HIM, BUT IT'S RIGGED WITH SOME KINDA SEALANT.
AMBULANCE
AMBULANCE
GOTHAM CITY EMERGENCY
721
"THEY'RE GONNA TRY TO CUT HIM OUT OF HIS COSTUME AT THE MORGUE FOR THE AUTOPSY."
ZZZZ
ZZZZiip
LAWTON.
UHN...

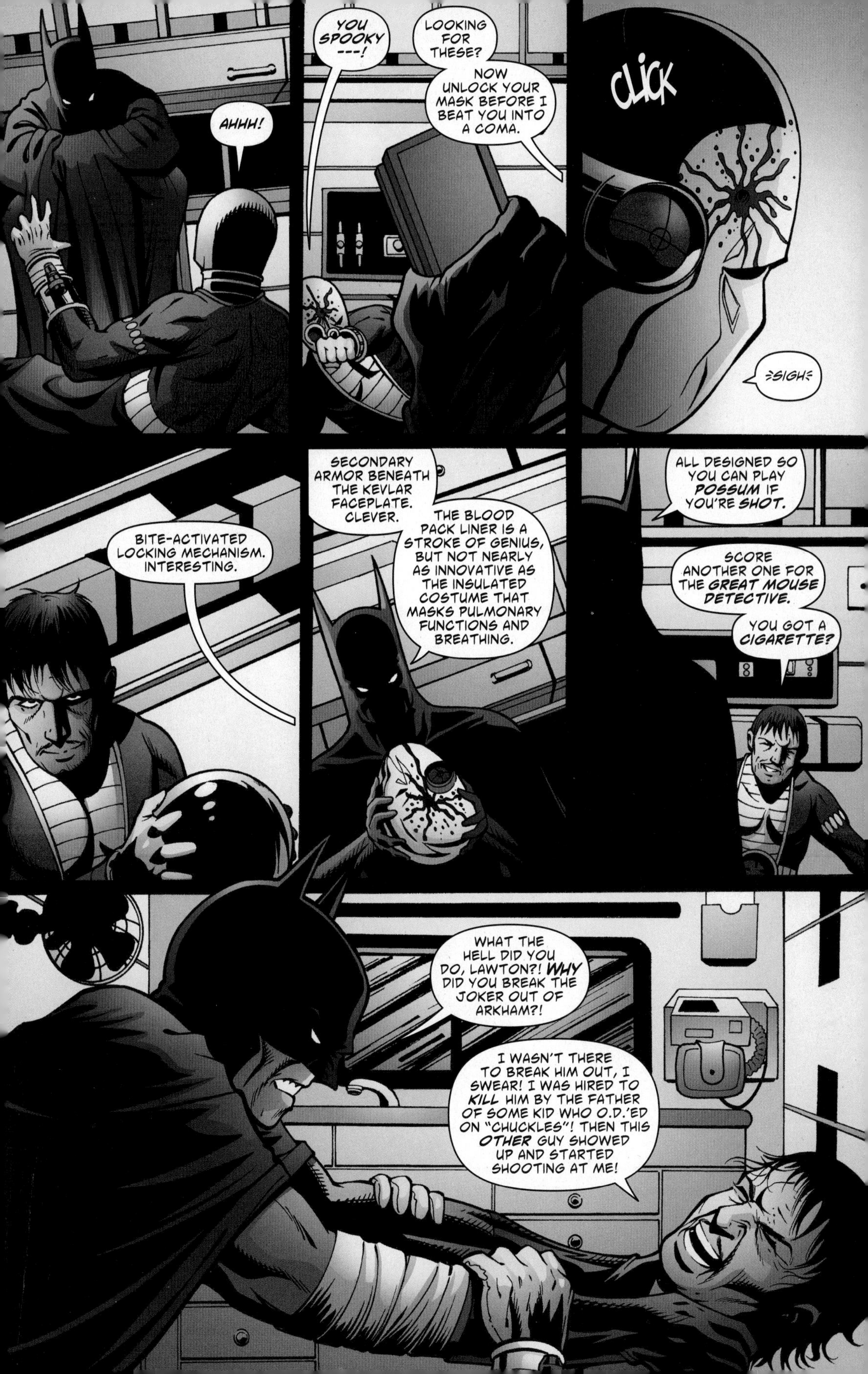
AHHH!
YOU SPOOKY ---!
LOOKING FOR THESE?
NOW UNLOCK YOUR MASK BEFORE I BEAT YOU INTO A COMA.
CLICK
SIGH
BITE-ACTIVATED LOCKING MECHANISM. INTERESTING.
SECONDARY ARMOR BENEATH THE KEVLAR FACEPLATE. CLEVER.
THE BLOOD PACK LINER IS A STROKE OF GENIUS, BUT NOT NEARLY AS INNOVATIVE AS THE INSULATED COSTUME THAT MASKS PULMONARY FUNCTIONS AND BREATHING.
ALL DESIGNED SO YOU CAN PLAY POSSUM IF YOU'RE SHOT.
SCORE ANOTHER ONE FOR THE GREAT MOUSE DETECTIVE.
YOU GOT A CIGARETTE?
WHAT THE HELL DID YOU DO, LAWTON?! WHY DID YOU BREAK THE JOKER OUT OF ARKHAM?!
I WASN'T THERE TO BREAK HIM OUT, I SWEAR! I WAS HIRED TO KILL HIM BY THE FATHER OF SOME KID WHO O.D.'ED ON "CHUCKLES"! THEN THIS OTHER GUY SHOWED UP AND STARTED SHOOTING AT ME!

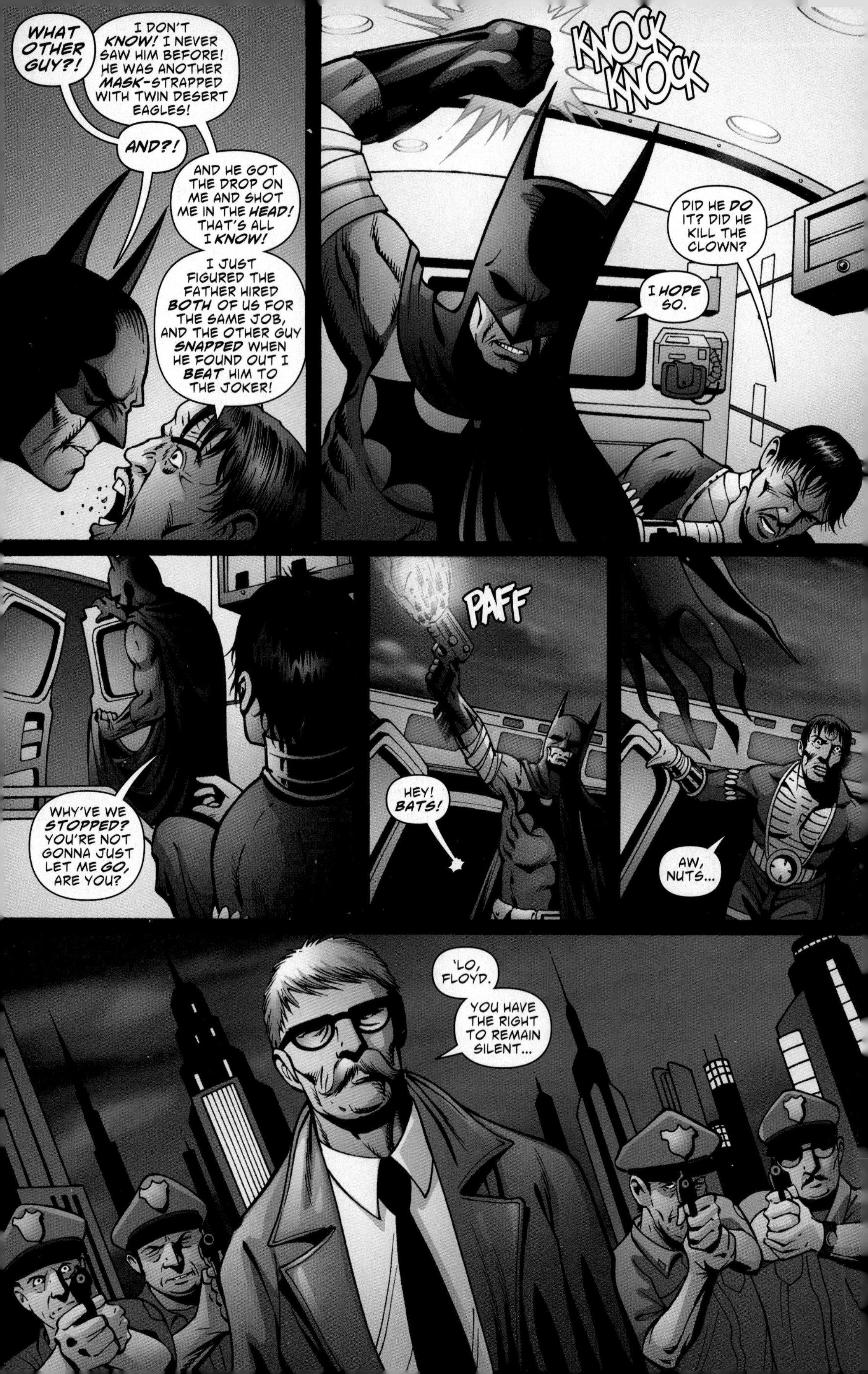
WHAT OTHER GUY?!
I DON'T KNOW! I NEVER SAW HIM BEFORE! HE WAS ANOTHER MASK-STRAPPED WITH TWIN DESERT EAGLES!
AND?!
AND HE GOT THE DROP ON ME AND SHOT ME IN THE HEAD! THAT'S ALL I KNOW!
I JUST FIGURED THE FATHER HIRED BOTH OF US FOR THE SAME JOB, AND THE OTHER GUY SNAPPED WHEN HE FOUND OUT I BEAT HIM TO THE JOKER!
KNOCK KNOCK
DID HE DO IT? DID HE KILL THE CLOWN?
I HOPE SO.
WHY'VE WE STOPPED? YOU'RE NOT GONNA JUST LET ME GO, ARE YOU?
PAFF
HEY! BATS!
AW, NUTS...
'LO, FLOYD.
YOU HAVE THE RIGHT TO REMAIN SILENT...

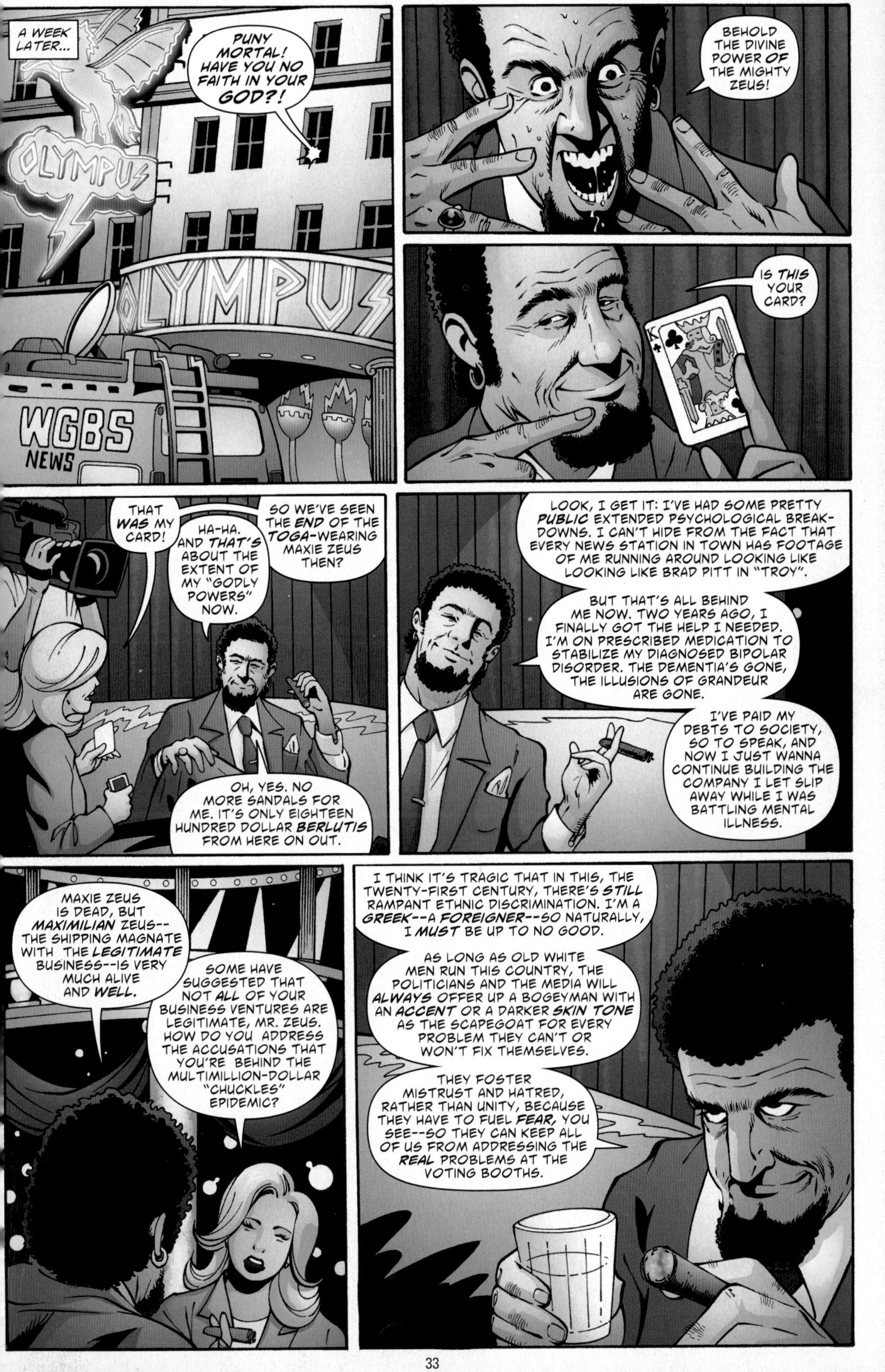
A WEEK LATER...
PUNY MORTAL! HAVE YOU NO FAITH IN YOUR GOD?!
OLYMPUS
OLYMPUS
WGBS NEWS
BEHOLD THE DIVINE POWER OF THE MIGHTY ZEUS!
IS THIS YOUR CARD?
THAT WAS MY CARD!
HA-HA. AND THAT'S ABOUT THE EXTENT OF MY "GODLY POWERS" NOW.
SO WE'VE SEEN THE END OF THE TOGA-WEARING MAXIE ZEUS THEN?
OH, YES. NO MORE SANDALS FOR ME. IT'S ONLY EIGHTEEN HUNDRED DOLLAR BERLUTIS FROM HERE ON OUT.
LOOK, I GET IT: I'VE HAD SOME PRETTY PUBLIC EXTENDED PSYCHOLOGICAL BREAK-DOWNS. I CAN'T HIDE FROM THE FACT THAT EVERY NEWS STATION IN TOWN HAS FOOTAGE OF ME RUNNING AROUND LOOKING LIKE LOOKING LIKE BRAD PITT IN "TROY".
BUT THAT'S ALL BEHIND ME NOW. TWO YEARS AGO, I FINALLY GOT THE HELP I NEEDED. I'M ON PRESCRIBED MEDICATION TO STABILIZE MY DIAGNOSED BIPOLAR DISORDER. THE DEMENTIA'S GONE, THE ILLUSIONS OF GRANDEUR ARE GONE.
I'VE PAID MY DEBTS TO SOCIETY, SO TO SPEAK, AND NOW I JUST WANNA CONTINUE BUILDING THE COMPANY I LET SLIP AWAY WHILE I WAS BATTLING MENTAL ILLNESS.
MAXIE ZEUS IS DEAD, BUT MAXIMILIAN ZEUS--THE SHIPPING MAGNATE WITH THE LEGITIMATE BUSINESS--IS VERY MUCH ALIVE AND WELL.
SOME HAVE SUGGESTED THAT NOT ALL OF YOUR BUSINESS VENTURES ARE LEGITIMATE, MR. ZEUS. HOW DO YOU ADDRESS THE ACCUSATIONS THAT YOU'RE BEHIND THE MULTIMILLION-DOLLAR "CHUCKLES" EPIDEMIC?
I THINK IT'S TRAGIC THAT IN THIS, THE TWENTY-FIRST CENTURY, THERE'S STILL RAMPANT ETHNIC DISCRIMINATION. I'M A GREEK--A FOREIGNER--SO NATURALLY, I MUST BE UP TO NO GOOD.
AS LONG AS OLD WHITE MEN RUN THIS COUNTRY, THE POLITICIANS AND THE MEDIA WILL ALWAYS OFFER UP A BOGEYMAN WITH AN ACCENT OR A DARKER SKIN TONE AS THE SCAPEGOAT FOR EVERY PROBLEM THEY CAN'T OR WON'T FIX THEMSELVES.
THEY FOSTER MISTRUST AND HATRED, RATHER THAN UNITY, BECAUSE THEY HAVE TO FUEL FEAR, YOU SEE--SO THEY CAN KEEP ALL OF US FROM ADDRESSING THE REAL PROBLEMS AT THE VOTING BOOTHS.

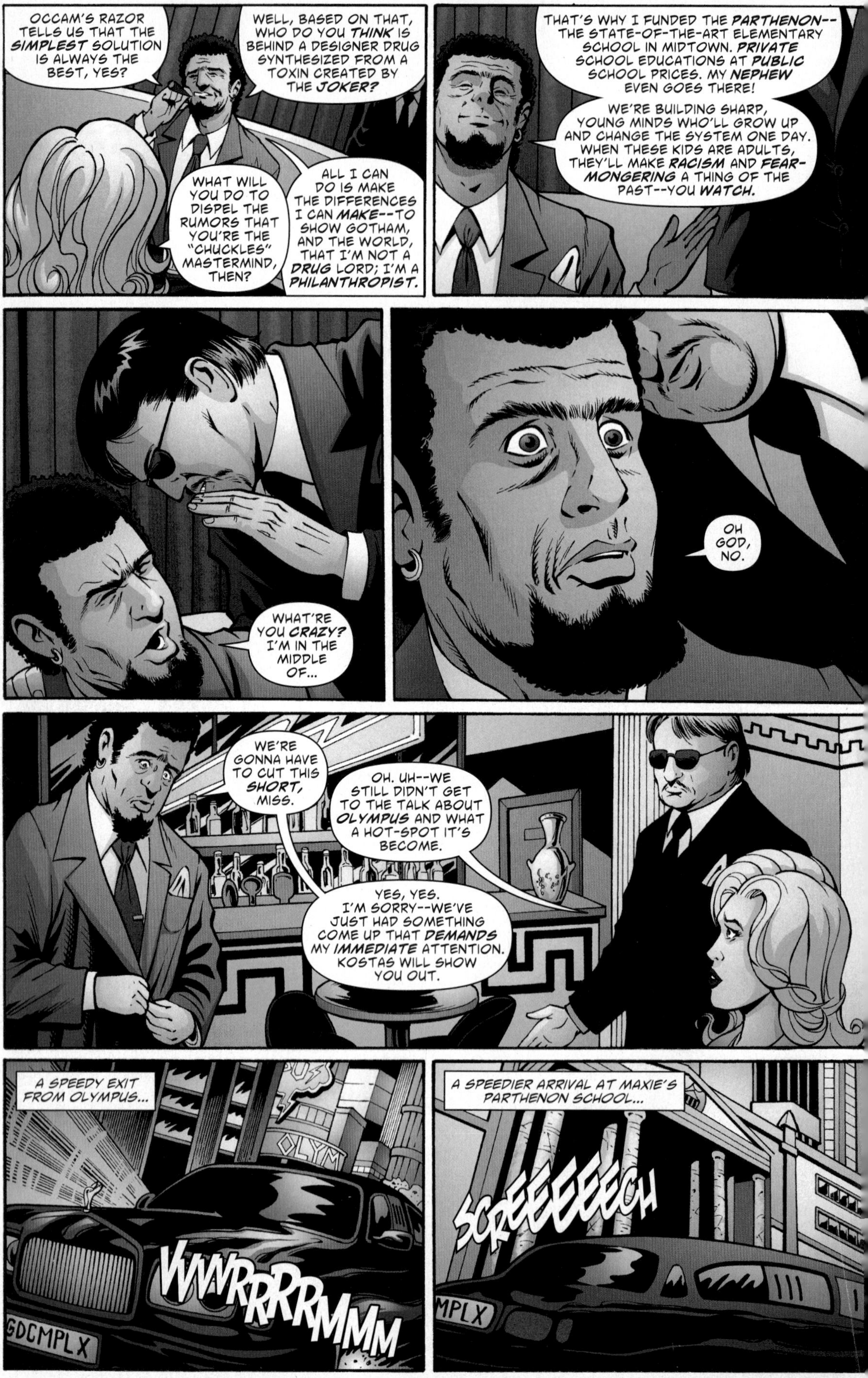
OCCAM'S RAZOR TELLS US THAT THE SIMPLEST SOLUTION IS ALWAYS THE BEST, YES?
WELL, BASED ON THAT, WHO DO YOU THINK IS BEHIND A DESIGNER DRUG SYNTHESIZED FROM A TOXIN CREATED BY THE JOKER?
WHAT WILL YOU DO TO DISPEL THE RUMORS THAT YOU'RE THE "CHUCKLES" MASTERMIND, THEN?
ALL I CAN DO IS MAKE THE DIFFERENCES I CAN MAKE--TO SHOW GOTHAM, AND THE WORLD, THAT I'M NOT A DRUG LORD; I'M A PHILANTHROPIST.
THAT'S WHY I FUNDED THE PARTHENON-- THE STATE-OF-THE-ART ELEMENTARY SCHOOL IN MIDTOWN. PRIVATE SCHOOL EDUCATIONS AT PUBLIC SCHOOL PRICES. MY NEPHEW EVEN GOES THERE!
WE'RE BUILDING SHARP, YOUNG MINDS WHO'LL GROW UP AND CHANGE THE SYSTEM ONE DAY. WHEN THESE KIDS ARE ADULTS, THEY'LL MAKE RACISM AND FEAR-MONGERING A THING OF THE PAST--YOU WATCH.
WHAT'RE YOU CRAZY? I'M IN THE MIDDLE OF...
OH GOD, NO.
WE'RE GONNA HAVE TO CUT THIS SHORT, MISS.
OH. UH--WE STILL DIDN'T GET TO THE TALK ABOUT OLYMPUS AND WHAT A HOT-SPOT IT'S BECOME.
YES, YES. I'M SORRY--WE'VE JUST HAD SOMETHING COME UP THAT DEMANDS MY IMMEDIATE ATTENTION. KOSTAS WILL SHOW YOU OUT.
A SPEEDY EXIT FROM OLYMPUS...
VVVVRRRRRMMMM
GDCMPLX
A SPEEDIER ARRIVAL AT MAXIE'S PARTHENON SCHOOL...
SCREEEEEECH
MPLX

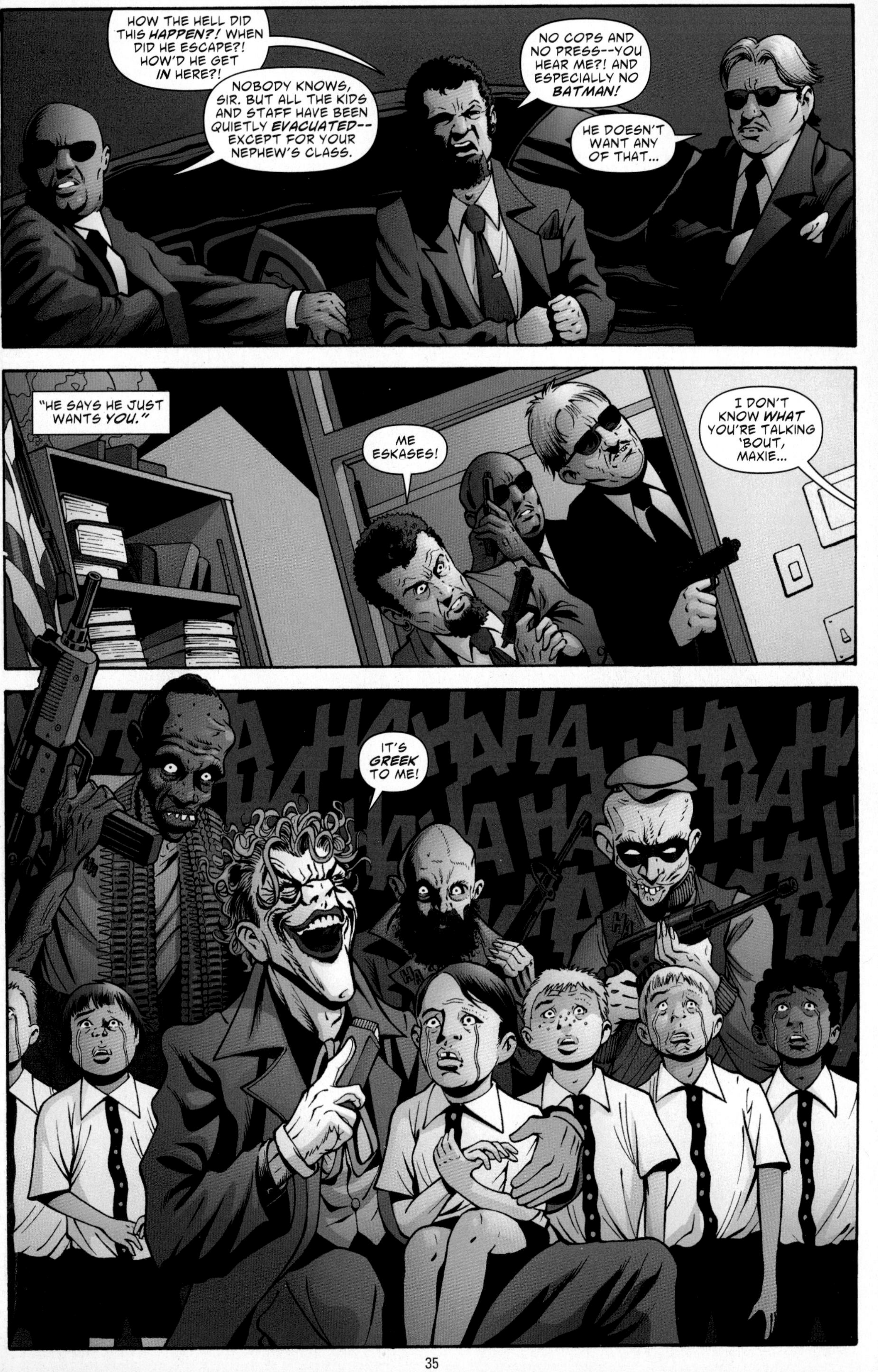
HOW THE HELL DID THIS HAPPEN?! WHEN DID HE ESCAPE?! HOW'D HE GET IN HERE?!
NOBODY KNOWS, SIR. BUT ALL THE KIDS AND STAFF HAVE BEEN QUIETLY EVACUATED-- EXCEPT FOR YOUR NEPHEW'S CLASS.
NO COPS AND NO PRESS--YOU HEAR ME?! AND ESPECIALLY NO BATMAN!
HE DOESN'T WANT ANY OF THAT...
"HE SAYS HE JUST WANTS YOU."
ME ESKASES!
I DON'T KNOW WHAT YOU'RE TALKING 'BOUT, MAXIE...
IT'S GREEK TO ME!

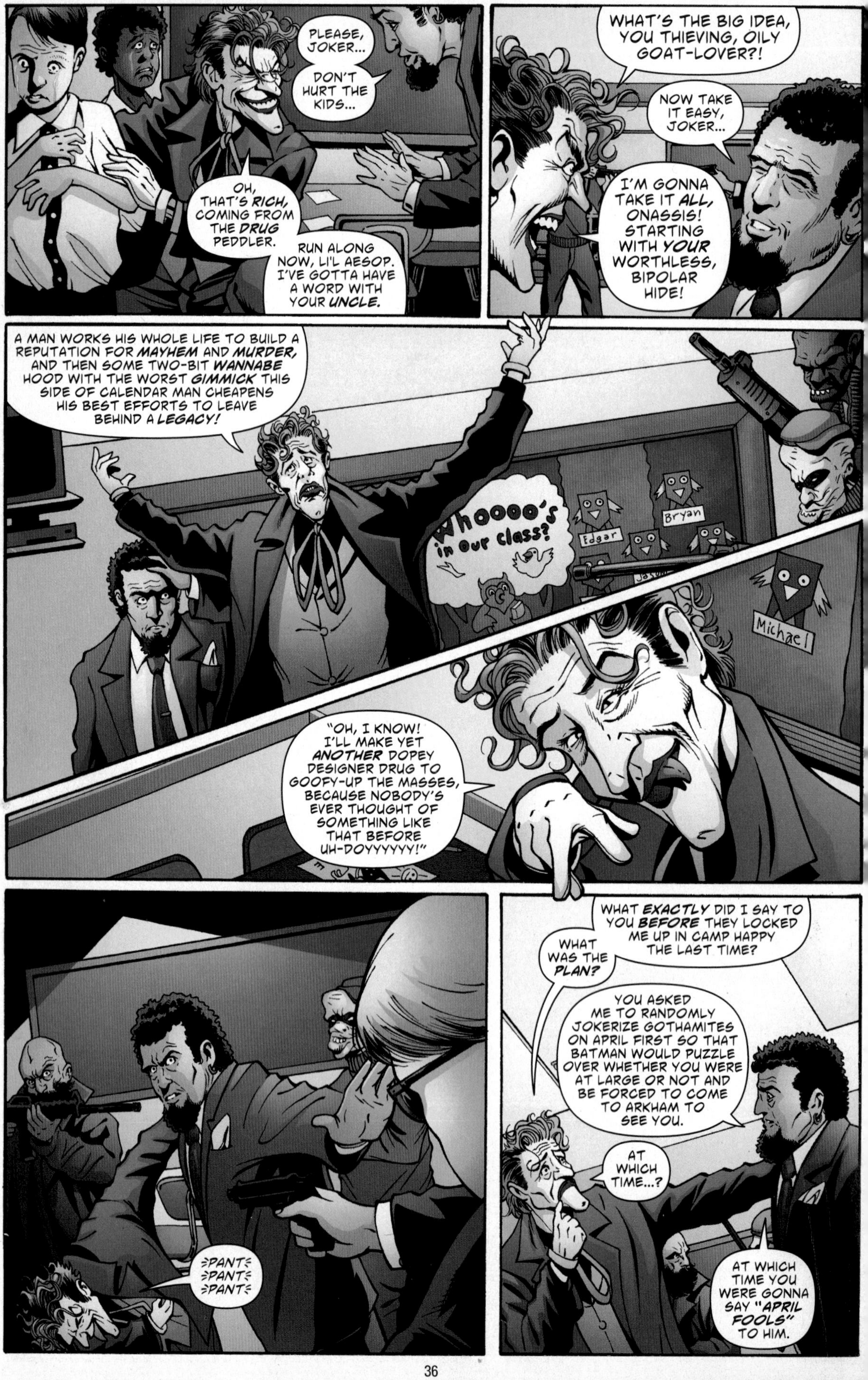
PLEASE, JOKER...
DON'T HURT THE KIDS...
OH, THAT'S RICH, COMING FROM THE DRUG PEDDLER.
RUN ALONG NOW, LI'L AESOP. I'VE GOTTA HAVE A WORD WITH YOUR UNCLE.
WHAT'S THE BIG IDEA, YOU THIEVING, OILY GOAT-LOVER?!
NOW TAKE IT EASY, JOKER...
I'M GONNA TAKE IT ALL, ONASSIS! STARTING WITH YOUR WORTHLESS, BIPOLAR HIDE!
A MAN WORKS HIS WHOLE LIFE TO BUILD A REPUTATION FOR MAYHEM AND MURDER, AND THEN SOME TWO-BIT WANNABE HOOD WITH THE WORST GIMMICK THIS SIDE OF CALENDAR MAN CHEAPENS HIS BEST EFFORTS TO LEAVE BEHIND A LEGACY!
Whoooo's in our class?
Edgar
Bryan
Michael
"OH, I KNOW! I'LL MAKE YET ANOTHER DOPEY DESIGNER DRUG TO GOOFY-UP THE MASSES, BECAUSE NOBODY'S EVER THOUGHT OF SOMETHING LIKE THAT BEFORE UH-DOYYYYYY!"
PANT PANT PANT
WHAT WAS THE PLAN?
WHAT EXACTLY DID I SAY TO YOU BEFORE THEY LOCKED ME UP IN CAMP HAPPY THE LAST TIME?
YOU ASKED ME TO RANDOMLY JOKERIZE GOTHAMITES ON APRIL FIRST SO THAT BATMAN WOULD PUZZLE OVER WHETHER YOU WERE AT LARGE OR NOT AND BE FORCED TO COME TO ARKHAM TO SEE YOU.
AT WHICH TIME...?
AT WHICH TIME YOU WERE GONNA SAY "APRIL FOOLS" TO HIM.

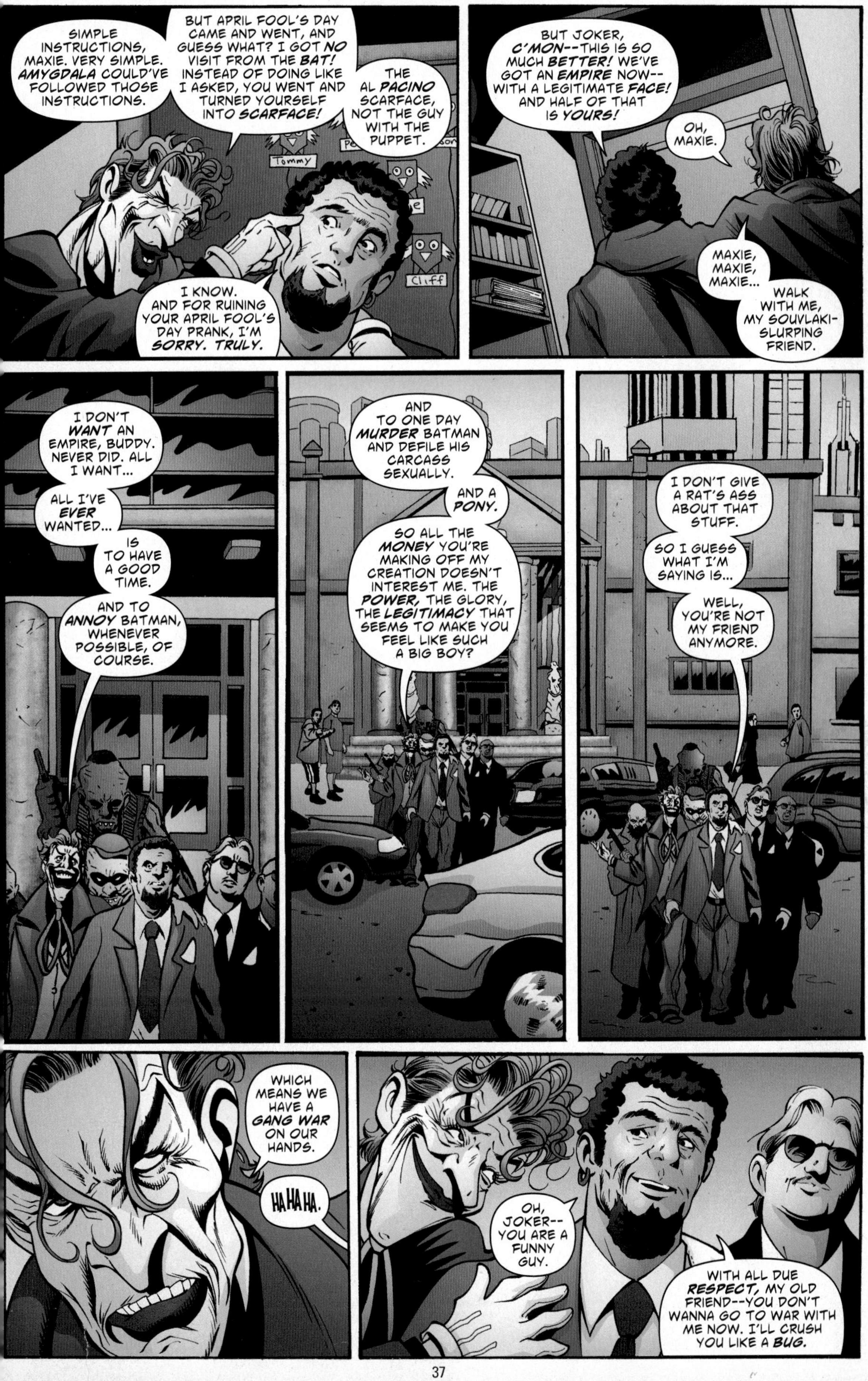
SIMPLE INSTRUCTIONS, MAXIE. VERY SIMPLE. AMYGDALA COULD'VE FOLLOWED THOSE INSTRUCTIONS.
BUT APRIL FOOL'S DAY CAME AND WENT, AND GUESS WHAT? I GOT NO VISIT FROM THE BAT! INSTEAD OF DOING LIKE I ASKED, YOU WENT AND TURNED YOURSELF INTO SCARFACE!
THE AL PACINO SCARFACE, NOT THE GUY WITH THE PUPPET.
Tommy
Cliff
I KNOW. AND FOR RUINING YOUR APRIL FOOL'S DAY PRANK, I'M SORRY. TRULY.
BUT JOKER, C'MON--THIS IS SO MUCH BETTER! WE'VE GOT AN EMPIRE NOW--WITH A LEGITIMATE FACE! AND HALF OF THAT IS YOURS!
OH, MAXIE.
MAXIE, MAXIE, MAXIE...
WALK WITH ME, MY SOUVLAKI-SLURPING FRIEND.
I DON'T WANT AN EMPIRE, BUDDY. NEVER DID. ALL I WANT...
ALL I'VE EVER WANTED...
IS TO HAVE A GOOD TIME.
AND TO ANNOY BATMAN, WHENEVER POSSIBLE, OF COURSE.
AND TO ONE DAY MURDER BATMAN AND DEFILE HIS CARCASS SEXUALLY.
AND A PONY.
SO ALL THE MONEY YOU'RE MAKING OFF MY CREATION DOESN'T INTEREST ME. THE POWER, THE GLORY, THE LEGITIMACY THAT SEEMS TO MAKE YOU FEEL LIKE SUCH A BIG BOY?
I DON'T GIVE A RAT'S ASS ABOUT THAT STUFF.
SO I GUESS WHAT I'M SAYING IS...
WELL, YOU'RE NOT MY FRIEND ANYMORE.
WHICH MEANS WE HAVE A GANG WAR ON OUR HANDS.
HA HA HA.
OH, JOKER--YOU ARE A FUNNY GUY.
WITH ALL DUE RESPECT, MY OLD FRIEND--YOU DON'T WANNA GO TO WAR WITH ME NOW. I'LL CRUSH YOU LIKE A BUG.

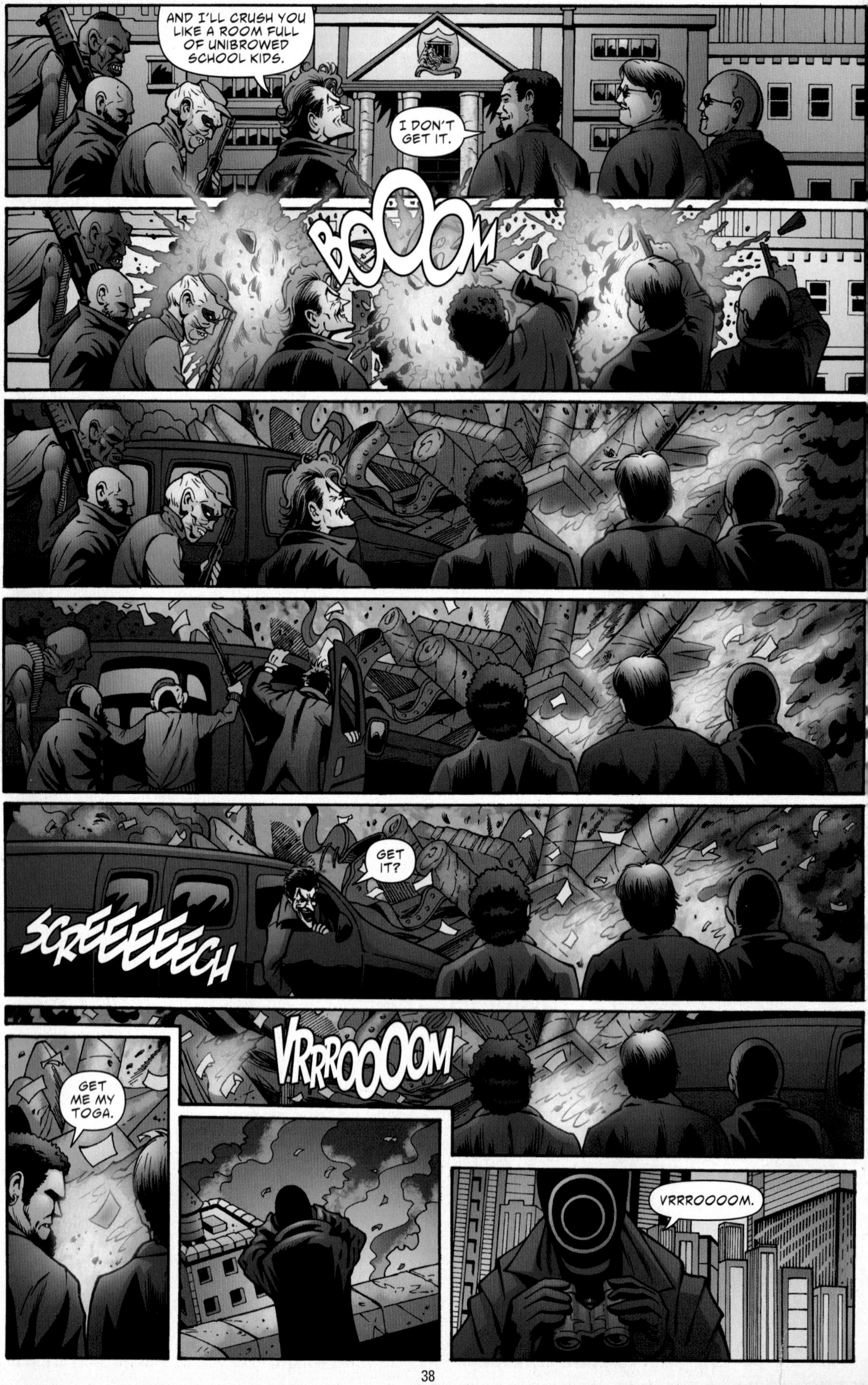
AND I'LL CRUSH YOU LIKE A ROOM FULL OF UNIBROWED SCHOOL KIDS.
I DON'T GET IT.
BOOOOM
GET IT?
SCREEEEEECH
VRRROOOOM
GET ME MY TOGA.
VRRROOOOM.

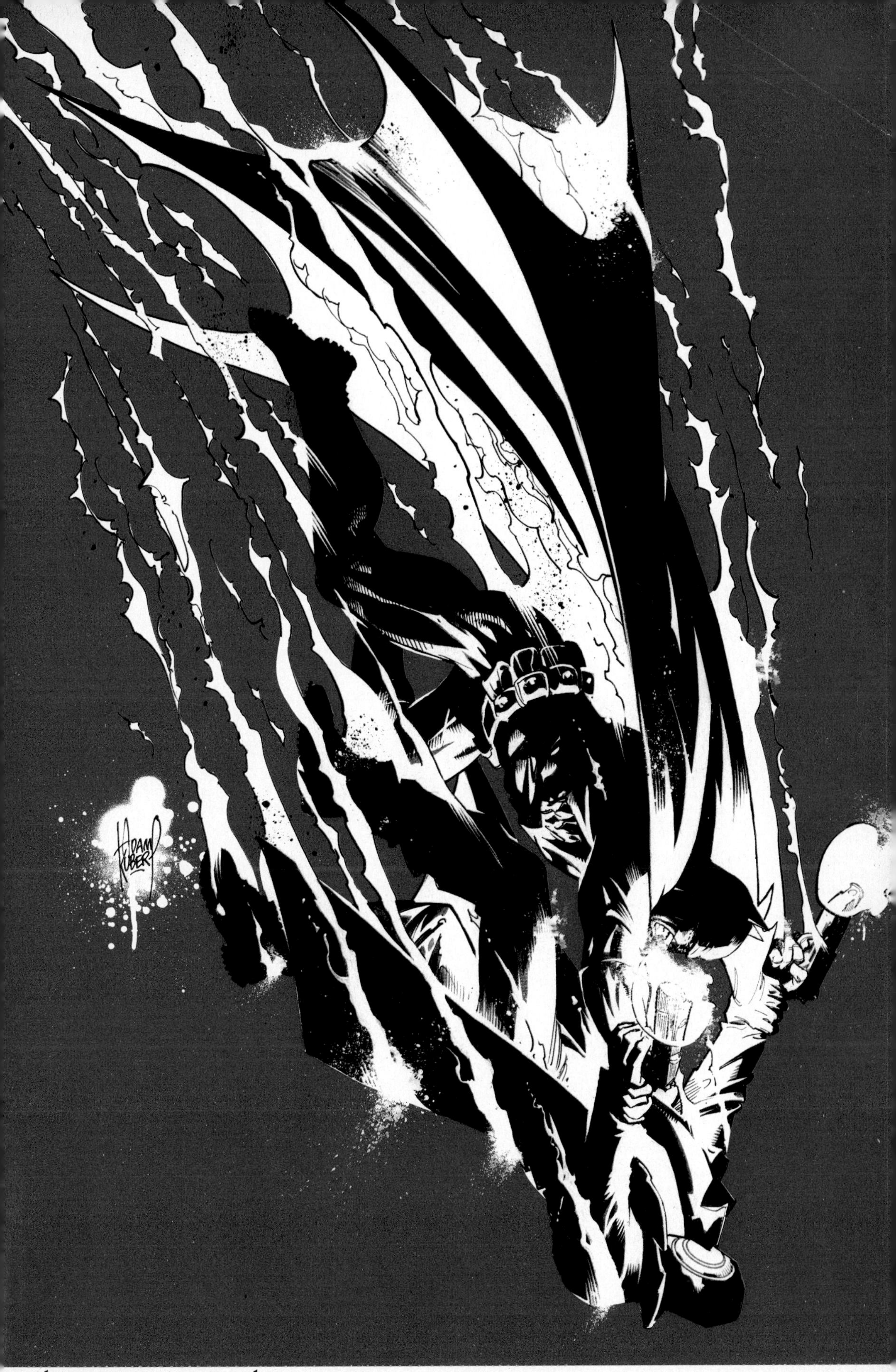
ADAM KUBERT

batman :: cacophony #2 *cover by* ADAM KUBERT

part two WIRED FOR SOUND

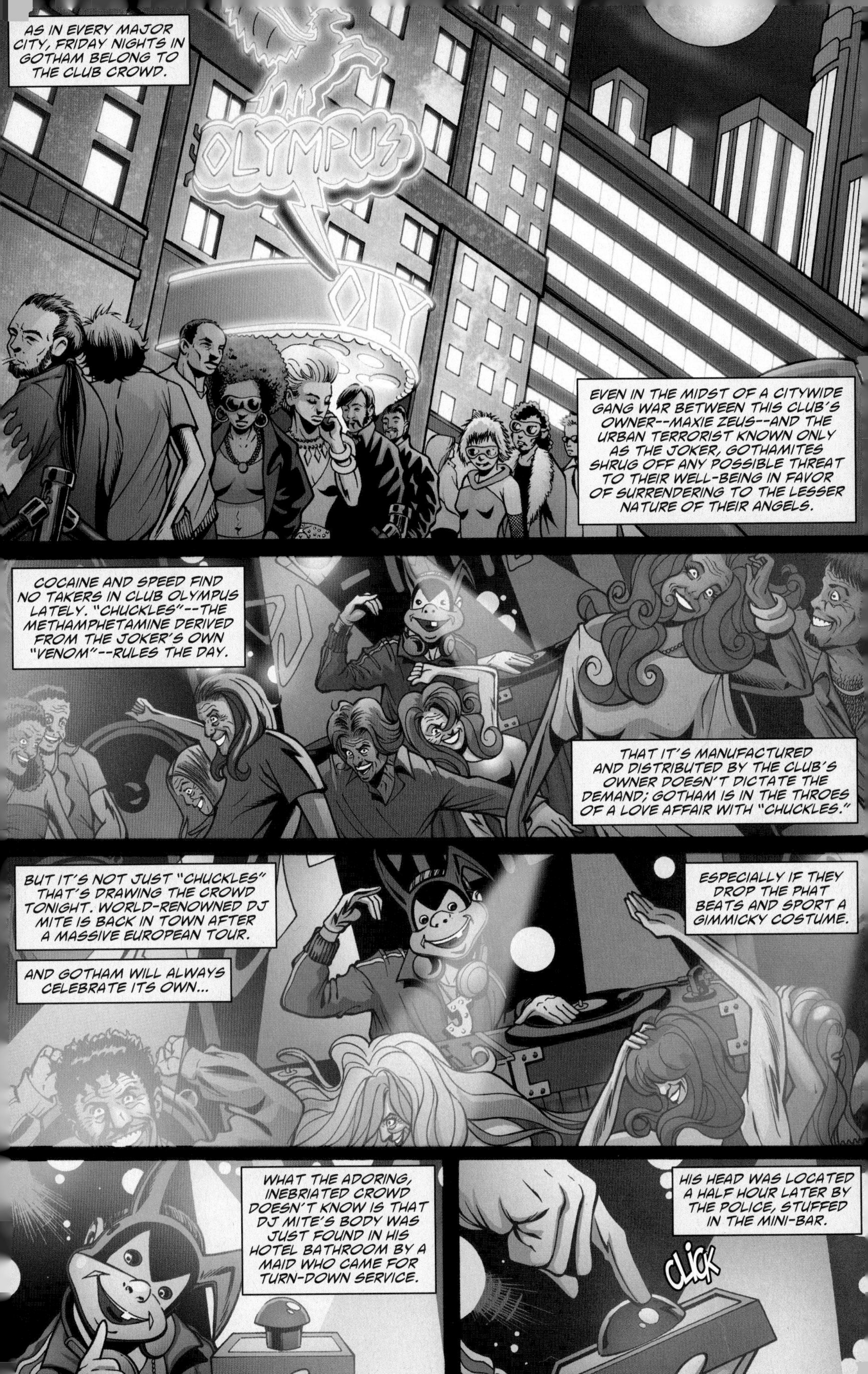
OLYMPUS
AS IN EVERY MAJOR CITY, FRIDAY NIGHTS IN GOTHAM BELONG TO THE CLUB CROWD.
EVEN IN THE MIDST OF A CITYWIDE GANG WAR BETWEEN THIS CLUB'S OWNER--MAXIE ZEUS--AND THE URBAN TERRORIST KNOWN ONLY AS THE JOKER, GOTHAMITES SHRUG OFF ANY POSSIBLE THREAT TO THEIR WELL-BEING IN FAVOR OF SURRENDERING TO THE LESSER NATURE OF THEIR ANGELS.
COCAINE AND SPEED FIND NO TAKERS IN CLUB OLYMPUS LATELY. "CHUCKLES"--THE METHAMPHETAMINE DERIVED FROM THE JOKER'S OWN "VENOM"--RULES THE DAY.
THAT IT'S MANUFACTURED AND DISTRIBUTED BY THE CLUB'S OWNER DOESN'T DICTATE THE DEMAND; GOTHAM IS IN THE THROES OF A LOVE AFFAIR WITH "CHUCKLES."
BUT IT'S NOT JUST "CHUCKLES" THAT'S DRAWING THE CROWD TONIGHT. WORLD-RENOWNED DJ MITE IS BACK IN TOWN AFTER A MASSIVE EUROPEAN TOUR.
AND GOTHAM WILL ALWAYS CELEBRATE ITS OWN...
ESPECIALLY IF THEY DROP THE PHAT BEATS AND SPORT A GIMMICKY COSTUME.
WHAT THE ADORING, INEBRIATED CROWD DOESN'T KNOW IS THAT DJ MITE'S BODY WAS JUST FOUND IN HIS HOTEL BATHROOM BY A MAID WHO CAME FOR TURN-DOWN SERVICE.
HIS HEAD WAS LOCATED A HALF HOUR LATER BY THE POLICE, STUFFED IN THE MINI-BAR.
CLICK

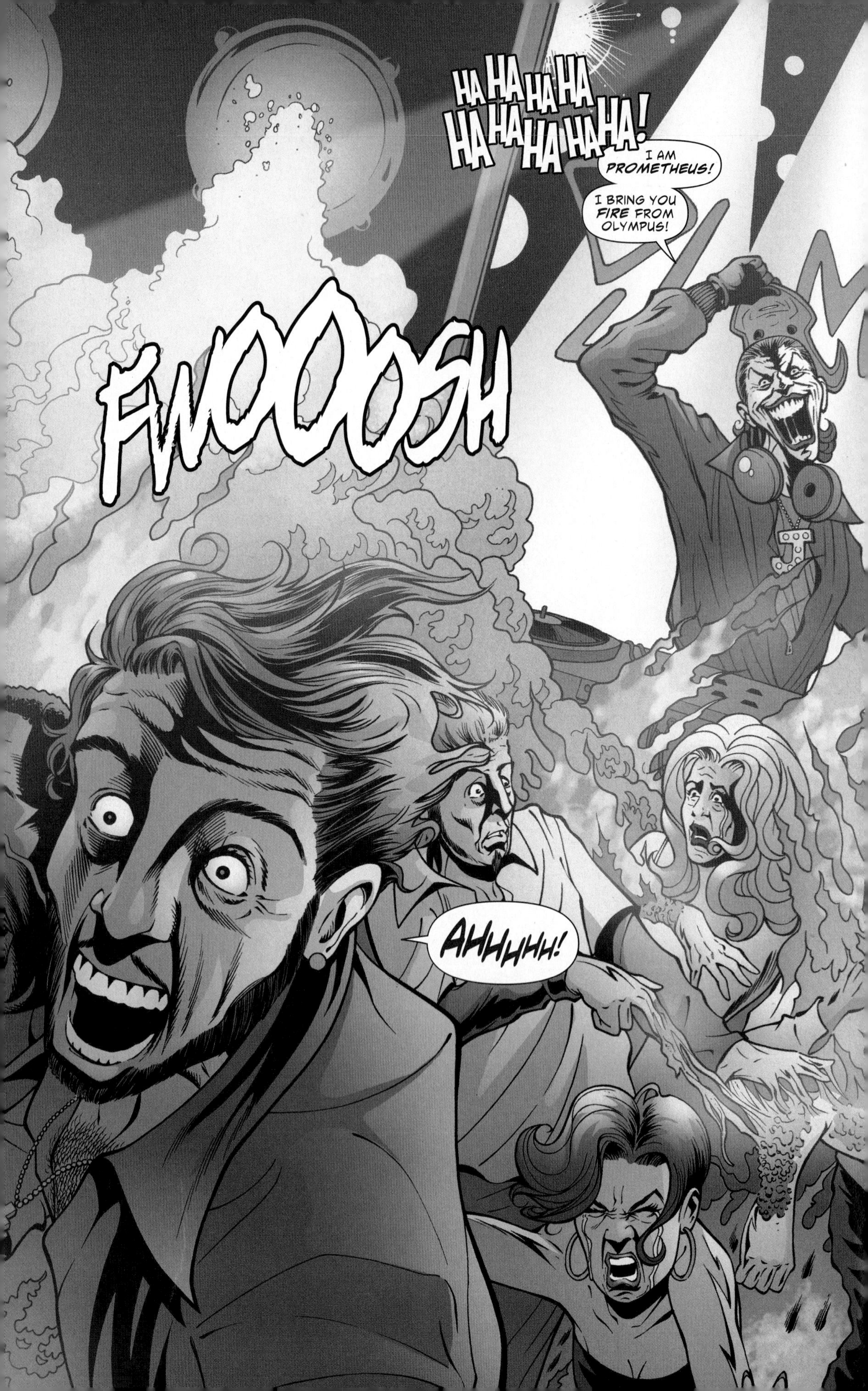
HA HA HA HA
HA HA HA HA HA!
I AM PROMETHEUS!
I BRING YOU FIRE FROM OLYMPUS!
FWOOOSH
AHHHHH!

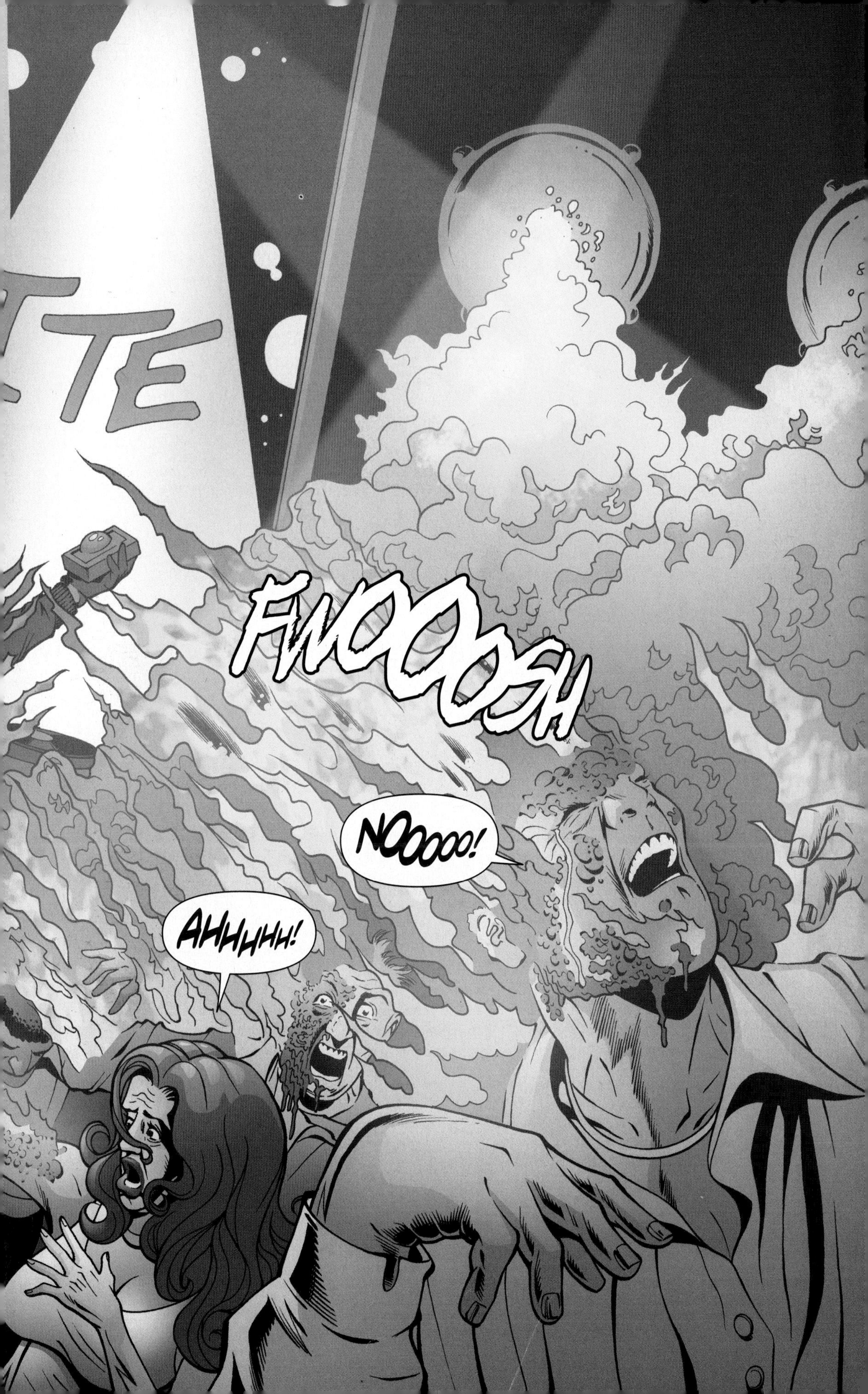
FWOOOSH
NOOOOO!
AHHHHH!

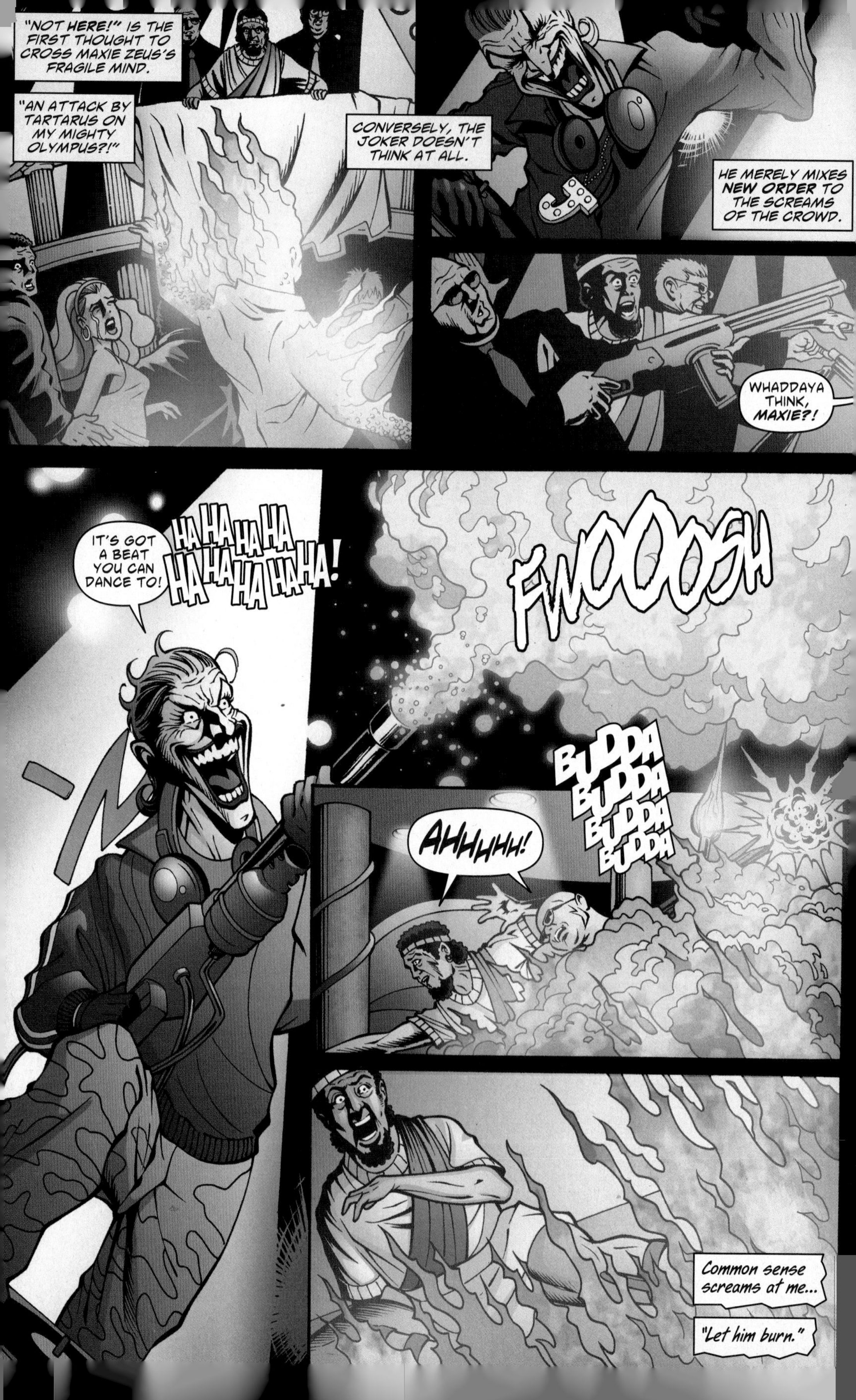
"NOT HERE!" IS THE FIRST THOUGHT TO CROSS MAXIE ZEUS'S FRAGILE MIND.
"AN ATTACK BY TARTARUS ON MY MIGHTY OLYMPUS?!"
CONVERSELY, THE JOKER DOESN'T THINK AT ALL.
HE MERELY MIXES NEW ORDER TO THE SCREAMS OF THE CROWD.
WHADDAYA THINK, MAXIE?!
IT'S GOT A BEAT YOU CAN DANCE TO!
HA HA HA HA HA HA HA HA HA HA!
FWOOOSH
BUDDA BUDDA BUDDA BUDDA
AHHHHH!
Common sense screams at me...
"Let him burn."

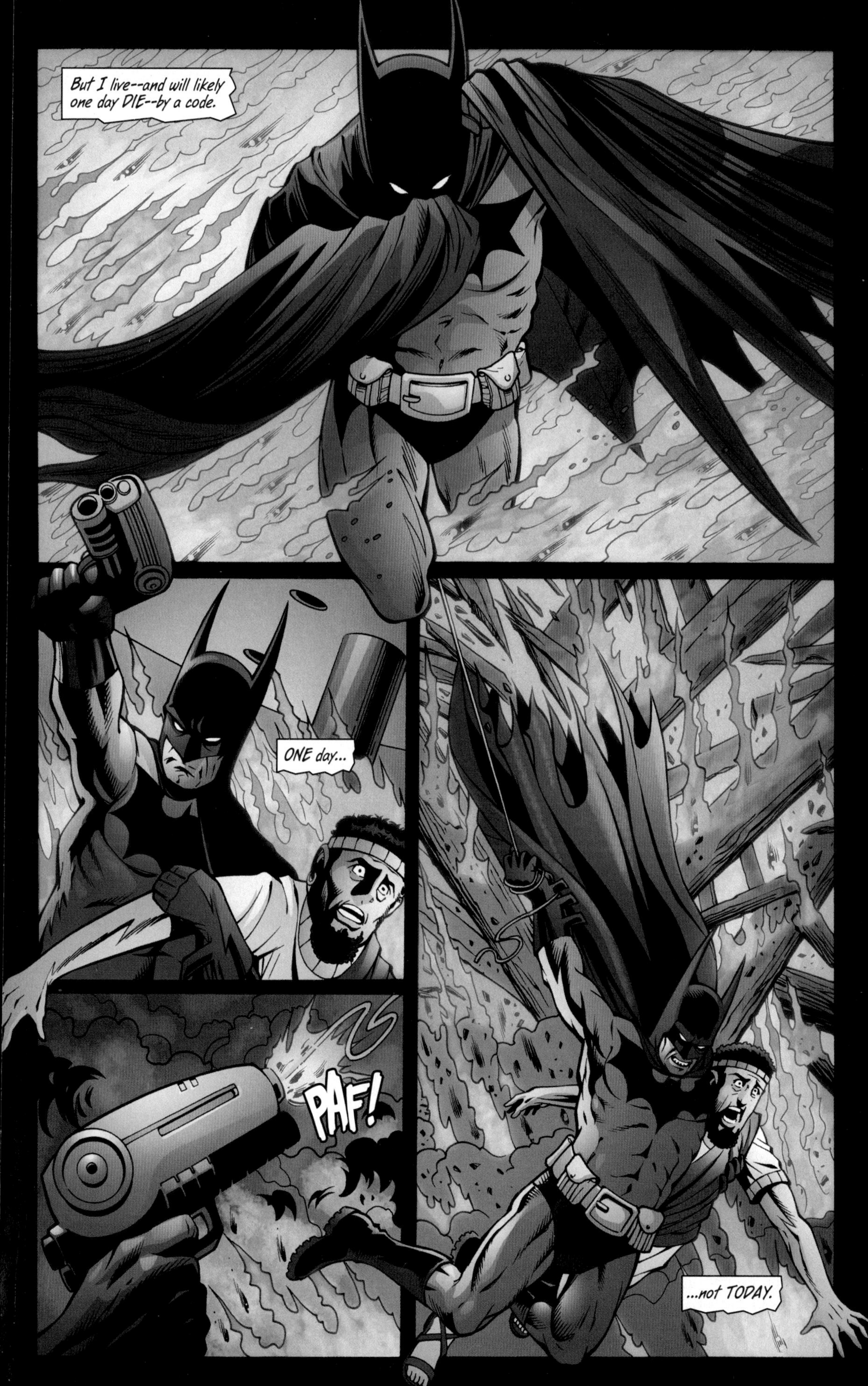
But I live--and will likely one day DIE--by a code.
ONE day...
PAF!
...not TODAY.

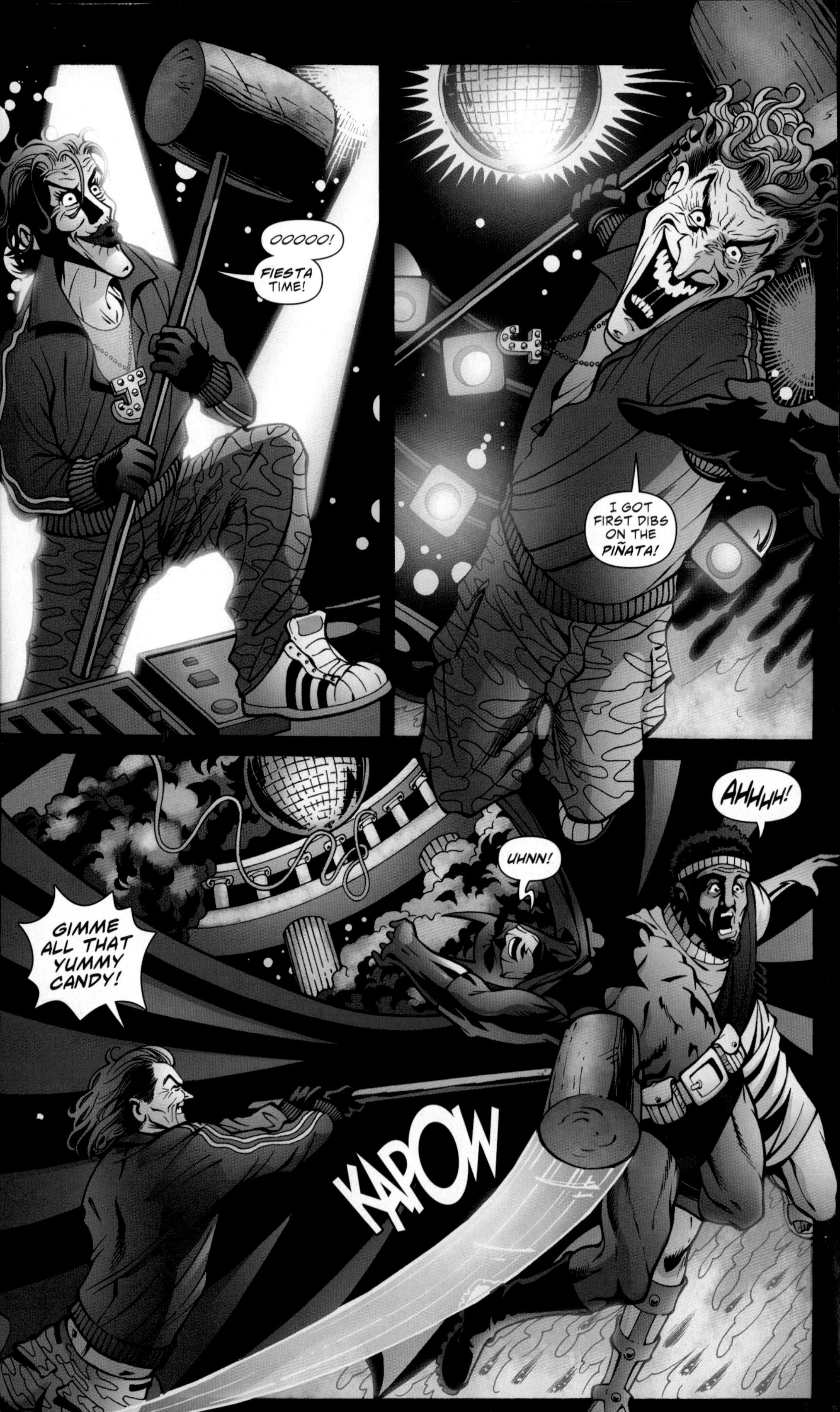
OOOOO!
FIESTA TIME!
I GOT FIRST DIBS ON THE PIÑATA!
GIMME ALL THAT YUMMY CANDY!
UHNN!
AHHHH!
KAPOW

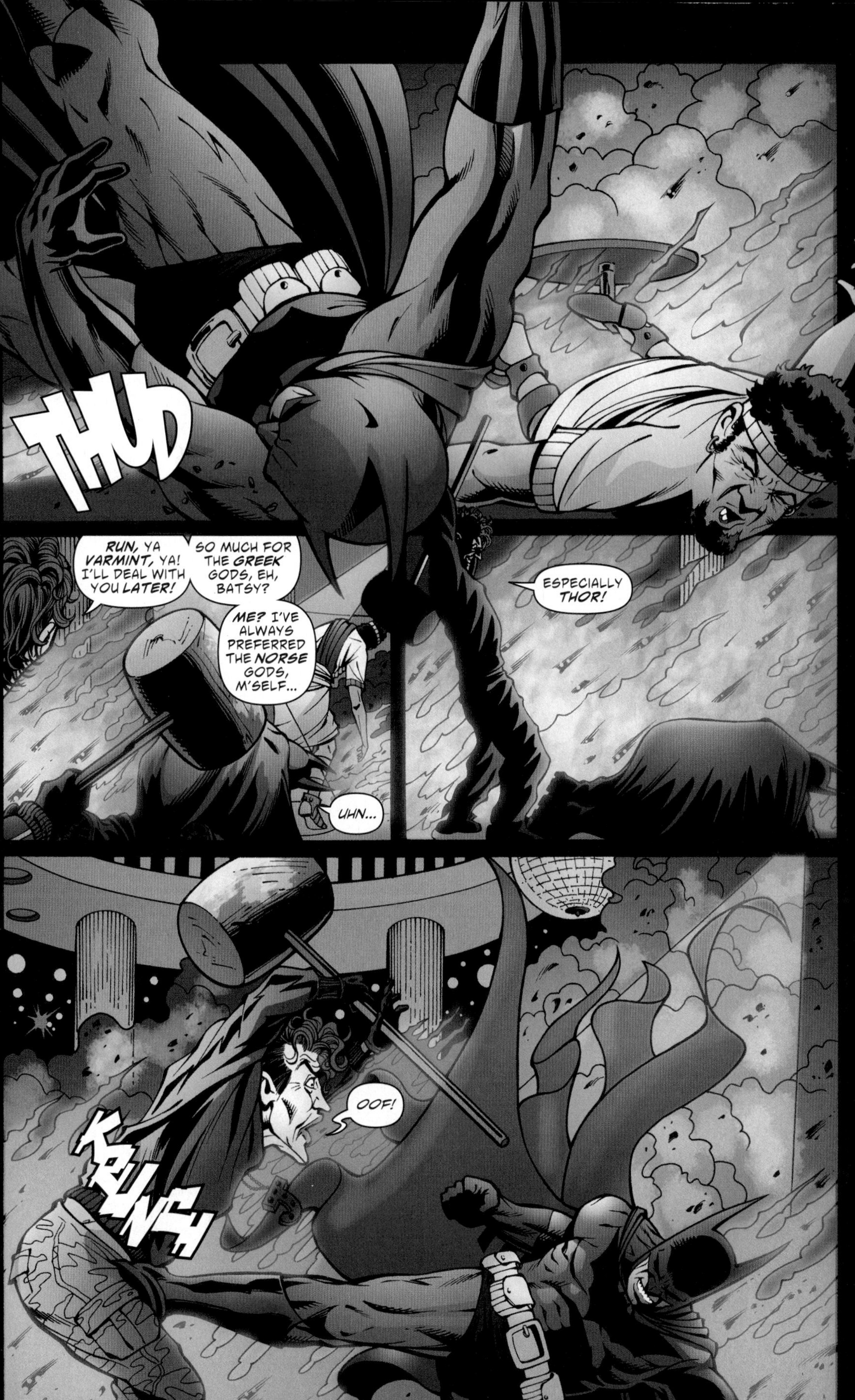
THUD
RUN, YA VARMINT, YA! I'LL DEAL WITH YOU LATER!
SO MUCH FOR THE GREEK GODS, EH, BATSY?
ME? I'VE ALWAYS PREFERRED THE NORSE GODS, M'SELF...
UHN...
ESPECIALLY THOR!
OOF!
KRUNCH

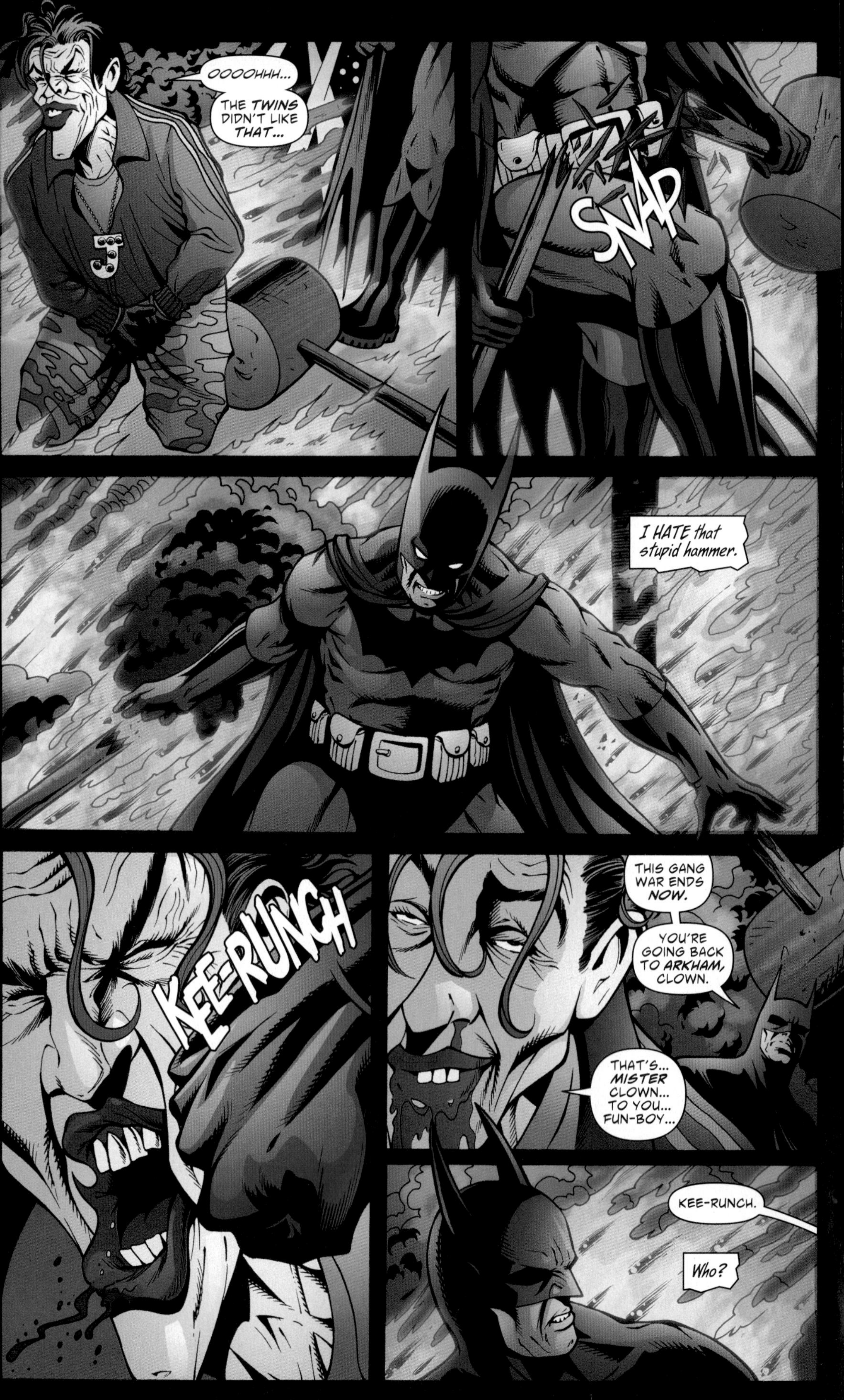
OOOOHHH...
THE TWINS DIDN'T LIKE THAT...
SNAP
I HATE that stupid hammer.
KEE-RUNCH
THIS GANG WAR ENDS NOW.
YOU'RE GOING BACK TO ARKHAM, CLOWN.
THAT'S... MISTER CLOWN... TO YOU... FUN-BOY...
KEE-RUNCH.
Who?

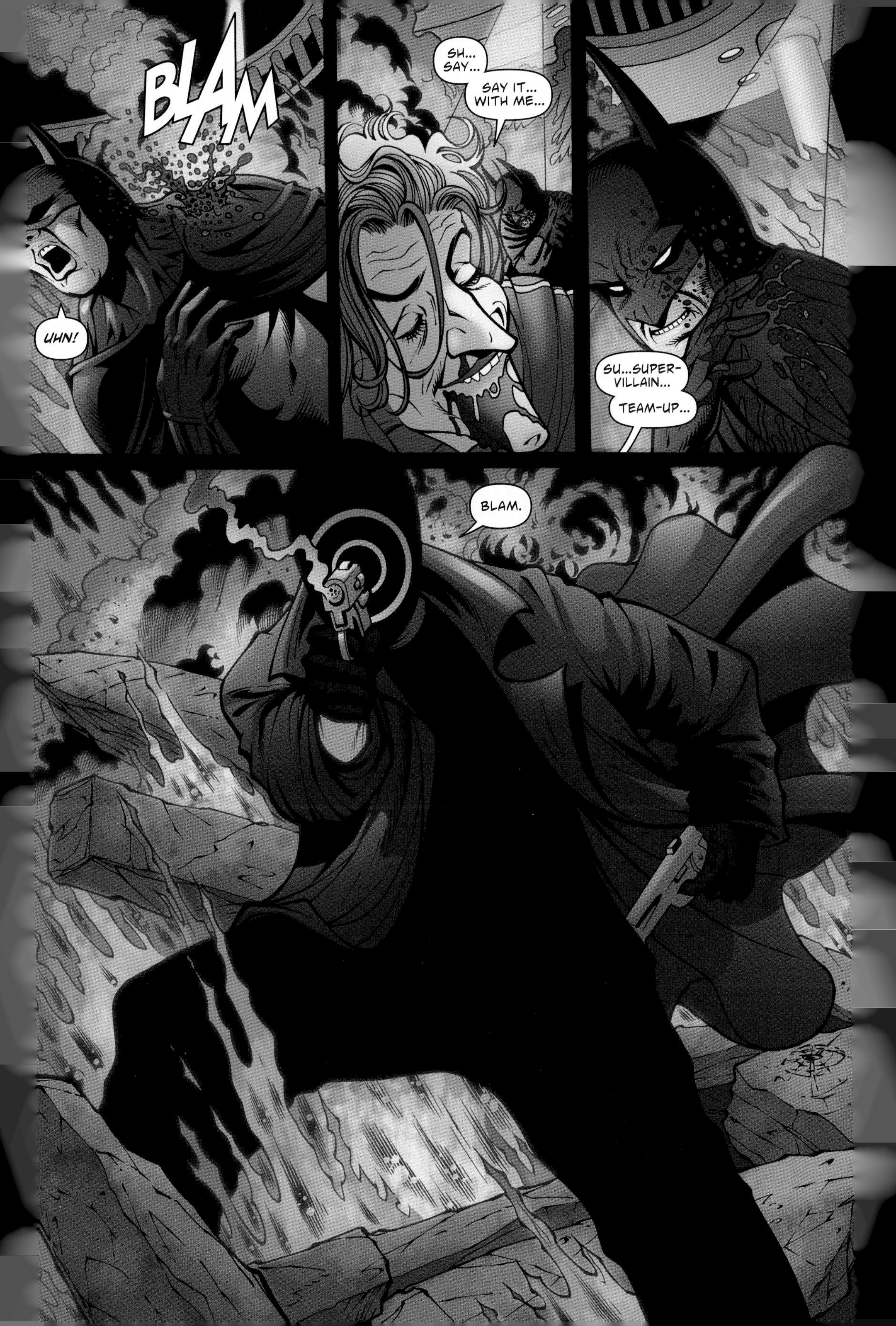
BLAM
UHN!
SH... SAY...
SAY IT... WITH ME...
SU...SUPER-VILLAIN...
TEAM-UP...
BLAM.

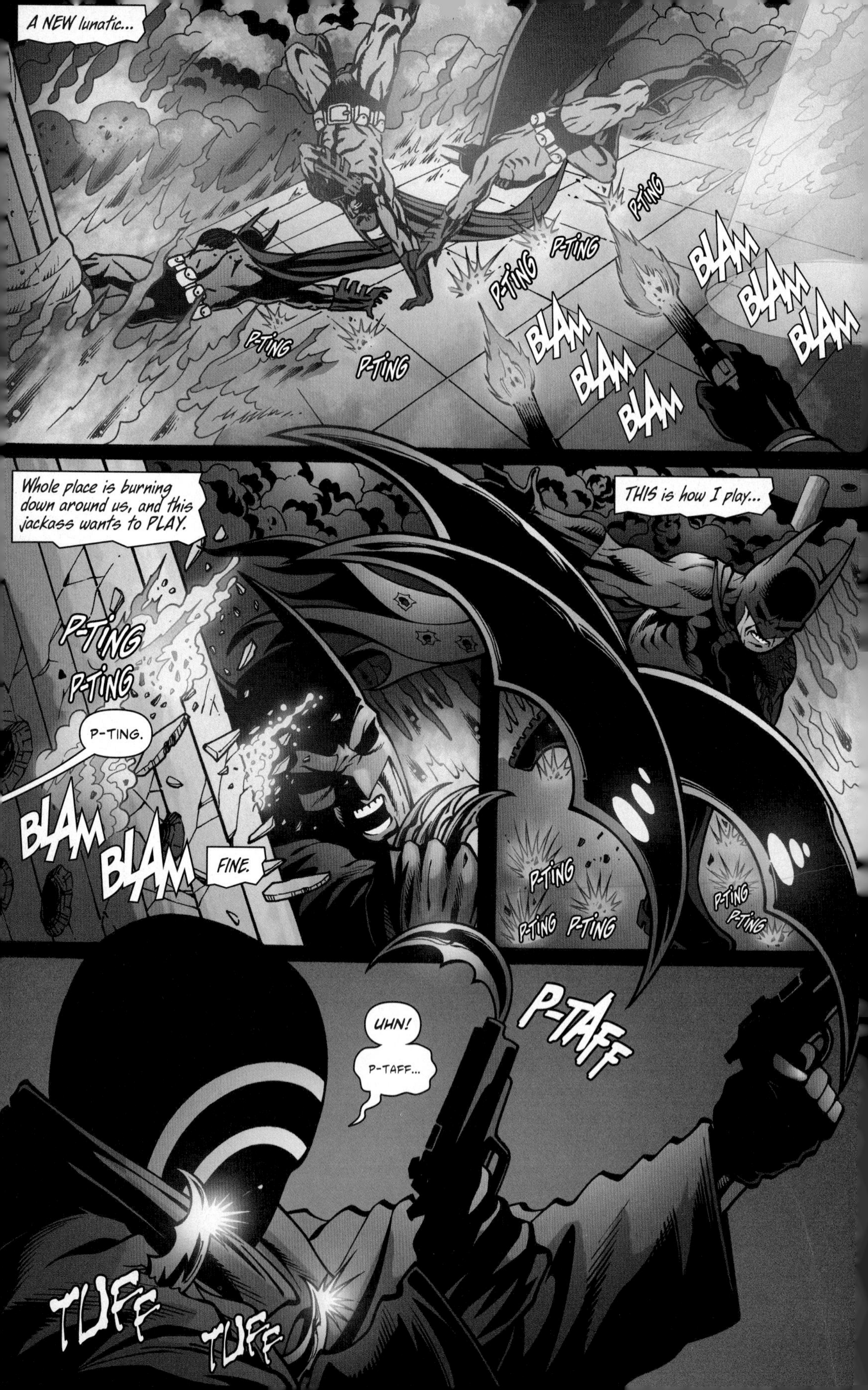

A NEW lunatic...
P-TING
P-TING
P-TING
P-TING
P-TING
P-TING
BLAM
BLAM
BLAM
BLAM
BLAM
BLAM
Whole place is burning down around us, and this jackass wants to PLAY.
P-TING
P-TING
P-TING.
BLAM
BLAM
FINE.
THIS is how I play...
P-TING
P-TING
P-TING
P-TING
P-TING
UHN!
P-TAFF...
P-TAFF
TUFF
TUFF

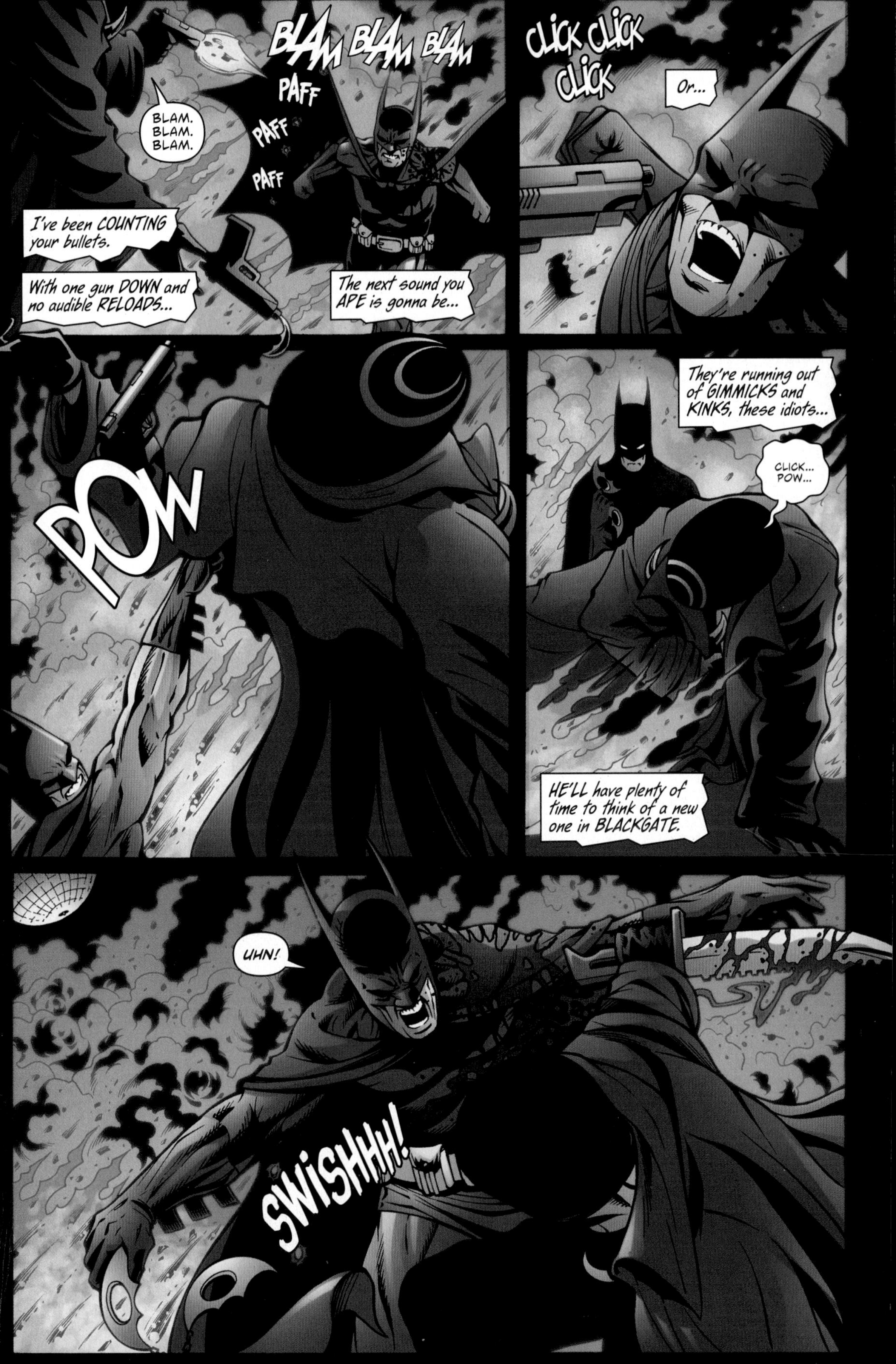
BLAM. BLAM. BLAM.
BLAM BLAM BLAM
PAFF
PAFF
PAFF
I've been COUNTING your bullets.
With one gun DOWN and no audible RELOADS...
The next sound you APE is gonna be...
CLICK CLICK CLICK
Or...
POW
They're running out of GIMMICKS and KINKS, these idiots...
CLICK... POW...
HE'LL have plenty of time to think of a new one in BLACKGATE.
UHN!
SWISHHH!

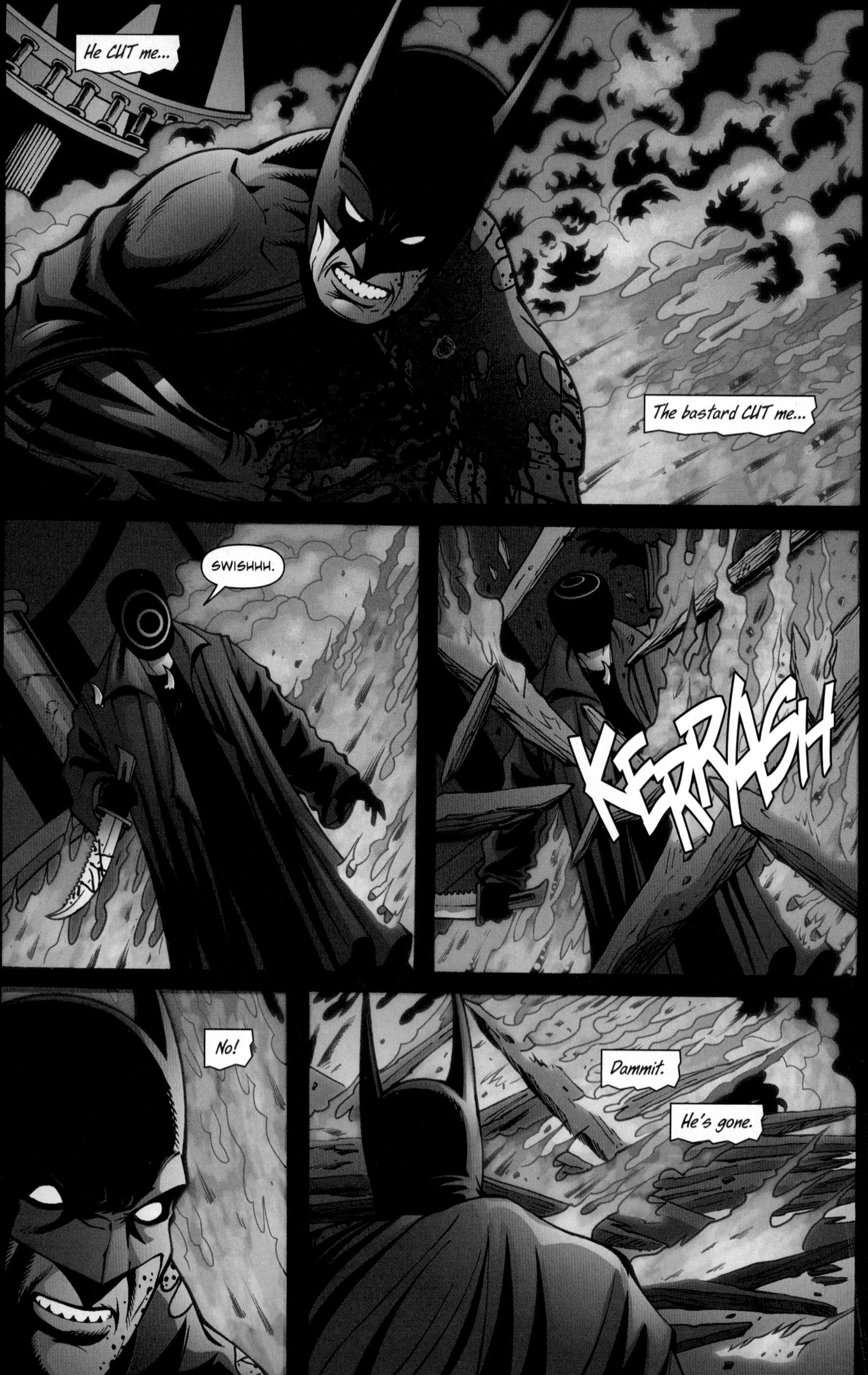
He CUT me...
The bastard CUT me...
SWISHHH.
KERRASH
No!
Dammit.
He's gone.

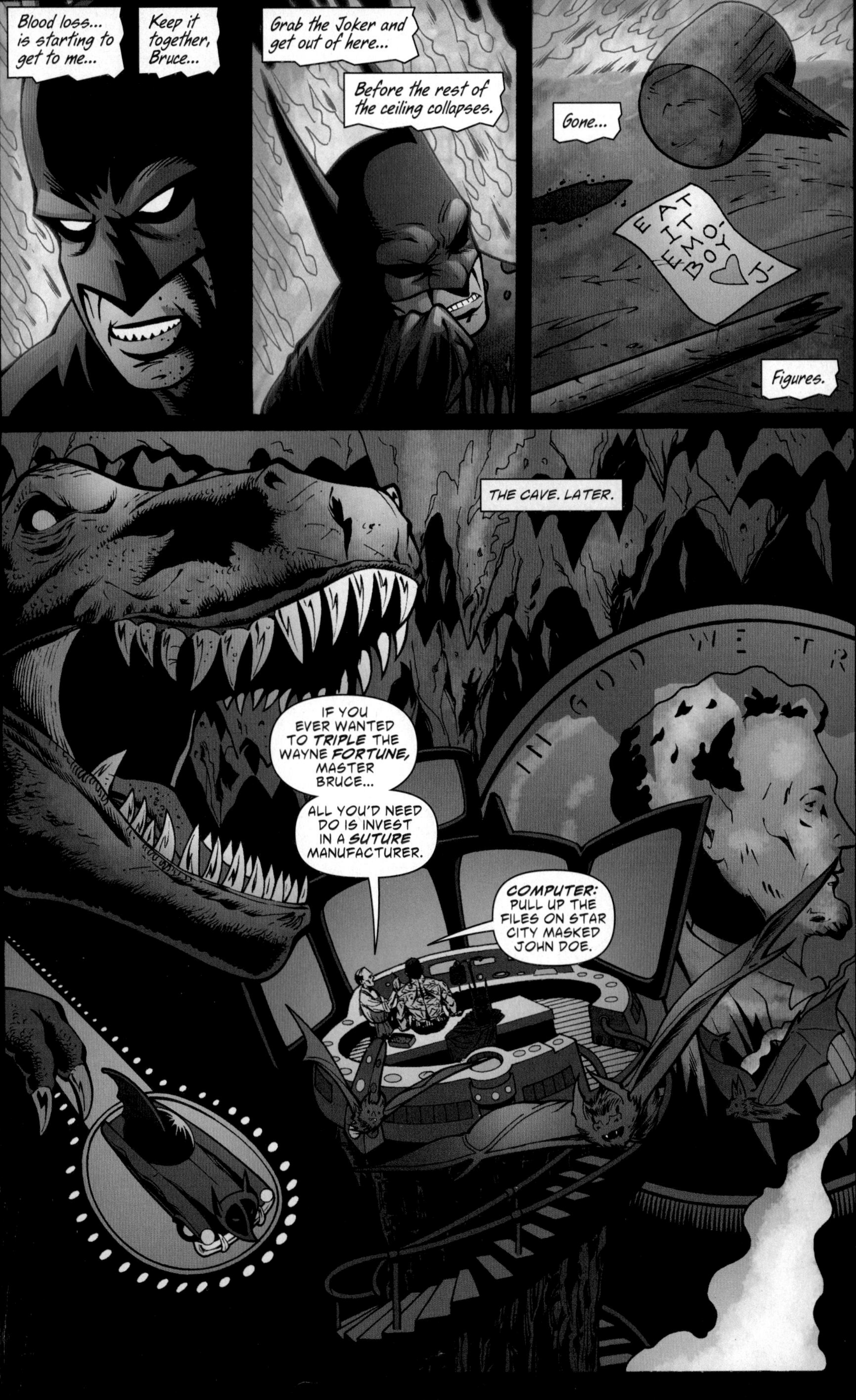
Blood loss... is starting to get to me...
Keep it together, Bruce...
Grab the Joker and get out of here...
Before the rest of the ceiling collapses.
Gone...
Figures.
THE CAVE. LATER.
IF YOU EVER WANTED TO TRIPLE THE WAYNE FORTUNE, MASTER BRUCE...
ALL YOU'D NEED DO IS INVEST IN A SUTURE MANUFACTURER.
COMPUTER: PULL UP THE FILES ON STAR CITY MASKED JOHN DOE.

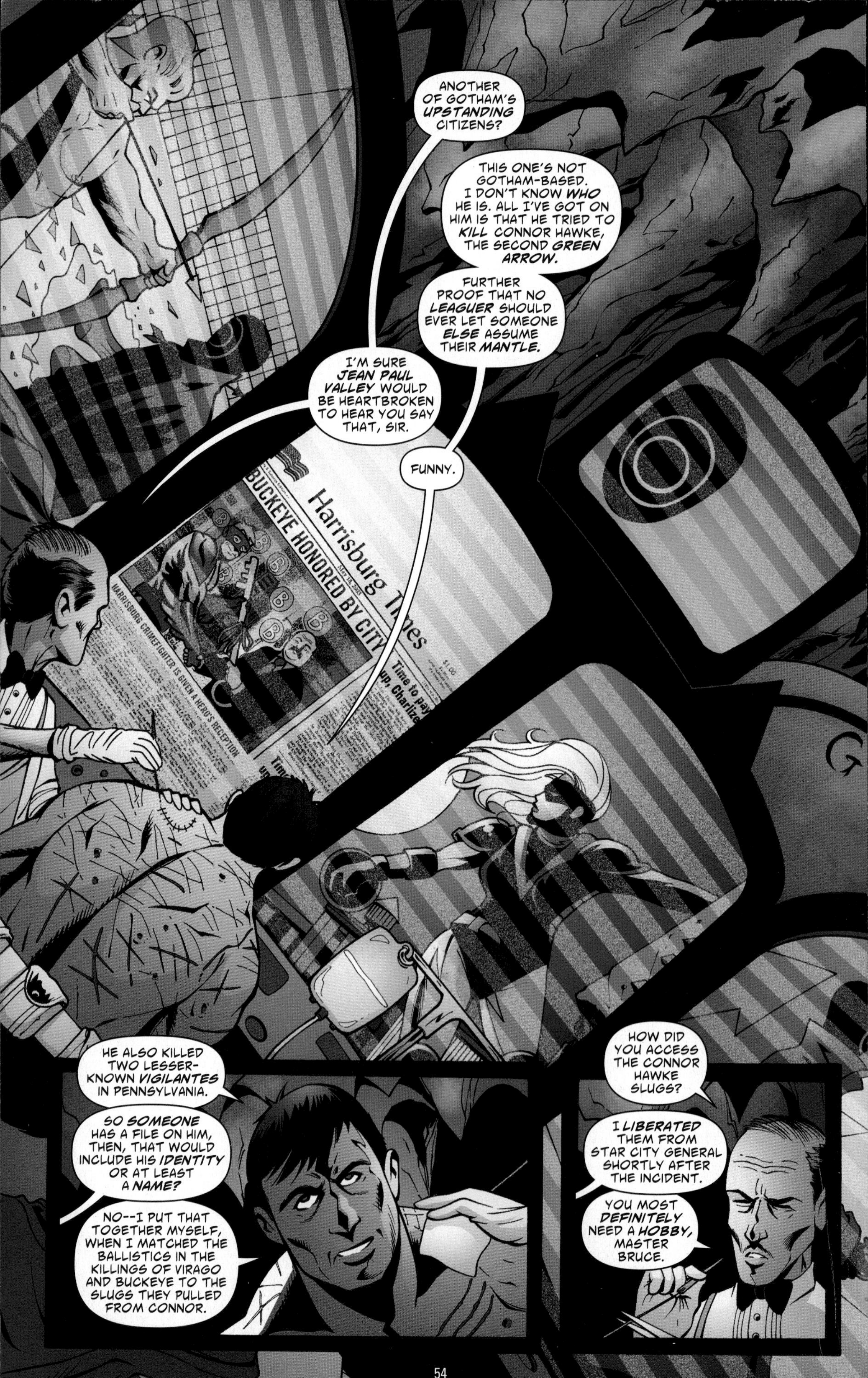
ANOTHER OF GOTHAM'S UPSTANDING CITIZENS?
THIS ONE'S NOT GOTHAM-BASED. I DON'T KNOW WHO HE IS. ALL I'VE GOT ON HIM IS THAT HE TRIED TO KILL CONNOR HAWKE, THE SECOND GREEN ARROW.
FURTHER PROOF THAT NO LEAGUER SHOULD EVER LET SOMEONE ELSE ASSUME THEIR MANTLE.
I'M SURE JEAN PAUL VALLEY WOULD BE HEARTBROKEN TO HEAR YOU SAY THAT, SIR.
FUNNY.
Harrisburg Times
BUCKEYE HONORED BY CITY
HARRISBURG CRIMEFIGHTER IS GIVEN A HERO'S RECEPTION
Time to pay up, Charlize
HE ALSO KILLED TWO LESSER-KNOWN VIGILANTES IN PENNSYLVANIA.
SO SOMEONE HAS A FILE ON HIM, THEN, THAT WOULD INCLUDE HIS IDENTITY OR AT LEAST A NAME?
NO--I PUT THAT TOGETHER MYSELF, WHEN I MATCHED THE BALLISTICS IN THE KILLINGS OF VIRAGO AND BUCKEYE TO THE SLUGS THEY PULLED FROM CONNOR.
HOW DID YOU ACCESS THE CONNOR HAWKE SLUGS?
I LIBERATED THEM FROM STAR CITY GENERAL SHORTLY AFTER THE INCIDENT.
YOU MOST DEFINITELY NEED A HOBBY, MASTER BRUCE.

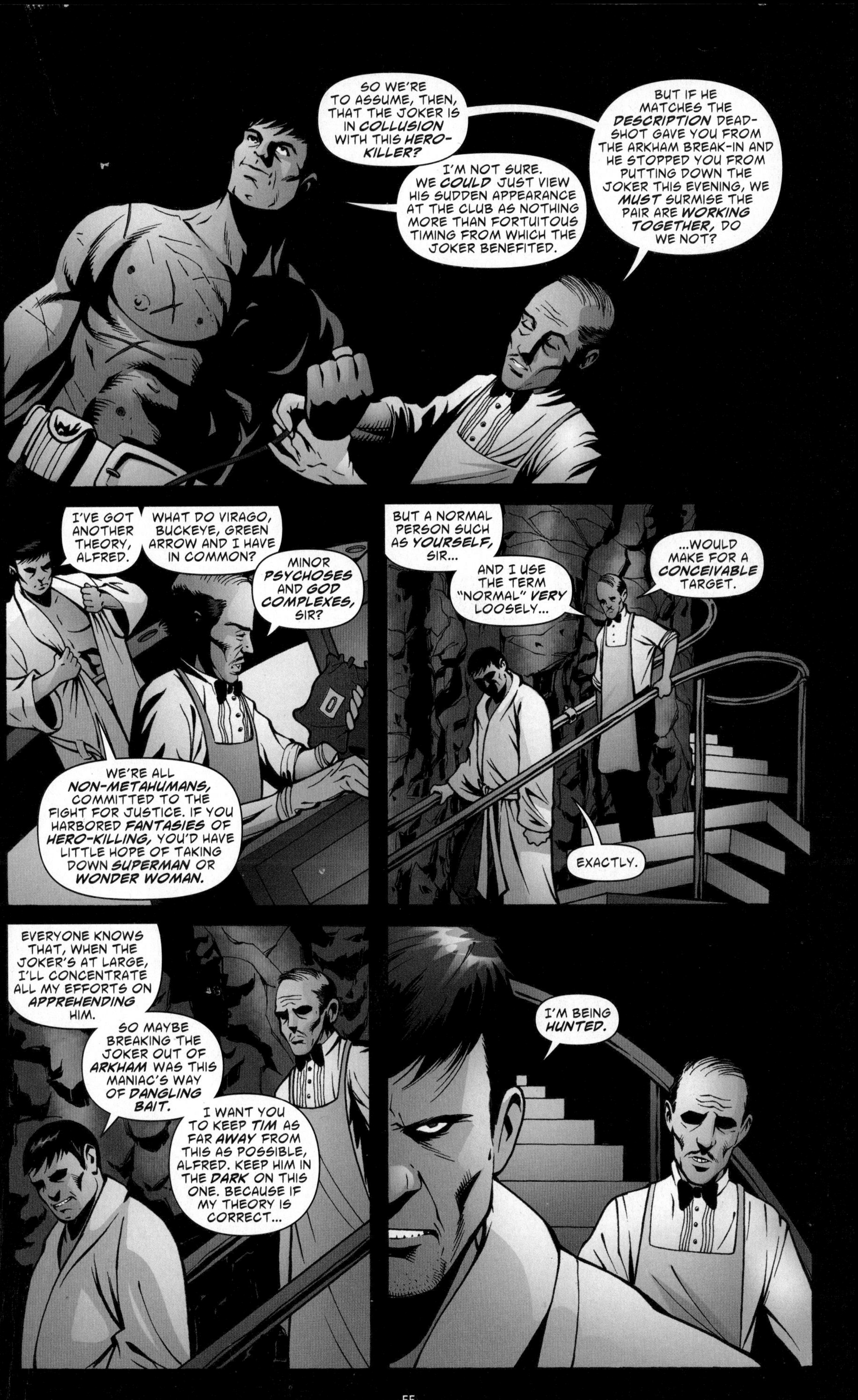
SO WE'RE TO ASSUME, THEN, THAT THE JOKER IS IN COLLUSION WITH THIS HERO-KILLER?
I'M NOT SURE. WE COULD JUST VIEW HIS SUDDEN APPEARANCE AT THE CLUB AS NOTHING MORE THAN FORTUITOUS TIMING FROM WHICH THE JOKER BENEFITED.
BUT IF HE MATCHES THE DESCRIPTION DEAD-SHOT GAVE YOU FROM THE ARKHAM BREAK-IN AND HE STOPPED YOU FROM PUTTING DOWN THE JOKER THIS EVENING, WE MUST SURMISE THE PAIR ARE WORKING TOGETHER, DO WE NOT?
I'VE GOT ANOTHER THEORY, ALFRED.
WHAT DO VIRAGO, BUCKEYE, GREEN ARROW AND I HAVE IN COMMON?
MINOR PSYCHOSES AND GOD COMPLEXES, SIR?
WE'RE ALL NON-METAHUMANS, COMMITTED TO THE FIGHT FOR JUSTICE. IF YOU HARBORED FANTASIES OF HERO-KILLING, YOU'D HAVE LITTLE HOPE OF TAKING DOWN SUPERMAN OR WONDER WOMAN.
BUT A NORMAL PERSON SUCH AS YOURSELF, SIR...
AND I USE THE TERM "NORMAL" VERY LOOSELY...
...WOULD MAKE FOR A CONCEIVABLE TARGET.
EXACTLY.
EVERYONE KNOWS THAT, WHEN THE JOKER'S AT LARGE, I'LL CONCENTRATE ALL MY EFFORTS ON APPREHENDING HIM.
SO MAYBE BREAKING THE JOKER OUT OF ARKHAM WAS THIS MANIAC'S WAY OF DANGLING BAIT.
I WANT YOU TO KEEP TIM AS FAR AWAY FROM THIS AS POSSIBLE, ALFRED. KEEP HIM IN THE DARK ON THIS ONE. BECAUSE IF MY THEORY IS CORRECT...
I'M BEING HUNTED.

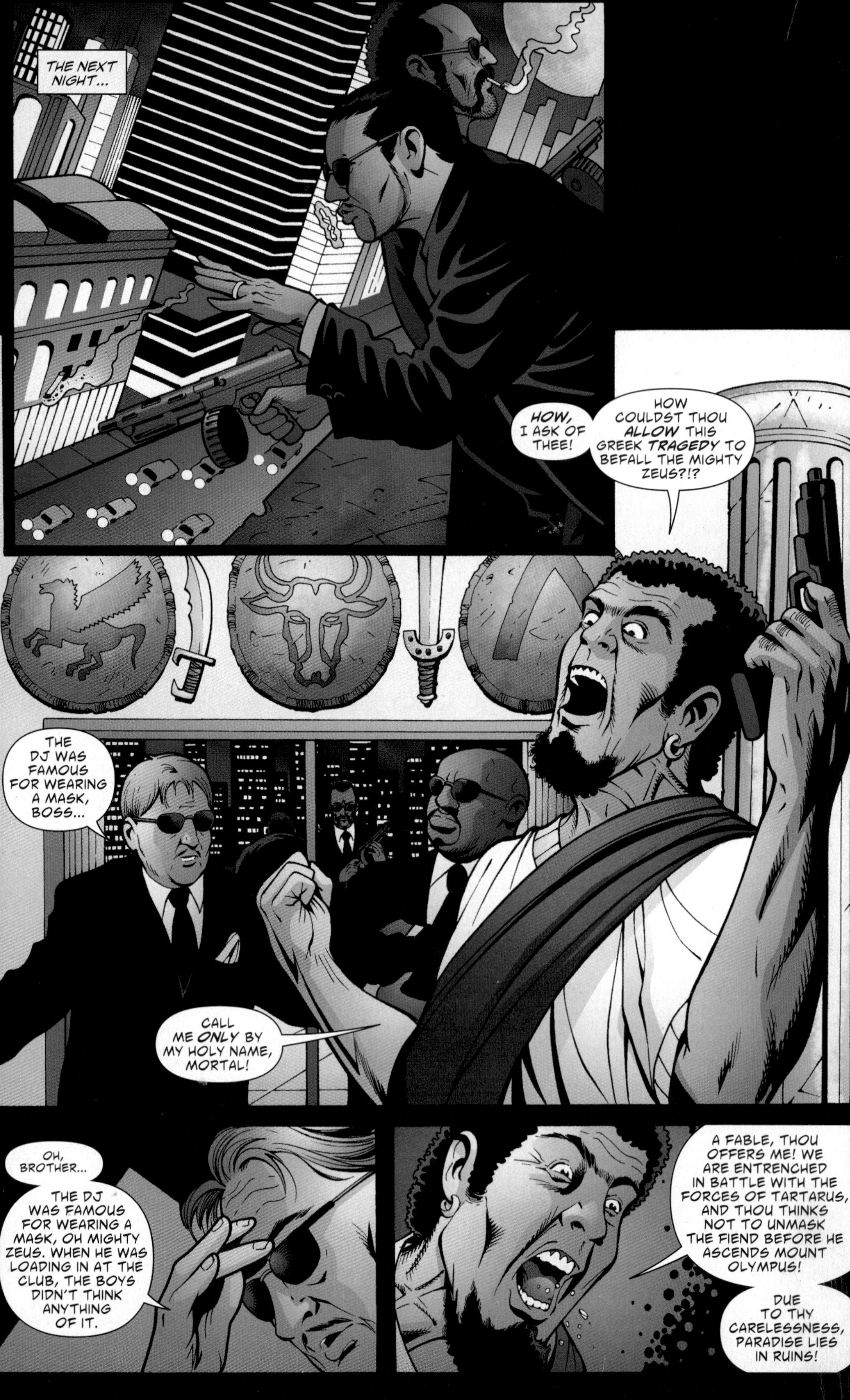
THE NEXT NIGHT...
HOW, I ASK OF THEE!
HOW COULDST THOU ALLOW THIS GREEK TRAGEDY TO BEFALL THE MIGHTY ZEUS?!?
THE DJ WAS FAMOUS FOR WEARING A MASK, BOSS...
CALL ME ONLY BY MY HOLY NAME, MORTAL!
OH, BROTHER...
THE DJ WAS FAMOUS FOR WEARING A MASK, OH MIGHTY ZEUS. WHEN HE WAS LOADING IN AT THE CLUB, THE BOYS DIDN'T THINK ANYTHING OF IT.
A FABLE, THOU OFFERS ME! WE ARE ENTRENCHED IN BATTLE WITH THE FORCES OF TARTARUS, AND THOU THINKS NOT TO UNMASK THE FIEND BEFORE HE ASCENDS MOUNT OLYMPUS!
DUE TO THY CARELESSNESS, PARADISE LIES IN RUINS!

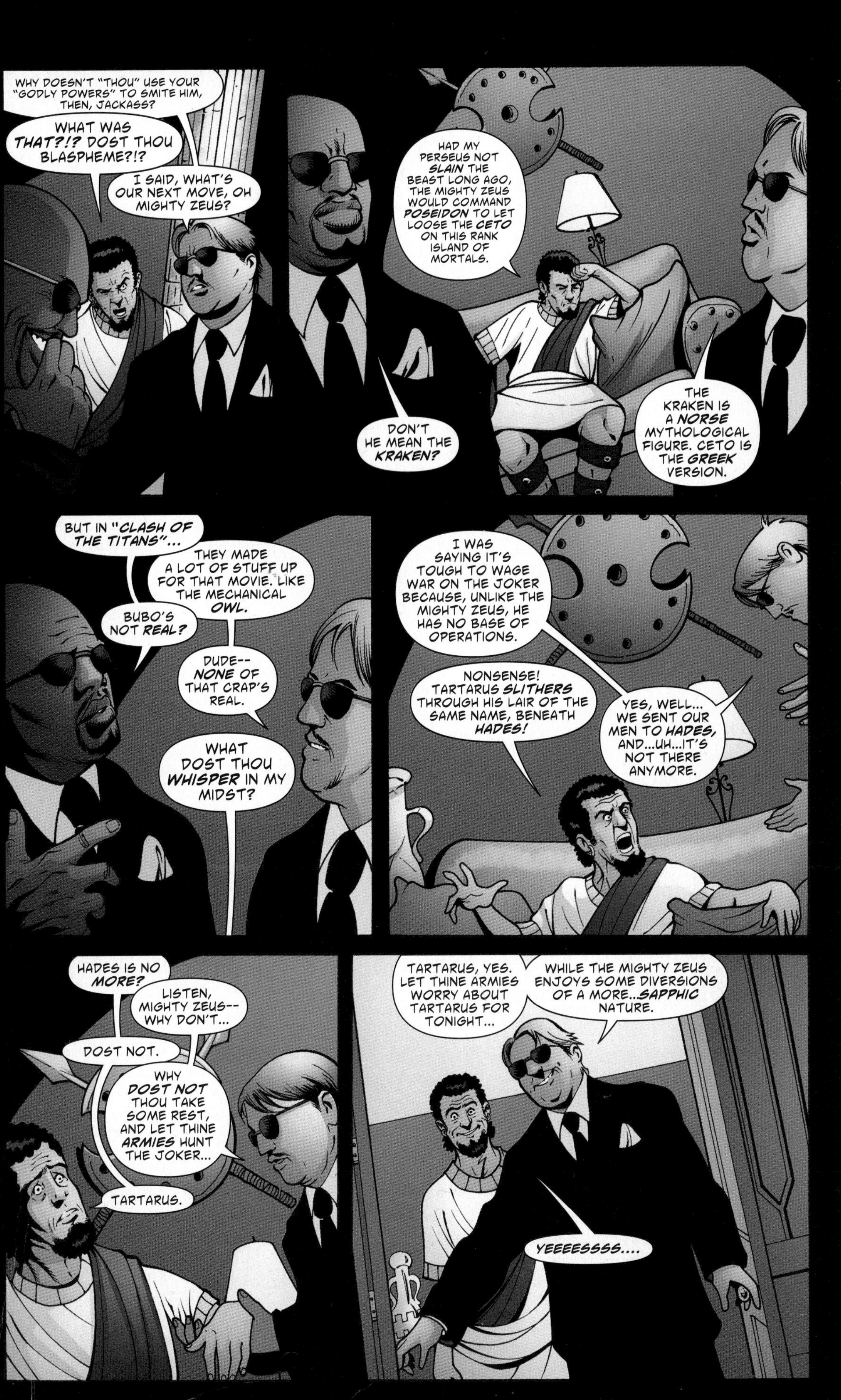

WHY DOESN'T "THOU" USE YOUR "GODLY POWERS" TO SMITE HIM, THEN, JACKASS?
WHAT WAS THAT?!? DOST THOU BLASPHEME?!?
I SAID, WHAT'S OUR NEXT MOVE, OH MIGHTY ZEUS?
HAD MY PERSEUS NOT SLAIN THE BEAST LONG AGO, THE MIGHTY ZEUS WOULD COMMAND POSEIDON TO LET LOOSE THE CETO ON THIS RANK ISLAND OF MORTALS.
DON'T HE MEAN THE KRAKEN?
THE KRAKEN IS A NORSE MYTHOLOGICAL FIGURE. CETO IS THE GREEK VERSION.
BUT IN "CLASH OF THE TITANS"...
THEY MADE A LOT OF STUFF UP FOR THAT MOVIE. LIKE THE MECHANICAL OWL.
BUBO'S NOT REAL?
DUDE-- NONE OF THAT CRAP'S REAL.
WHAT DOST THOU WHISPER IN MY MIDST?
I WAS SAYING IT'S TOUGH TO WAGE WAR ON THE JOKER BECAUSE, UNLIKE THE MIGHTY ZEUS, HE HAS NO BASE OF OPERATIONS.
NONSENSE! TARTARUS SLITHERS THROUGH HIS LAIR OF THE SAME NAME, BENEATH HADES!
YES, WELL... WE SENT OUR MEN TO HADES, AND...UH...IT'S NOT THERE ANYMORE.
HADES IS NO MORE?
LISTEN, MIGHTY ZEUS-- WHY DON'T...
DOST NOT.
WHY DOST NOT THOU TAKE SOME REST, AND LET THINE ARMIES HUNT THE JOKER...
TARTARUS.
TARTARUS, YES. LET THINE ARMIES WORRY ABOUT TARTARUS FOR TONIGHT...
WHILE THE MIGHTY ZEUS ENJOYS SOME DIVERSIONS OF A MORE...SAPPHIC NATURE.
YEEEESSSS....

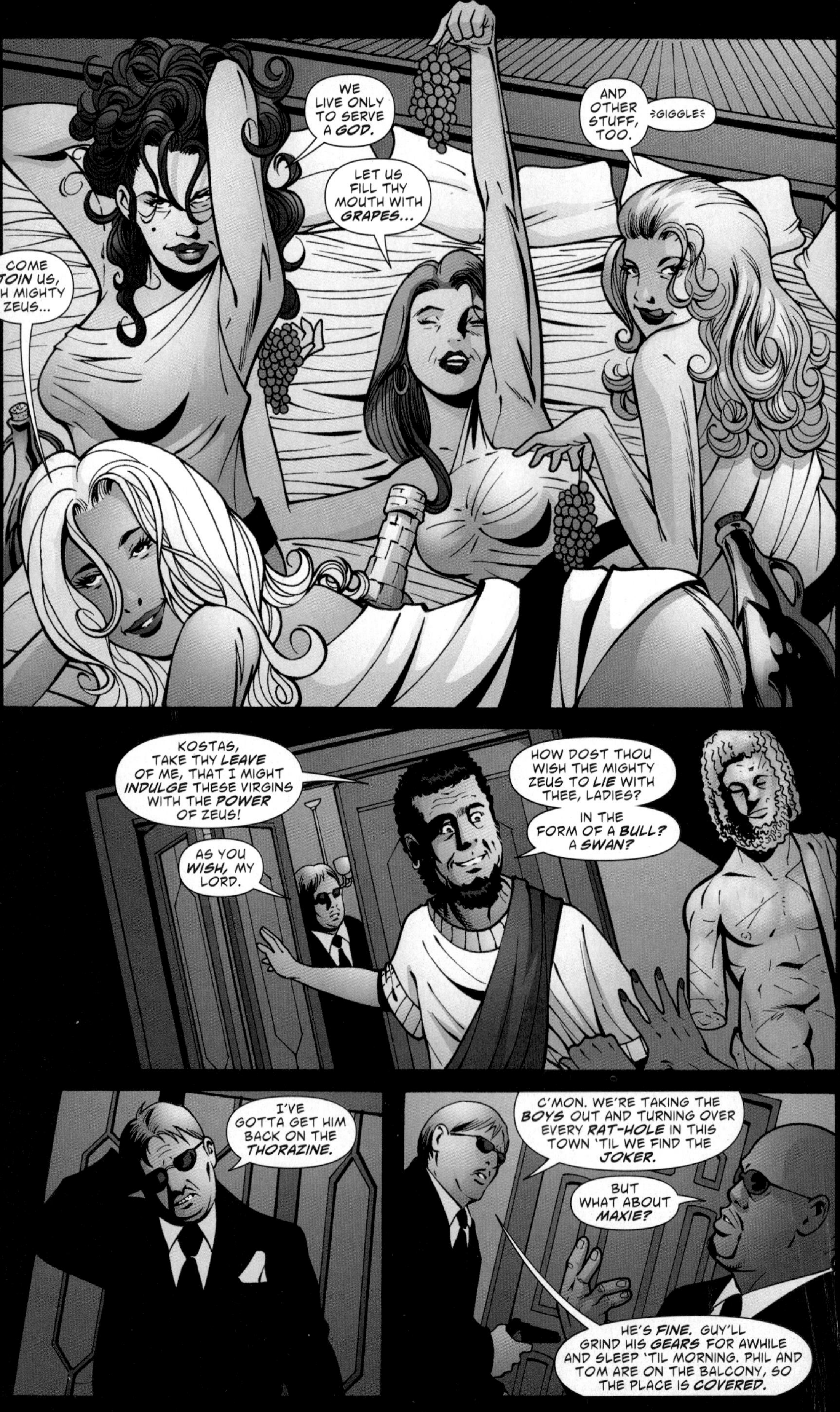
WE LIVE ONLY TO SERVE A GOD.
AND OTHER STUFF, TOO.
GIGGLE
LET US FILL THY MOUTH WITH GRAPES...
COME JOIN US, OH MIGHTY ZEUS...
KOSTAS, TAKE THY LEAVE OF ME, THAT I MIGHT INDULGE THESE VIRGINS WITH THE POWER OF ZEUS!
AS YOU WISH, MY LORD.
HOW DOST THOU WISH THE MIGHTY ZEUS TO LIE WITH THEE, LADIES?
IN THE FORM OF A BULL? A SWAN?
I'VE GOTTA GET HIM BACK ON THE THORAZINE.
C'MON. WE'RE TAKING THE BOYS OUT AND TURNING OVER EVERY RAT-HOLE IN THIS TOWN 'TIL WE FIND THE JOKER.
BUT WHAT ABOUT MAXIE?
HE'S FINE. GUY'LL GRIND HIS GEARS FOR AWHILE AND SLEEP 'TIL MORNING. PHIL AND TOM ARE ON THE BALCONY, SO THE PLACE IS COVERED.

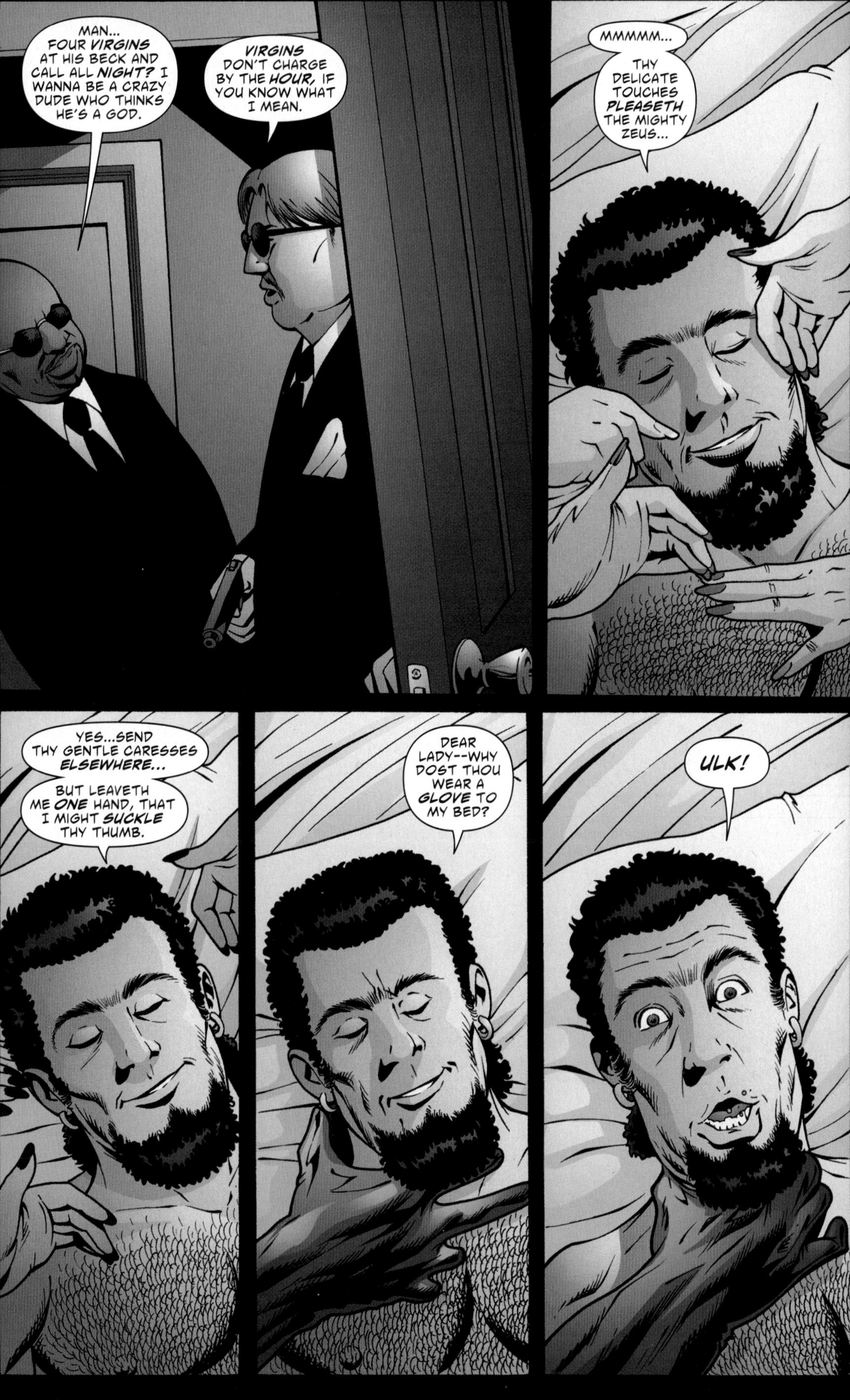
MAN... FOUR VIRGINS AT HIS BECK AND CALL ALL NIGHT? I WANNA BE A CRAZY DUDE WHO THINKS HE'S A GOD.
VIRGINS DON'T CHARGE BY THE HOUR, IF YOU KNOW WHAT I MEAN.
MMMMM...
THY DELICATE TOUCHES PLEASETH THE MIGHTY ZEUS...
YES...SEND THY GENTLE CARESSES ELSEWHERE...
BUT LEAVETH ME ONE HAND, THAT I MIGHT SUCKLE THY THUMB.
DEAR LADY--WHY DOST THOU WEAR A GLOVE TO MY BED?
ULK!

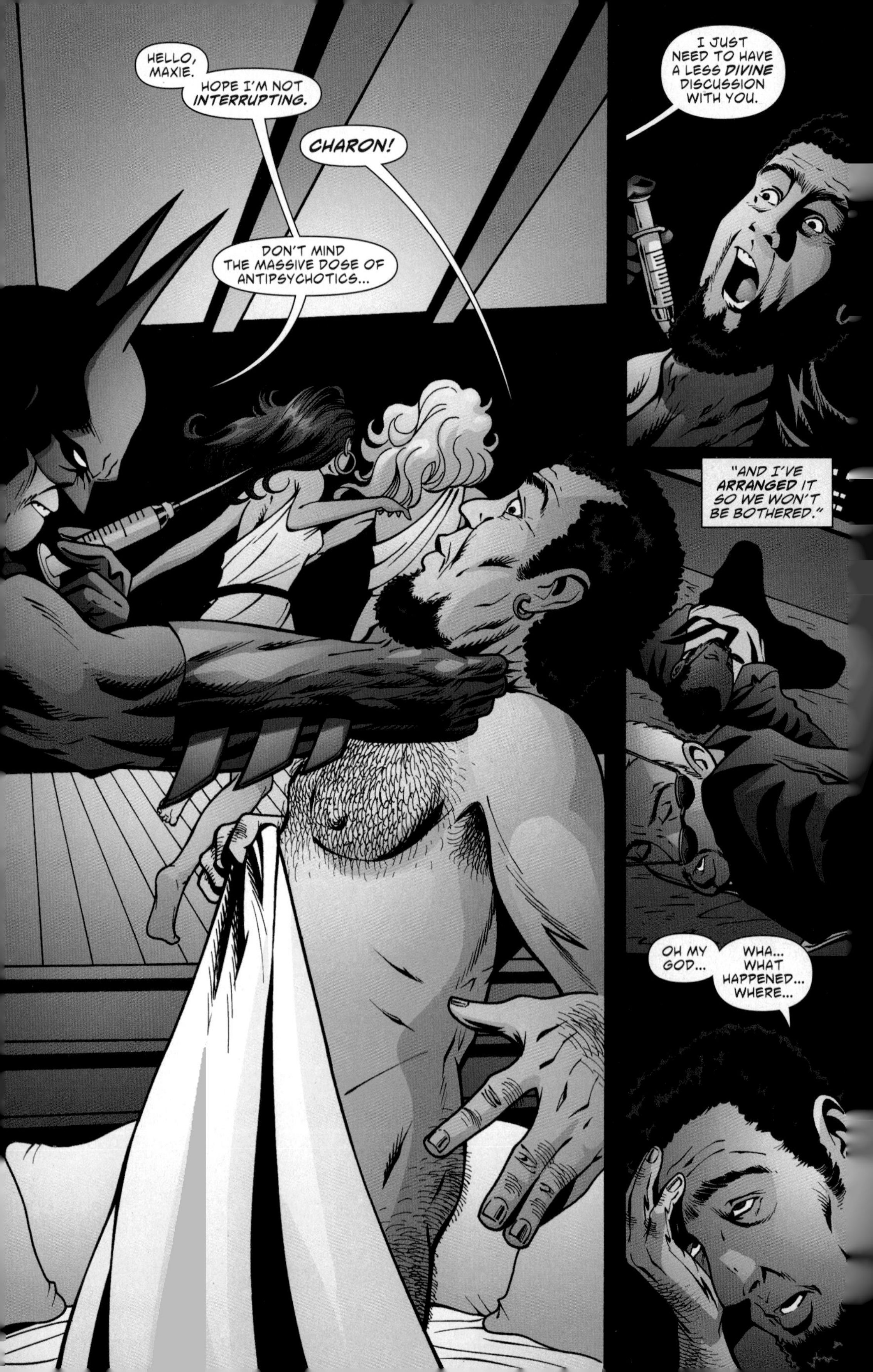
HELLO, MAXIE.
HOPE I'M NOT *INTERRUPTING.*
CHARON!
DON'T MIND THE MASSIVE DOSE OF ANTIPSYCHOTICS...
I JUST NEED TO HAVE A LESS *DIVINE* DISCUSSION WITH YOU.
"AND I'VE *ARRANGED* IT SO WE WON'T BE BOTHERED."
OH MY GOD...
WHA... WHAT HAPPENED... WHERE...

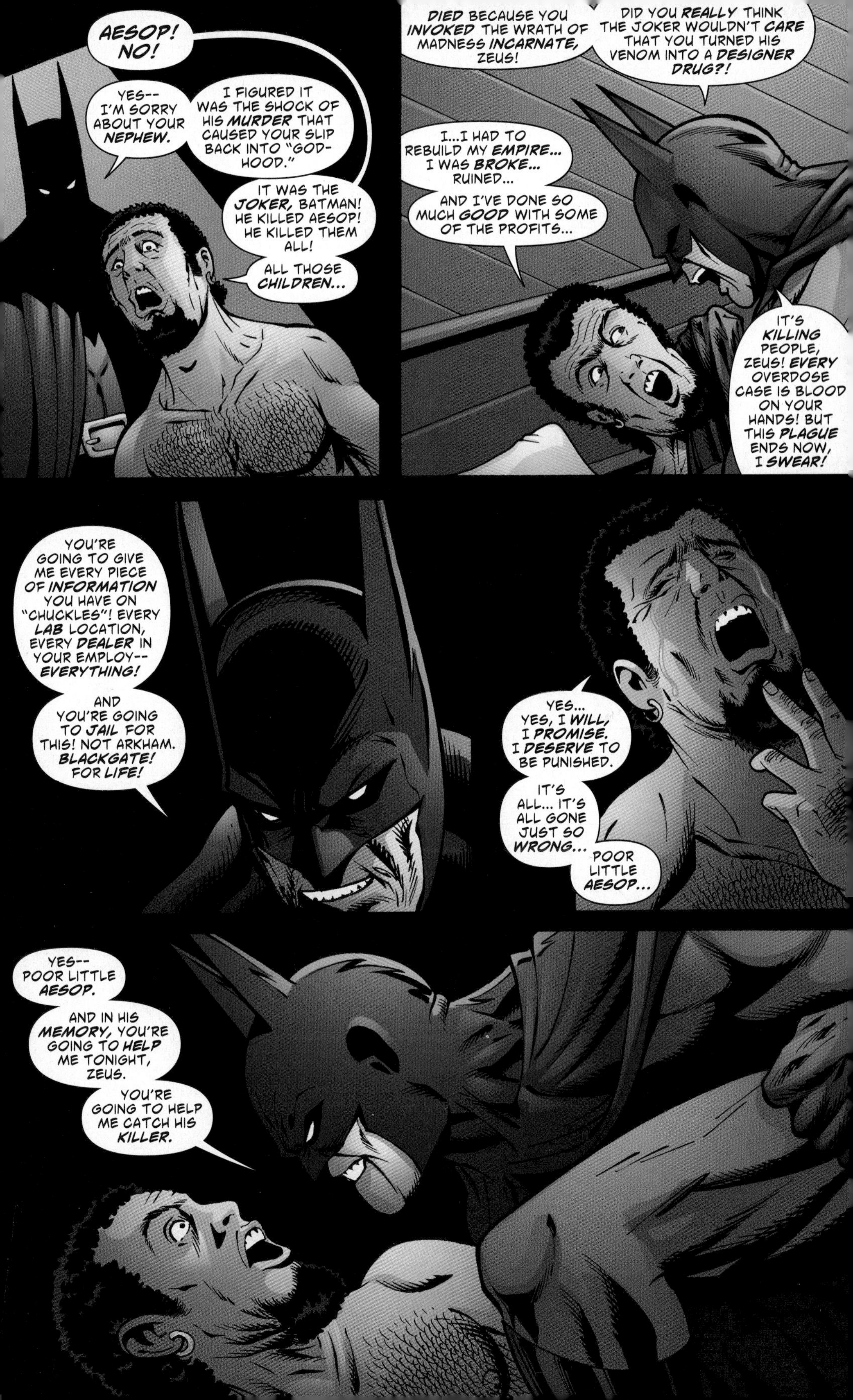
AESOP! NO!
YES-- I'M SORRY ABOUT YOUR NEPHEW.
I FIGURED IT WAS THE SHOCK OF HIS MURDER THAT CAUSED YOUR SLIP BACK INTO "GOD-HOOD."
IT WAS THE JOKER, BATMAN! HE KILLED AESOP! HE KILLED THEM ALL!
ALL THOSE CHILDREN...
DIED BECAUSE YOU INVOKED THE WRATH OF MADNESS INCARNATE, ZEUS!
DID YOU REALLY THINK THE JOKER WOULDN'T CARE THAT YOU TURNED HIS VENOM INTO A DESIGNER DRUG?!
I...I HAD TO REBUILD MY EMPIRE... I WAS BROKE... RUINED...
AND I'VE DONE SO MUCH GOOD WITH SOME OF THE PROFITS...
IT'S KILLING PEOPLE, ZEUS! EVERY OVERDOSE CASE IS BLOOD ON YOUR HANDS! BUT THIS PLAGUE ENDS NOW, I SWEAR!
YOU'RE GOING TO GIVE ME EVERY PIECE OF INFORMATION YOU HAVE ON "CHUCKLES"! EVERY LAB LOCATION, EVERY DEALER IN YOUR EMPLOY-- EVERYTHING!
AND YOU'RE GOING TO JAIL FOR THIS! NOT ARKHAM. BLACKGATE! FOR LIFE!
YES... YES, I WILL, I PROMISE. I DESERVE TO BE PUNISHED.
IT'S ALL... IT'S ALL GONE JUST SO WRONG...
POOR LITTLE AESOP...
YES-- POOR LITTLE AESOP.
AND IN HIS MEMORY, YOU'RE GOING TO HELP ME TONIGHT, ZEUS.
YOU'RE GOING TO HELP ME CATCH HIS KILLER.

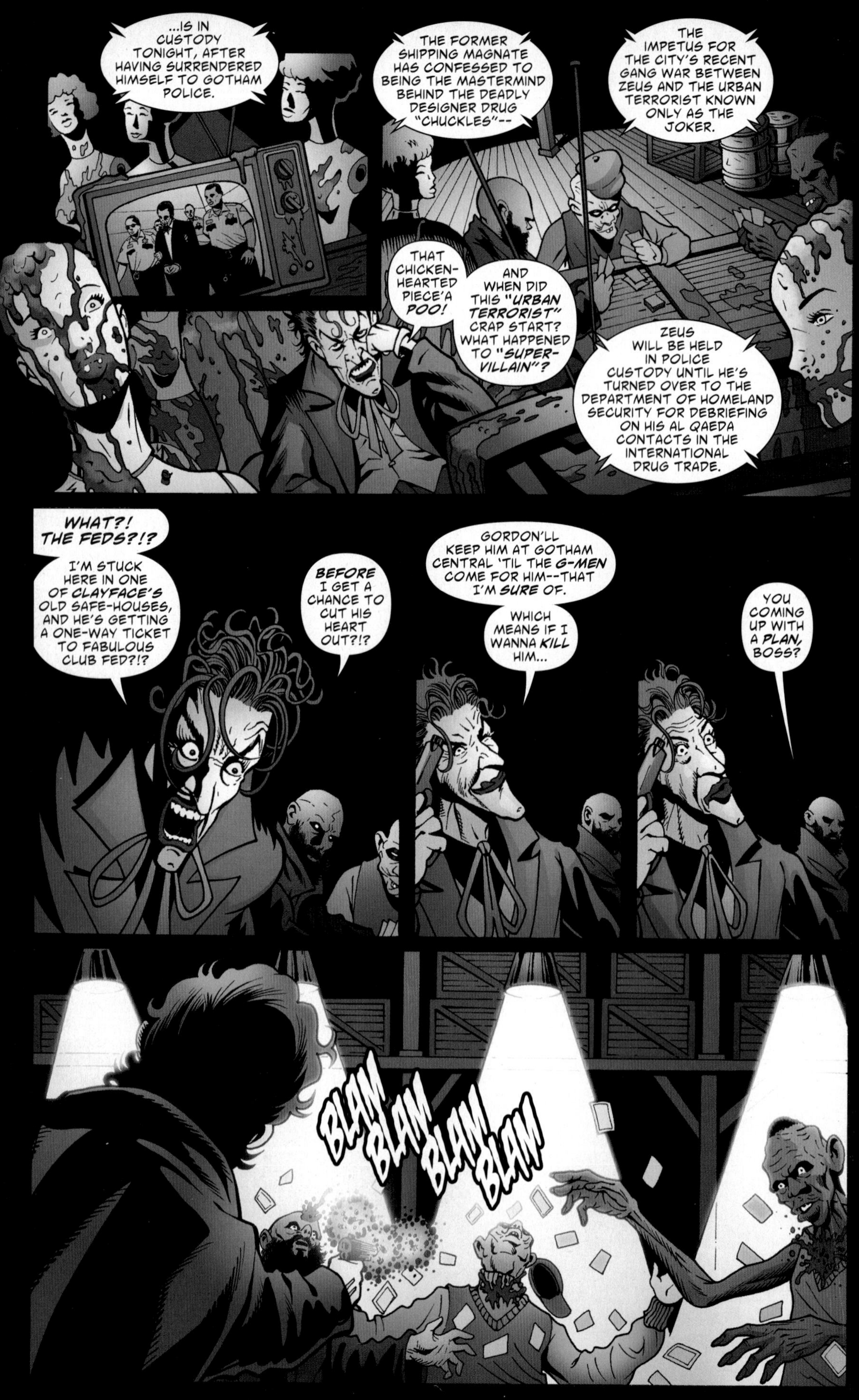
...IS IN CUSTODY TONIGHT, AFTER HAVING SURRENDERED HIMSELF TO GOTHAM POLICE.
THE FORMER SHIPPING MAGNATE HAS CONFESSED TO BEING THE MASTERMIND BEHIND THE DEADLY DESIGNER DRUG "CHUCKLES"--
THE IMPETUS FOR THE CITY'S RECENT GANG WAR BETWEEN ZEUS AND THE URBAN TERRORIST KNOWN ONLY AS THE JOKER.
THAT CHICKEN-HEARTED PIECE'A POO!
AND WHEN DID THIS "URBAN TERRORIST" CRAP START? WHAT HAPPENED TO "SUPER-VILLAIN"?
ZEUS WILL BE HELD IN POLICE CUSTODY UNTIL HE'S TURNED OVER TO THE DEPARTMENT OF HOMELAND SECURITY FOR DEBRIEFING ON HIS AL QAEDA CONTACTS IN THE INTERNATIONAL DRUG TRADE.
WHAT?! THE FEDS?!?
I'M STUCK HERE IN ONE OF CLAYFACE'S OLD SAFE-HOUSES, AND HE'S GETTING A ONE-WAY TICKET TO FABULOUS CLUB FED?!?
BEFORE I GET A CHANCE TO CUT HIS HEART OUT?!?
GORDON'LL KEEP HIM AT GOTHAM CENTRAL 'TIL THE G-MEN COME FOR HIM--THAT I'M SURE OF.
WHICH MEANS IF I WANNA KILL HIM...
YOU COMING UP WITH A PLAN, BOSS?
BLAM BLAM BLAM BLAM

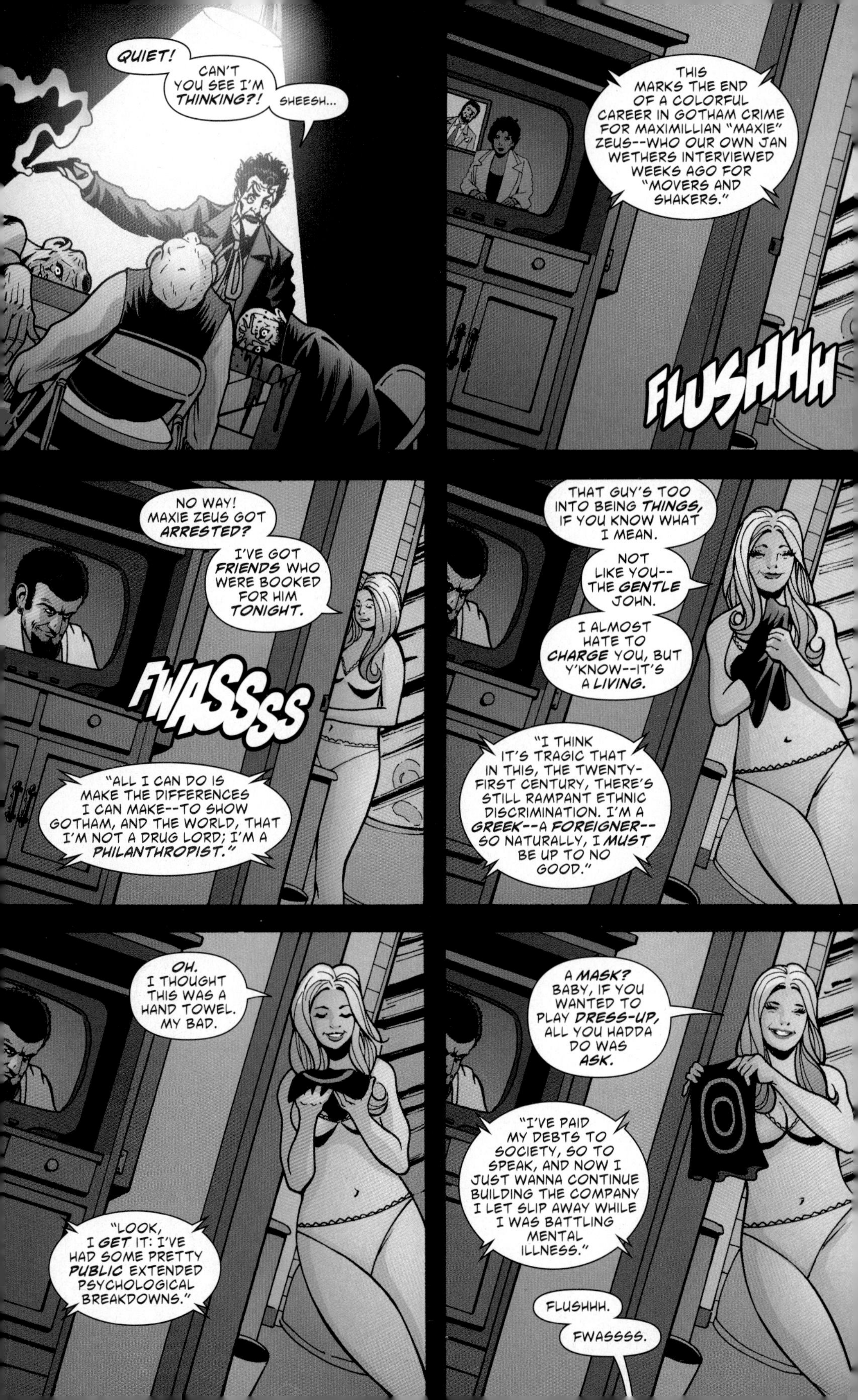
QUIET!
CAN'T YOU SEE I'M THINKING?!
SHEESH...
THIS MARKS THE END OF A COLORFUL CAREER IN GOTHAM CRIME FOR MAXIMILLIAN "MAXIE" ZEUS--WHO OUR OWN JAN WETHERS INTERVIEWED WEEKS AGO FOR "MOVERS AND SHAKERS."
FLUSHHH
NO WAY! MAXIE ZEUS GOT ARRESTED?
I'VE GOT FRIENDS WHO WERE BOOKED FOR HIM TONIGHT.
FWASSSSS
"ALL I CAN DO IS MAKE THE DIFFERENCES I CAN MAKE--TO SHOW GOTHAM, AND THE WORLD, THAT I'M NOT A DRUG LORD; I'M A PHILANTHROPIST."
THAT GUY'S TOO INTO BEING THINGS, IF YOU KNOW WHAT I MEAN.
NOT LIKE YOU--THE GENTLE JOHN.
I ALMOST HATE TO CHARGE YOU, BUT Y'KNOW--IT'S A LIVING.
"I THINK IT'S TRAGIC THAT IN THIS, THE TWENTY-FIRST CENTURY, THERE'S STILL RAMPANT ETHNIC DISCRIMINATION. I'M A GREEK--A FOREIGNER--SO NATURALLY, I MUST BE UP TO NO GOOD."
OH. I THOUGHT THIS WAS A HAND TOWEL. MY BAD.
"LOOK, I GET IT: I'VE HAD SOME PRETTY PUBLIC EXTENDED PSYCHOLOGICAL BREAKDOWNS."
A MASK? BABY, IF YOU WANTED TO PLAY DRESS-UP, ALL YOU HADDA DO WAS ASK.
"I'VE PAID MY DEBTS TO SOCIETY, SO TO SPEAK, AND NOW I JUST WANNA CONTINUE BUILDING THE COMPANY I LET SLIP AWAY WHILE I WAS BATTLING MENTAL ILLNESS."
FLUSHHH.
FWASSSS.

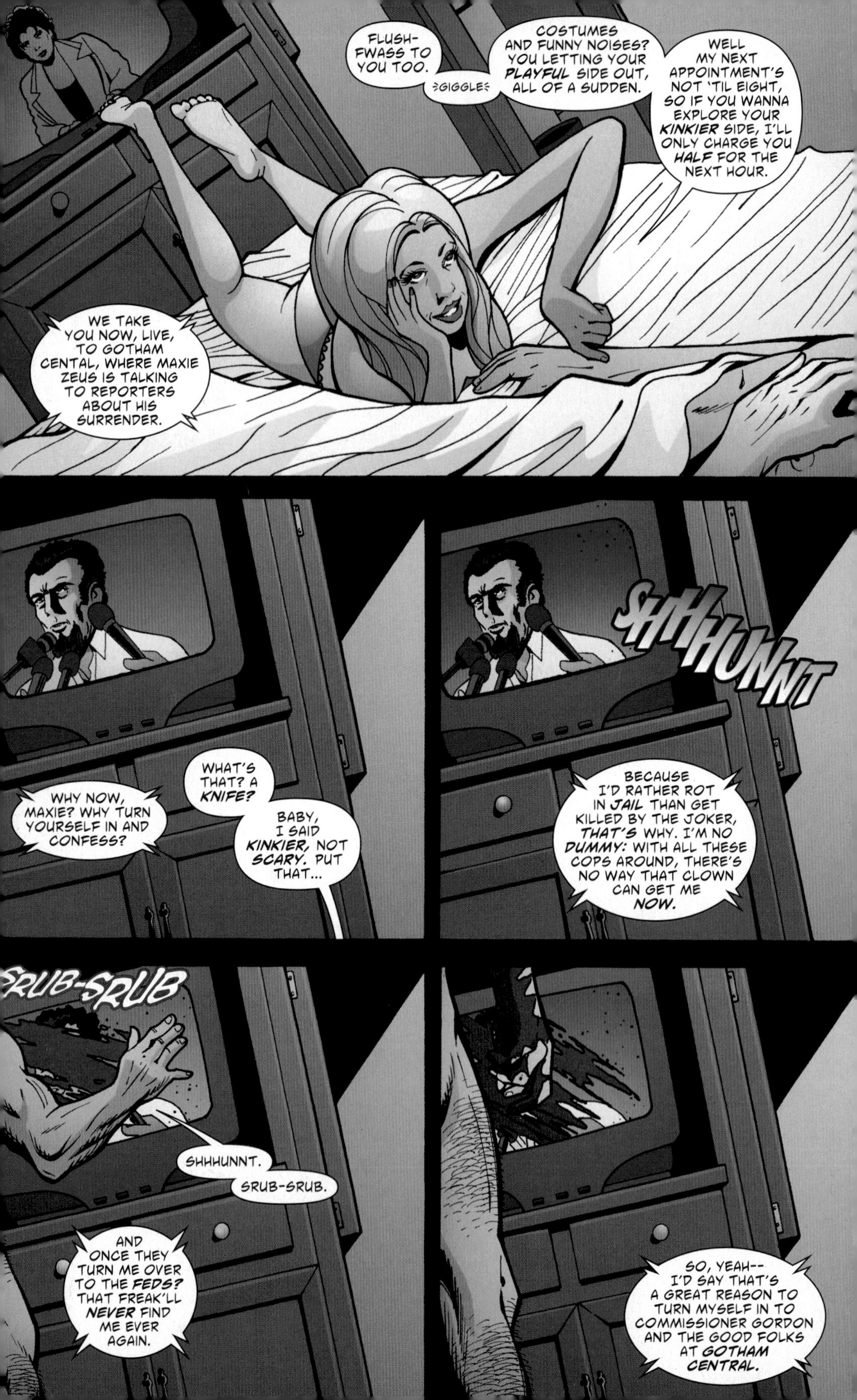

FLUSH-FWASS TO YOU TOO.
GIGGLE
COSTUMES AND FUNNY NOISES? YOU LETTING YOUR PLAYFUL SIDE OUT, ALL OF A SUDDEN.
WELL MY NEXT APPOINTMENT'S NOT 'TIL EIGHT, SO IF YOU WANNA EXPLORE YOUR KINKIER SIDE, I'LL ONLY CHARGE YOU HALF FOR THE NEXT HOUR.
WE TAKE YOU NOW, LIVE, TO GOTHAM CENTAL, WHERE MAXIE ZEUS IS TALKING TO REPORTERS ABOUT HIS SURRENDER.
WHY NOW, MAXIE? WHY TURN YOURSELF IN AND CONFESS?
WHAT'S THAT? A KNIFE?
BABY, I SAID KINKIER, NOT SCARY. PUT THAT...
SHHHUNNT
BECAUSE I'D RATHER ROT IN JAIL THAN GET KILLED BY THE JOKER, THAT'S WHY. I'M NO DUMMY: WITH ALL THESE COPS AROUND, THERE'S NO WAY THAT CLOWN CAN GET ME NOW.
SRUB-SRUB
SHHHUNNT.
SRUB-SRUB.
AND ONCE THEY TURN ME OVER TO THE FEDS? THAT FREAK'LL NEVER FIND ME EVER AGAIN.
SO, YEAH-- I'D SAY THAT'S A GREAT REASON TO TURN MYSELF IN TO COMMISSIONER GORDON AND THE GOOD FOLKS AT GOTHAM CENTRAL.

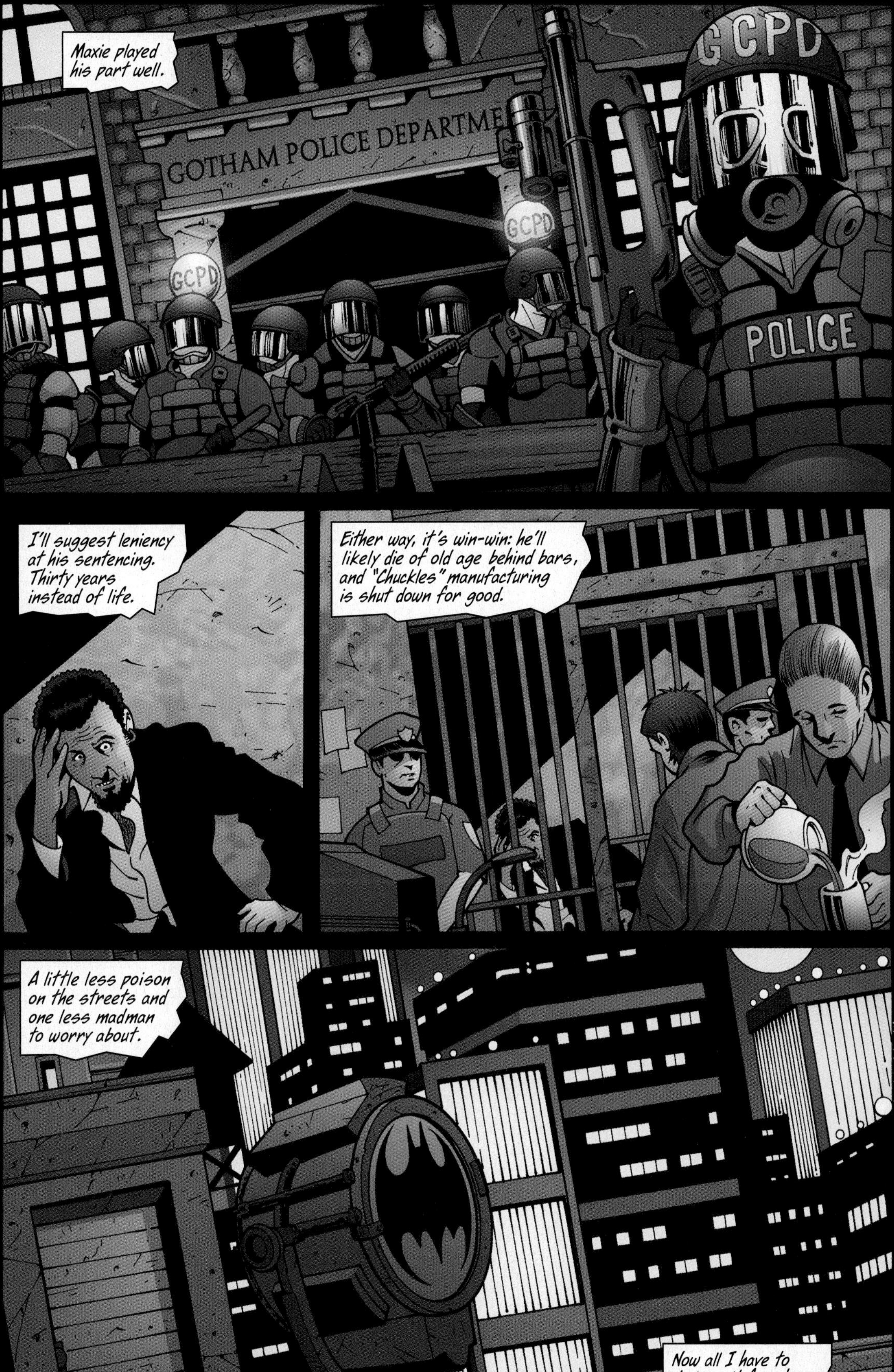
Maxie played his part well.
GCPD
GOTHAM POLICE DEPARTME
GCPD
GCPD
POLICE
I'll suggest leniency at his sentencing. Thirty years instead of life.
Either way, it's win-win: he'll likely die of old age behind bars, and "Chuckles" manufacturing is shut down for good.
A little less poison on the streets and one less madman to worry about.
Now all I have to do is wait for phase two to kick in.

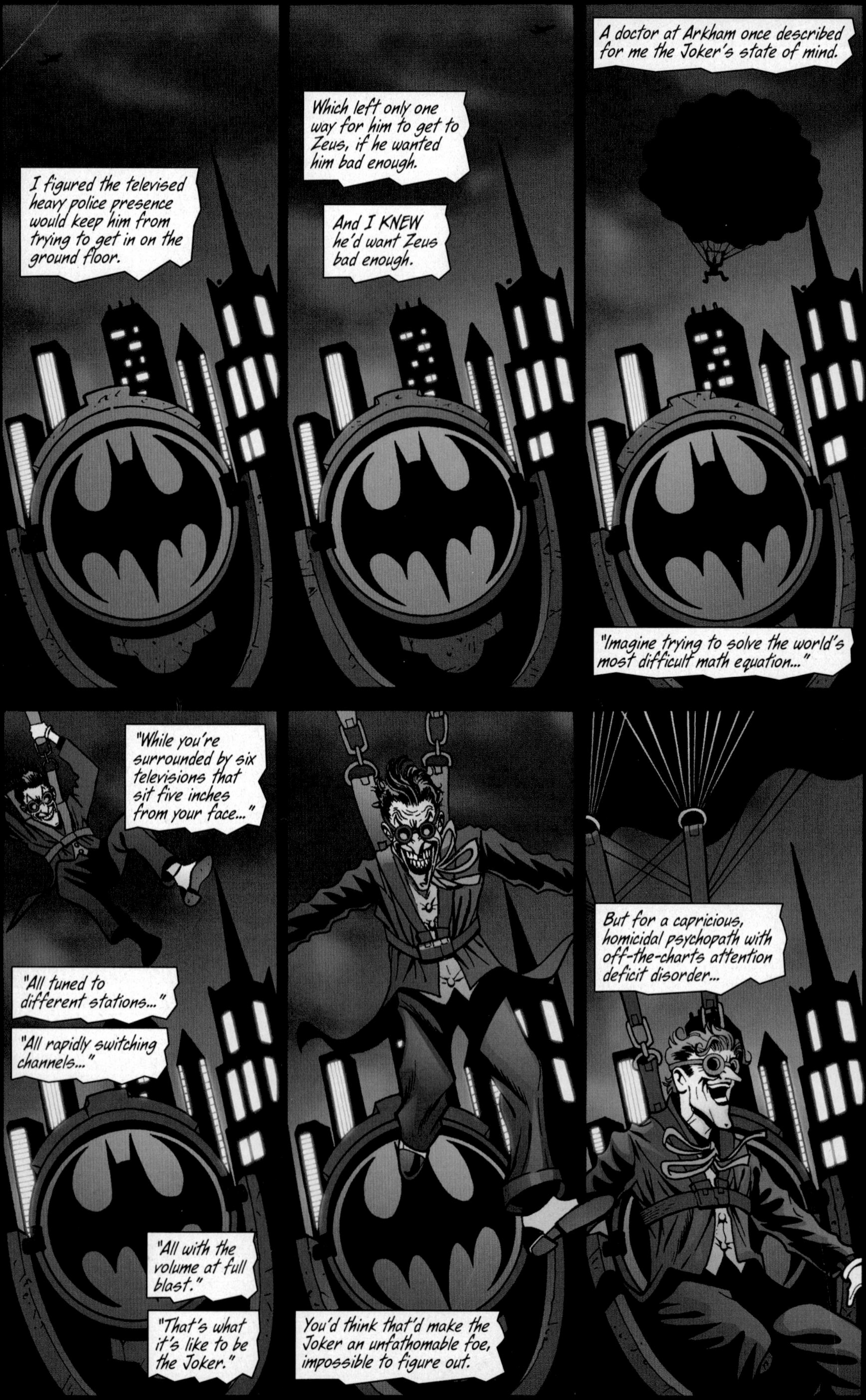
I figured the televised heavy police presence would keep him from trying to get in on the ground floor.
Which left only one way for him to get to Zeus, if he wanted him bad enough.
And I KNEW he'd want Zeus bad enough.
A doctor at Arkham once described for me the Joker's state of mind.
"Imagine trying to solve the world's most difficult math equation..."
"While you're surrounded by six televisions that sit five inches from your face..."
"All tuned to different stations..."
"All rapidly switching channels..."
"All with the volume at full blast."
"That's what it's like to be the Joker."
You'd think that'd make the Joker an unfathomable foe, impossible to figure out.
But for a capricious, homicidal psychopath with off-the-charts attention deficit disorder...

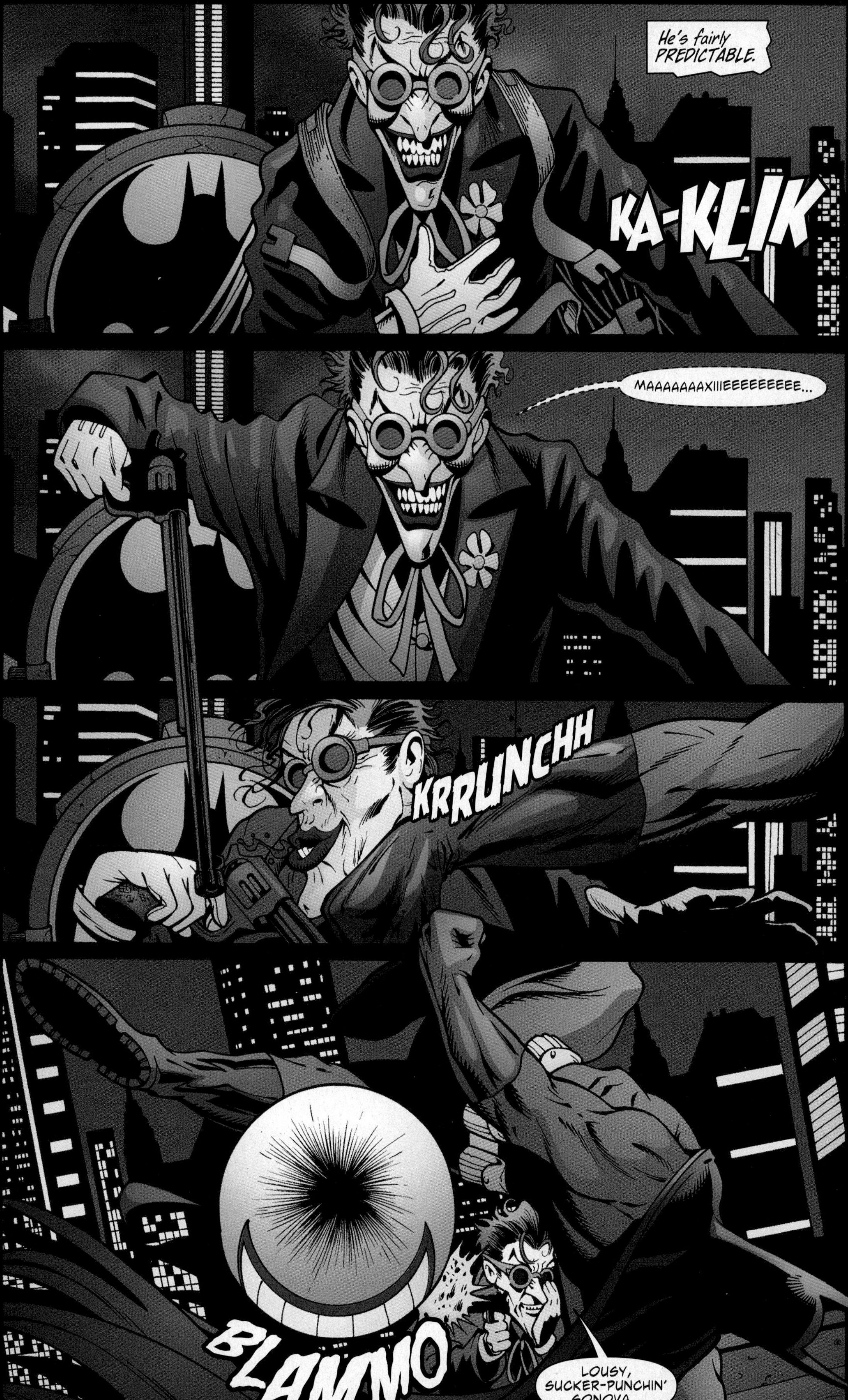
He's fairly PREDICTABLE.
KA-KLIK
MAAAAAAAXIIIEEEEEEEEE...
KRRUNCHH
BLAMMO
LOUSY, SUCKER-PUNCHIN' SONOVA...

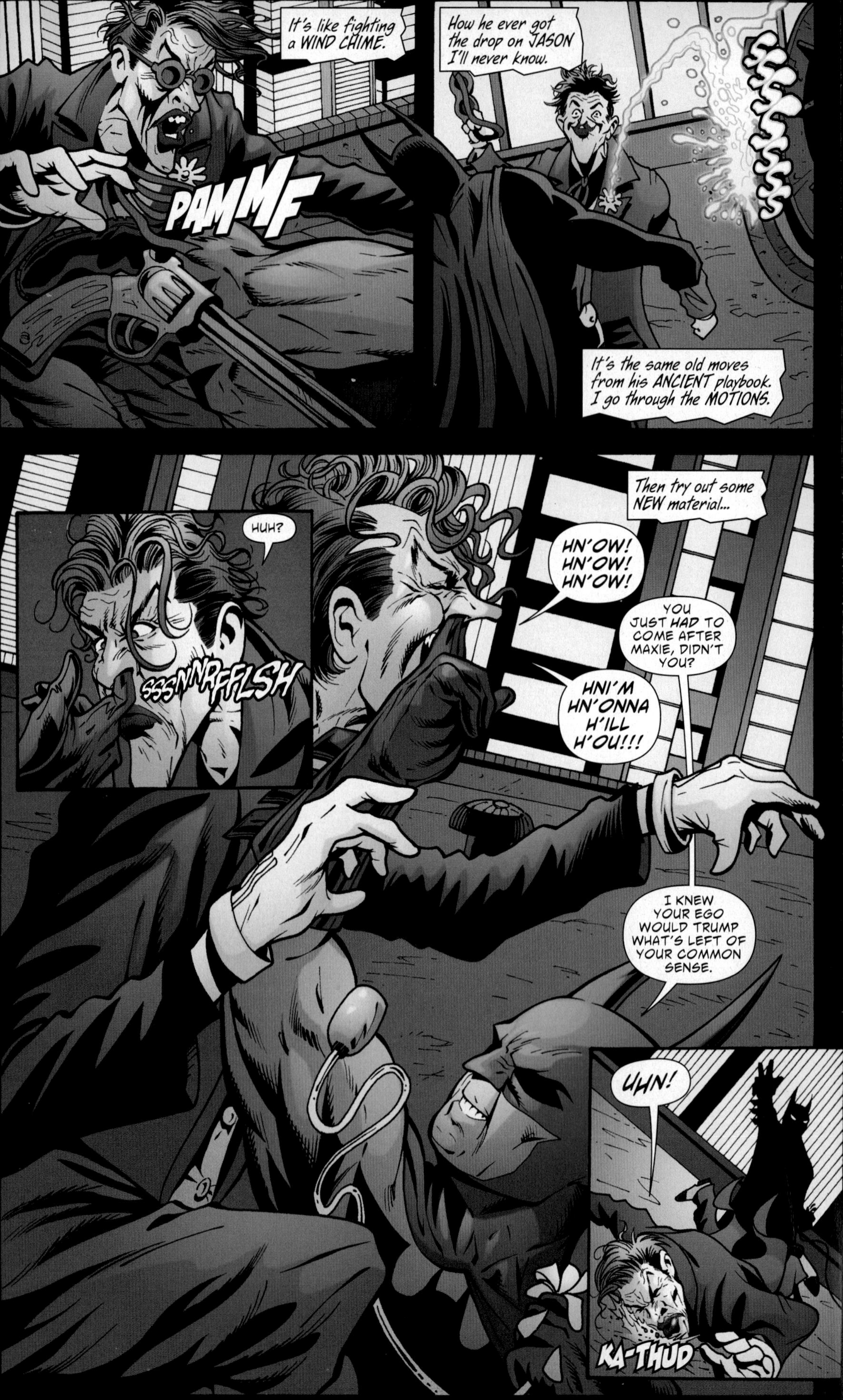

It's like fighting a WIND CHIME.
PAMMF
How he ever got the drop on JASON I'll never know.
SSSSSSSSS
It's the same old moves from his ANCIENT playbook. I go through the MOTIONS.
Then try out some NEW material...
HUH?
SSSNNRFFLSH
HN'OW! HN'OW! HN'OW!
HNI'M HN'ONNA H'ILL H'OU!!!
YOU JUST HAD TO COME AFTER MAXIE, DIDN'T YOU?
I KNEW YOUR EGO WOULD TRUMP WHAT'S LEFT OF YOUR COMMON SENSE.
UHN!
KA-THUD

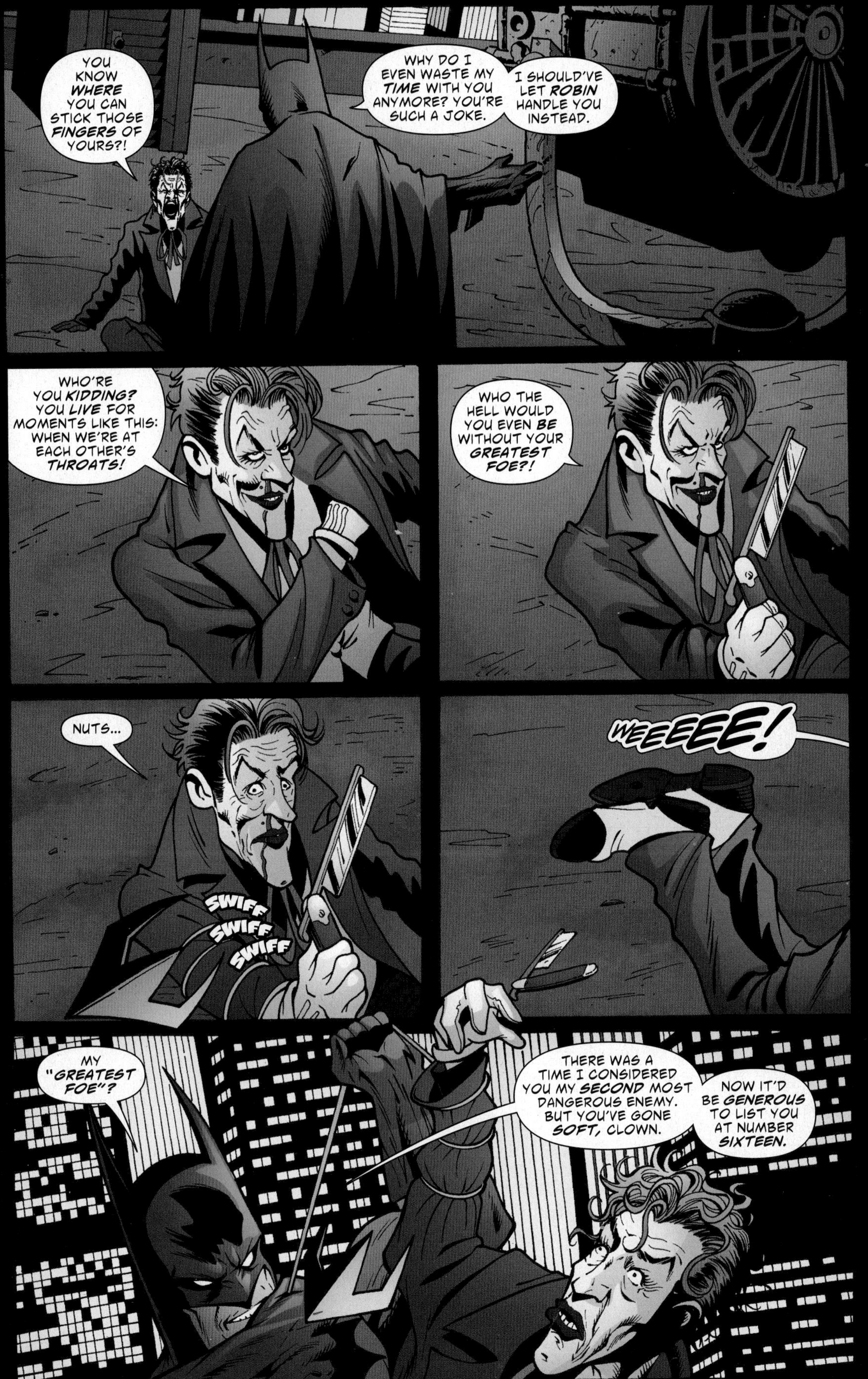

YOU KNOW WHERE YOU CAN STICK THOSE FINGERS OF YOURS?!
WHY DO I EVEN WASTE MY TIME WITH YOU ANYMORE? YOU'RE SUCH A JOKE.
I SHOULD'VE LET ROBIN HANDLE YOU INSTEAD.
WHO'RE YOU KIDDING? YOU LIVE FOR MOMENTS LIKE THIS: WHEN WE'RE AT EACH OTHER'S THROATS!
WHO THE HELL WOULD YOU EVEN BE WITHOUT YOUR GREATEST FOE?!
NUTS...
SWIFF SWIFF SWIFF
WEEEEEE!
MY "GREATEST FOE"?
THERE WAS A TIME I CONSIDERED YOU MY SECOND MOST DANGEROUS ENEMY. BUT YOU'VE GONE SOFT, CLOWN.
NOW IT'D BE GENEROUS TO LIST YOU AT NUMBER SIXTEEN.

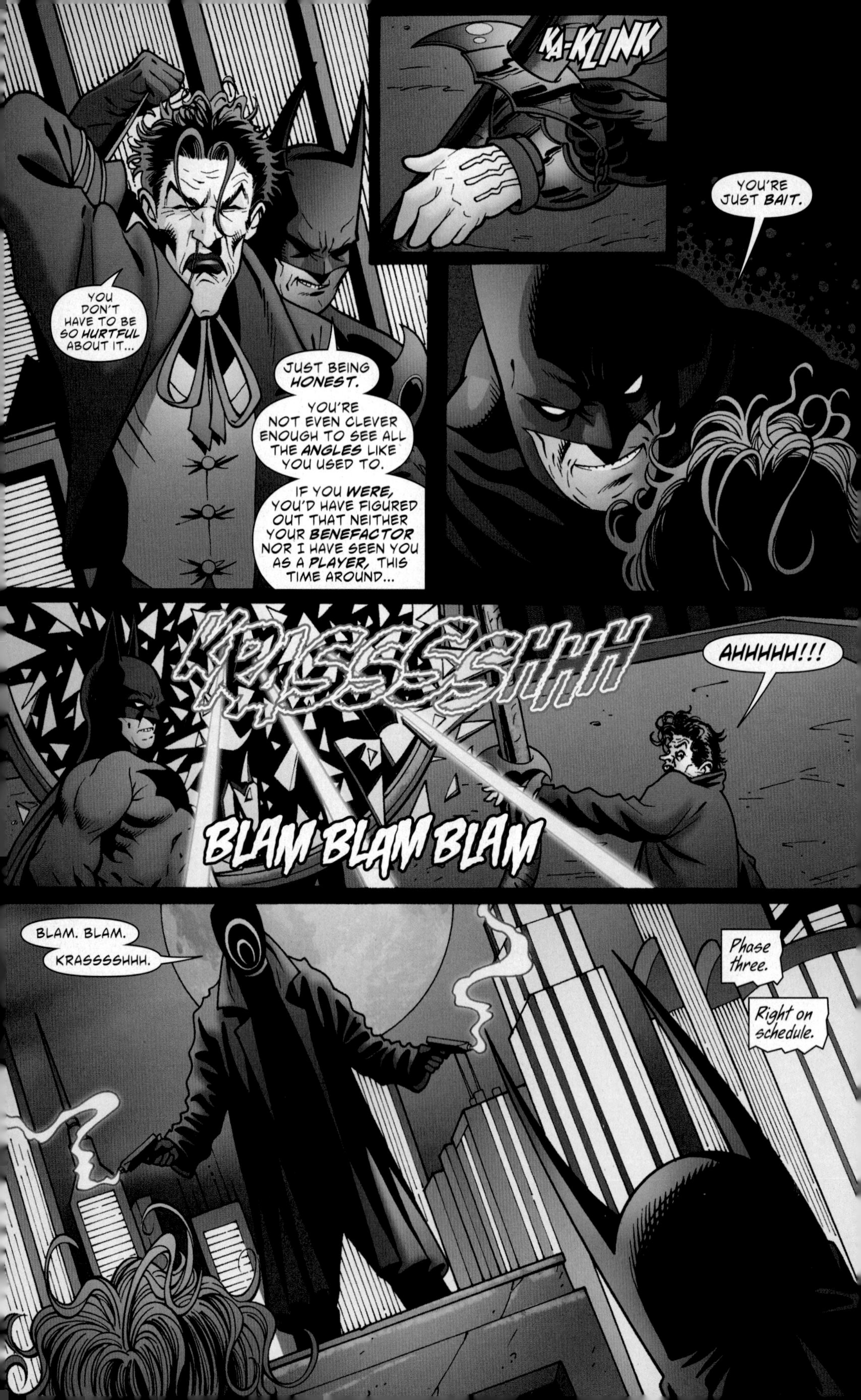
KA-KLINK
YOU DON'T HAVE TO BE SO HURTFUL ABOUT IT...
JUST BEING HONEST.
YOU'RE NOT EVEN CLEVER ENOUGH TO SEE ALL THE ANGLES LIKE YOU USED TO.
IF YOU WERE, YOU'D HAVE FIGURED OUT THAT NEITHER YOUR BENEFACTOR NOR I HAVE SEEN YOU AS A PLAYER, THIS TIME AROUND...
YOU'RE JUST BAIT.
KRASSSSHHH
AHHHHH!!!
BLAM BLAM BLAM
BLAM. BLAM. KRASSSSHHH.
Phase three.
Right on schedule.

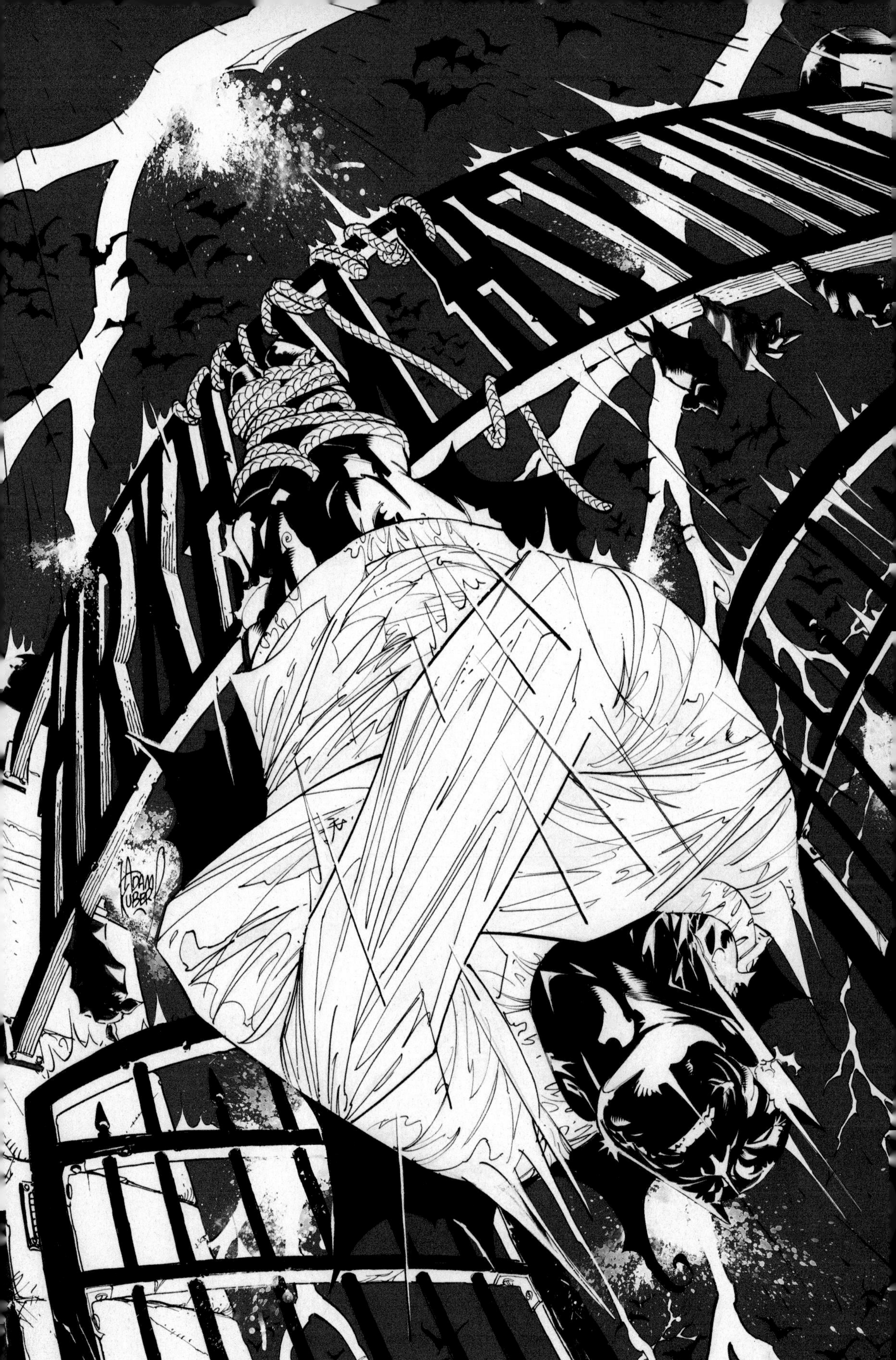
ADAM KUBERT

batman :: cacophony #3 *cover by* ADAM KUBERT

part three BAFFLES

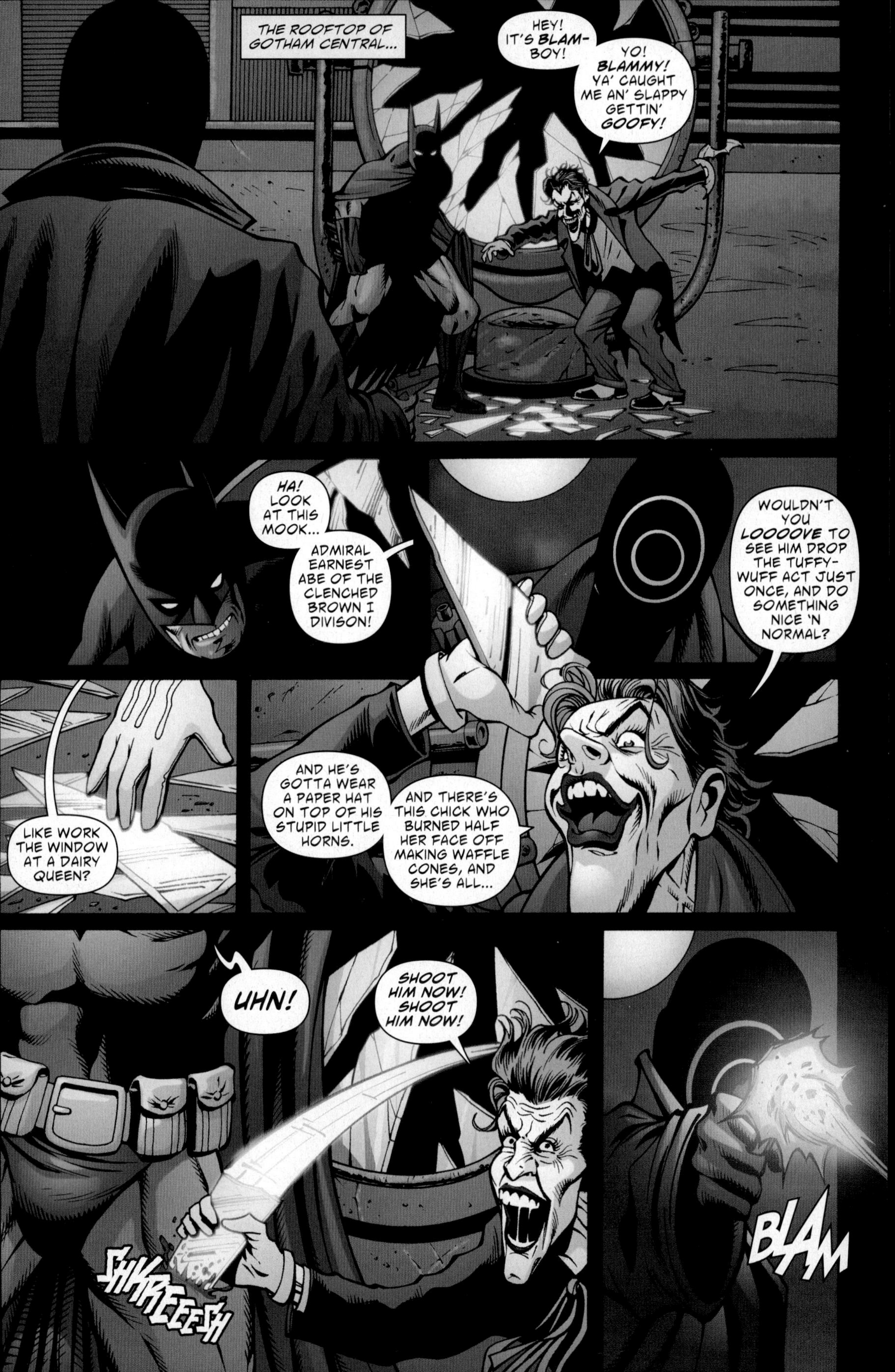
THE ROOFTOP OF GOTHAM CENTRAL...
HEY! IT'S BLAM-BOY!
YO! BLAMMY! YA' CAUGHT ME AN' SLAPPY GETTIN' GOOFY!
HA! LOOK AT THIS MOOK...
ADMIRAL EARNEST ABE OF THE CLENCHED BROWN I DIVISON!
WOULDN'T YOU LOOOOVE TO SEE HIM DROP THE TUFFY-WUFF ACT JUST ONCE, AND DO SOMETHING NICE 'N NORMAL?
LIKE WORK THE WINDOW AT A DAIRY QUEEN?
AND HE'S GOTTA WEAR A PAPER HAT ON TOP OF HIS STUPID LITTLE HORNS.
AND THERE'S THIS CHICK WHO BURNED HALF HER FACE OFF MAKING WAFFLE CONES, AND SHE'S ALL...
UHN!
SHOOT HIM NOW! SHOOT HIM NOW!
SHKREEEESH
BLAM

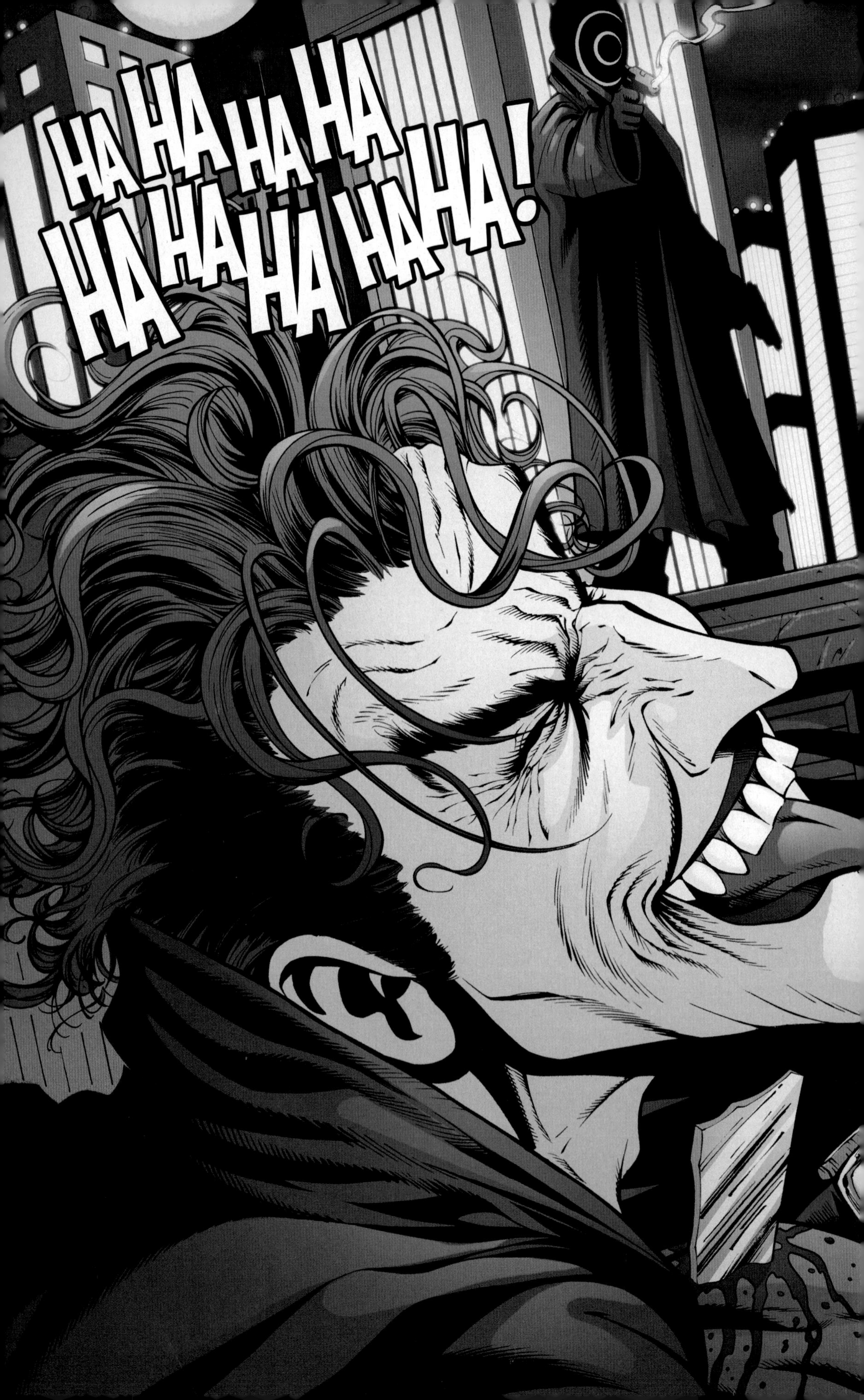
HA HA HA HA HA
HA HA HA HA HA HA HA!

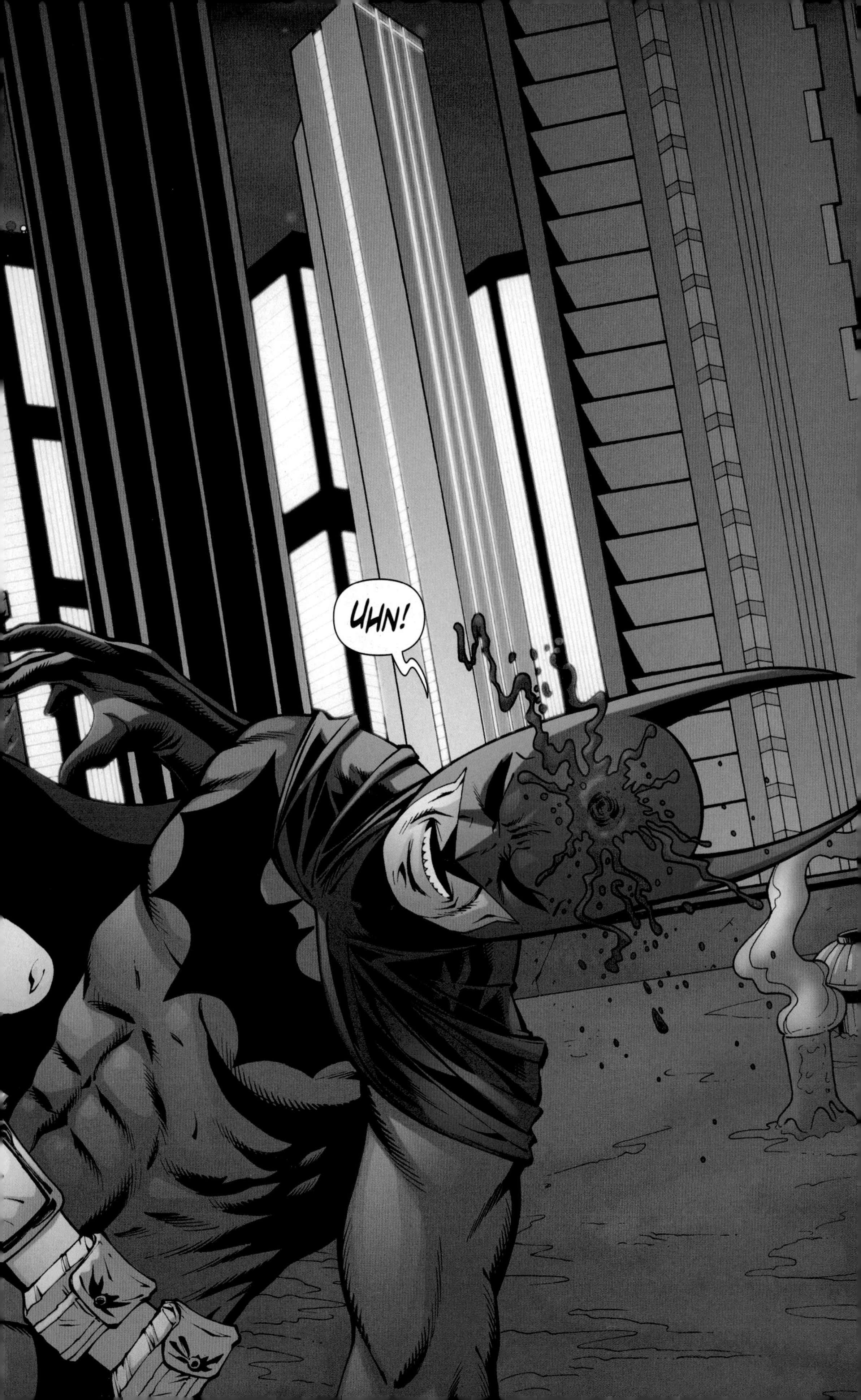
UHN!

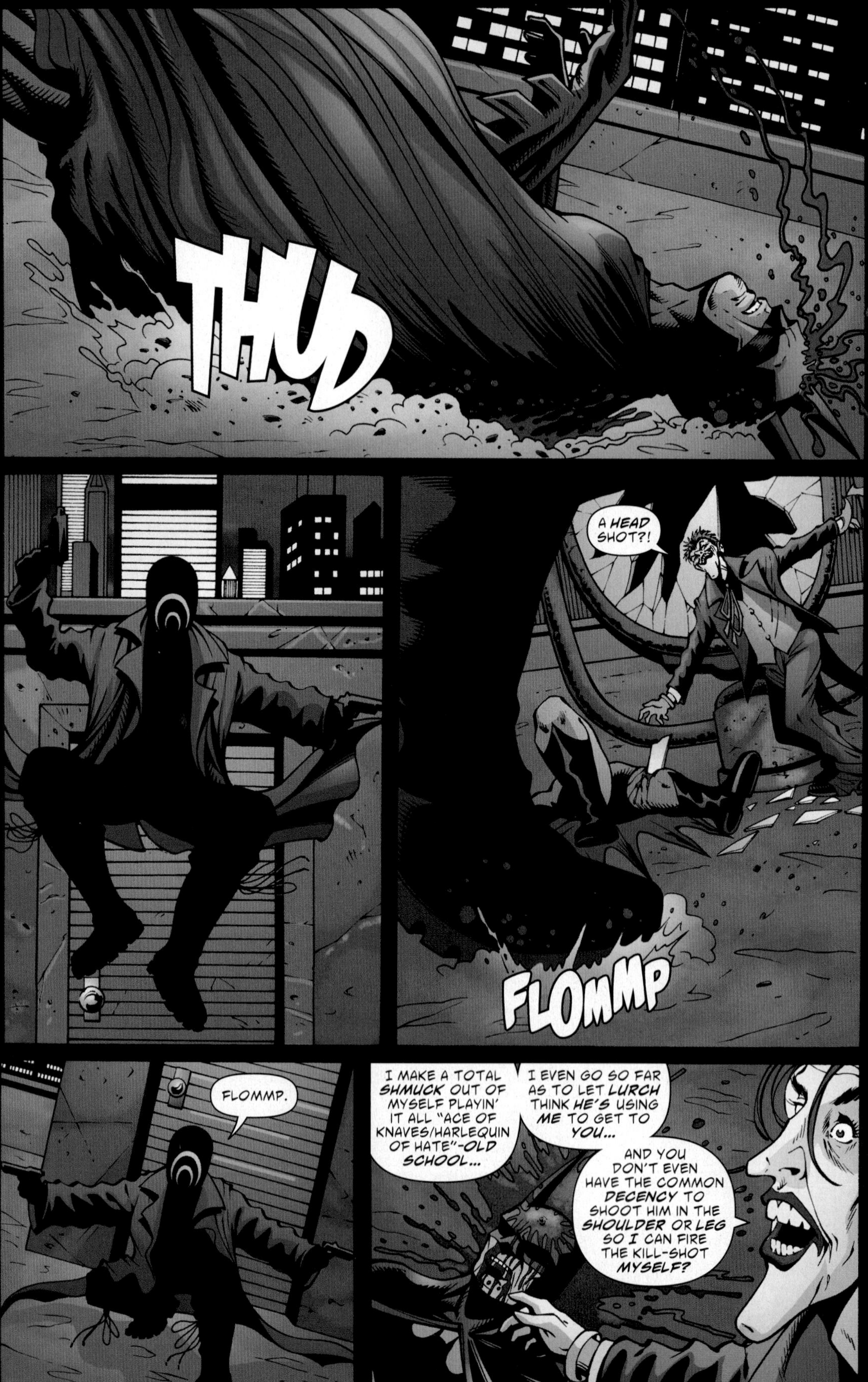
THUD
A HEAD SHOT?!
FLOMMP
FLOMMP.
I MAKE A TOTAL SHMUCK OUT OF MYSELF PLAYIN' IT ALL "ACE OF KNAVES/HARLEQUIN OF HATE"-OLD SCHOOL...
I EVEN GO SO FAR AS TO LET LURCH THINK HE'S USING ME TO GET TO YOU...
AND YOU DON'T EVEN HAVE THE COMMON DECENCY TO SHOOT HIM IN THE SHOULDER OR LEG SO I CAN FIRE THE KILL-SHOT MYSELF?

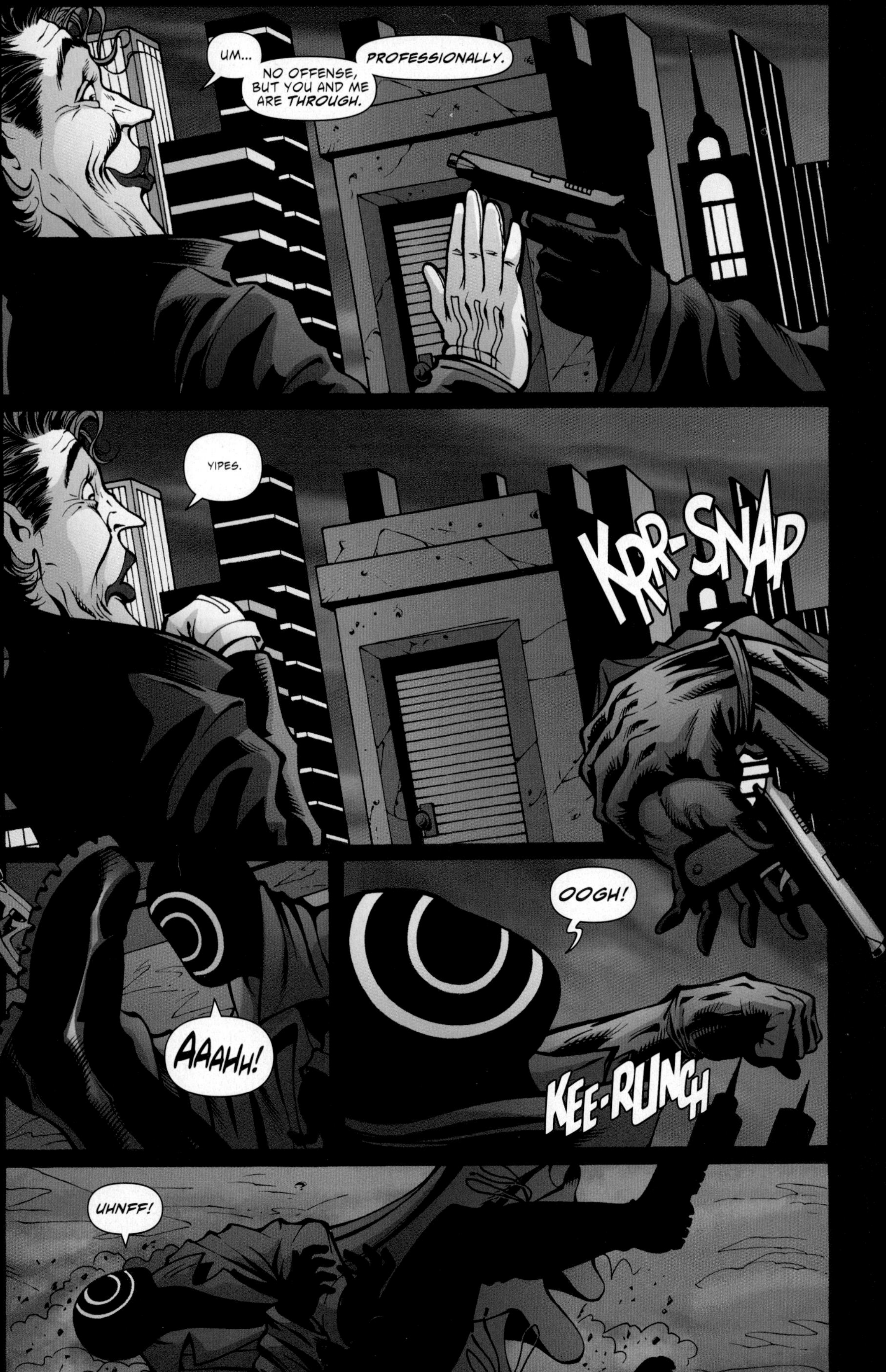
UM...
NO OFFENSE, BUT YOU AND ME ARE THROUGH.
PROFESSIONALLY.
YIPES.
KRR-SNAP
OOGH!
AAAHH!
KEE-RUNCH
UHNFF!

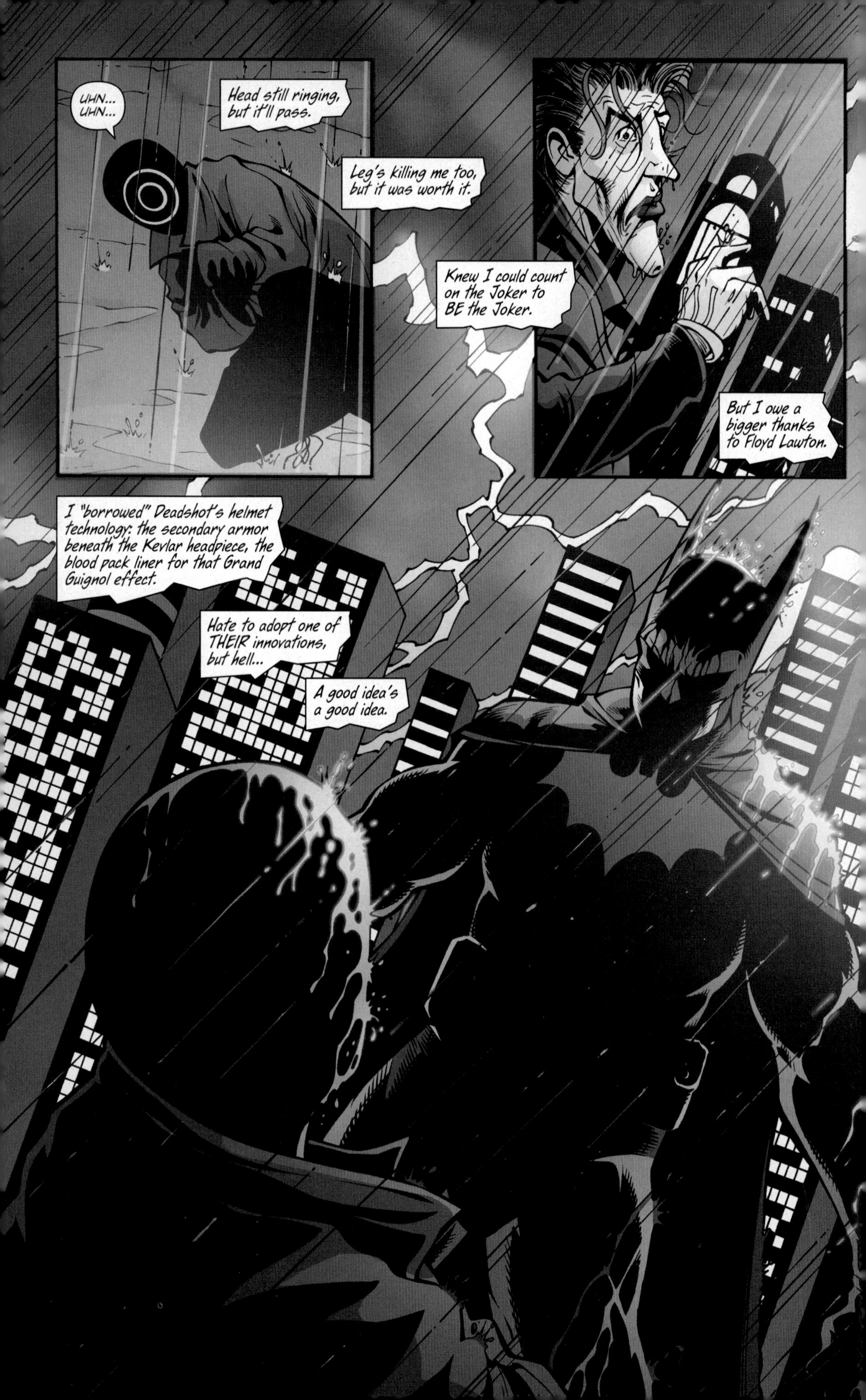
UHN... UHN...
Head still ringing, but it'll pass.
Leg's killing me too, but it was worth it.
Knew I could count on the Joker to BE the Joker.
But I owe a bigger thanks to Floyd Lawton.
I "borrowed" Deadshot's helmet technology: the secondary armor beneath the Kevlar headpiece, the blood pack liner for that Grand Guignol effect.
Hate to adopt one of THEIR innovations, but hell...
A good idea's a good idea.

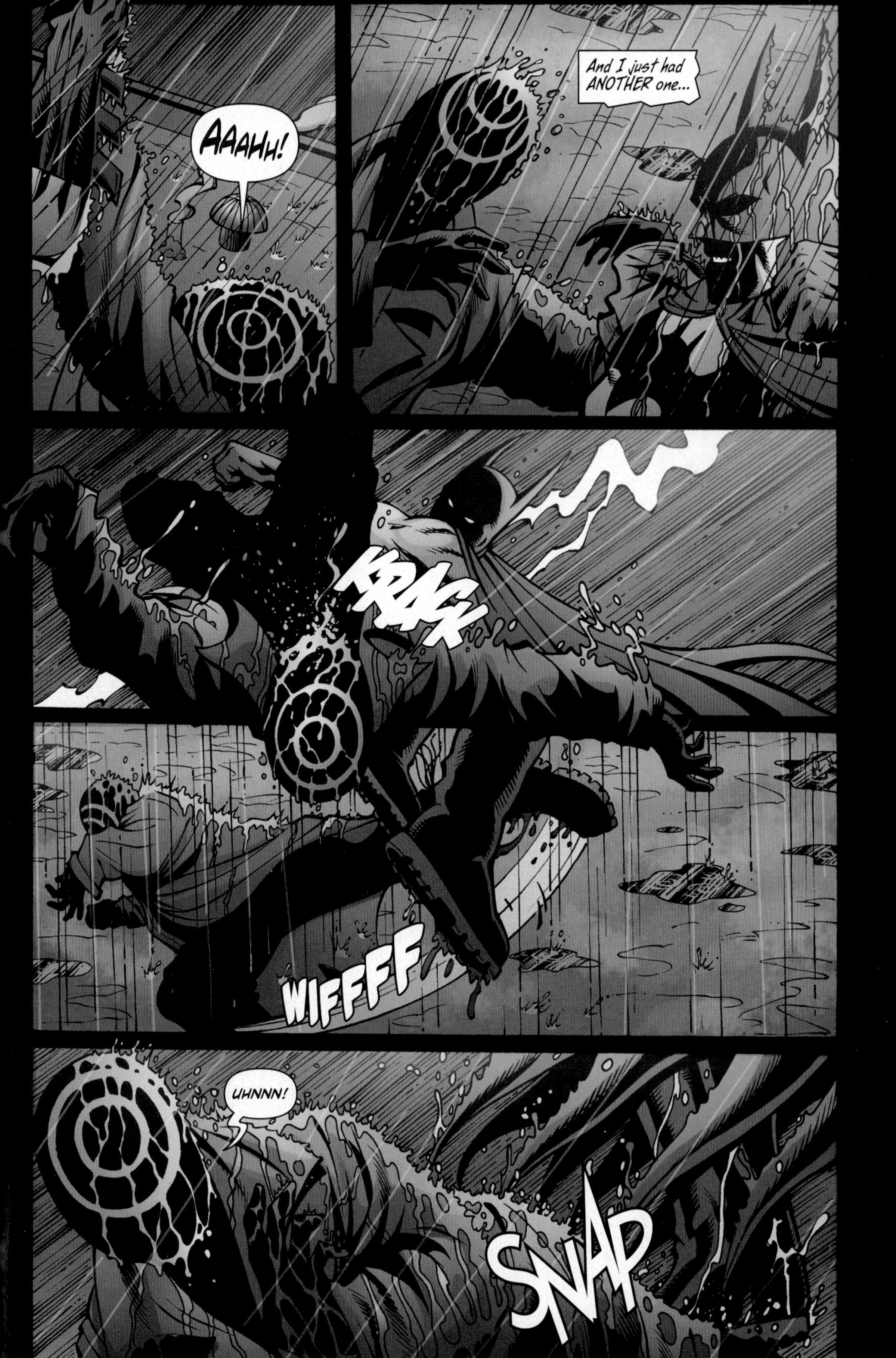
AAAHH!
And I just had ANOTHER one...
KRACK
WIFFFF
UHNNN!
SNAP

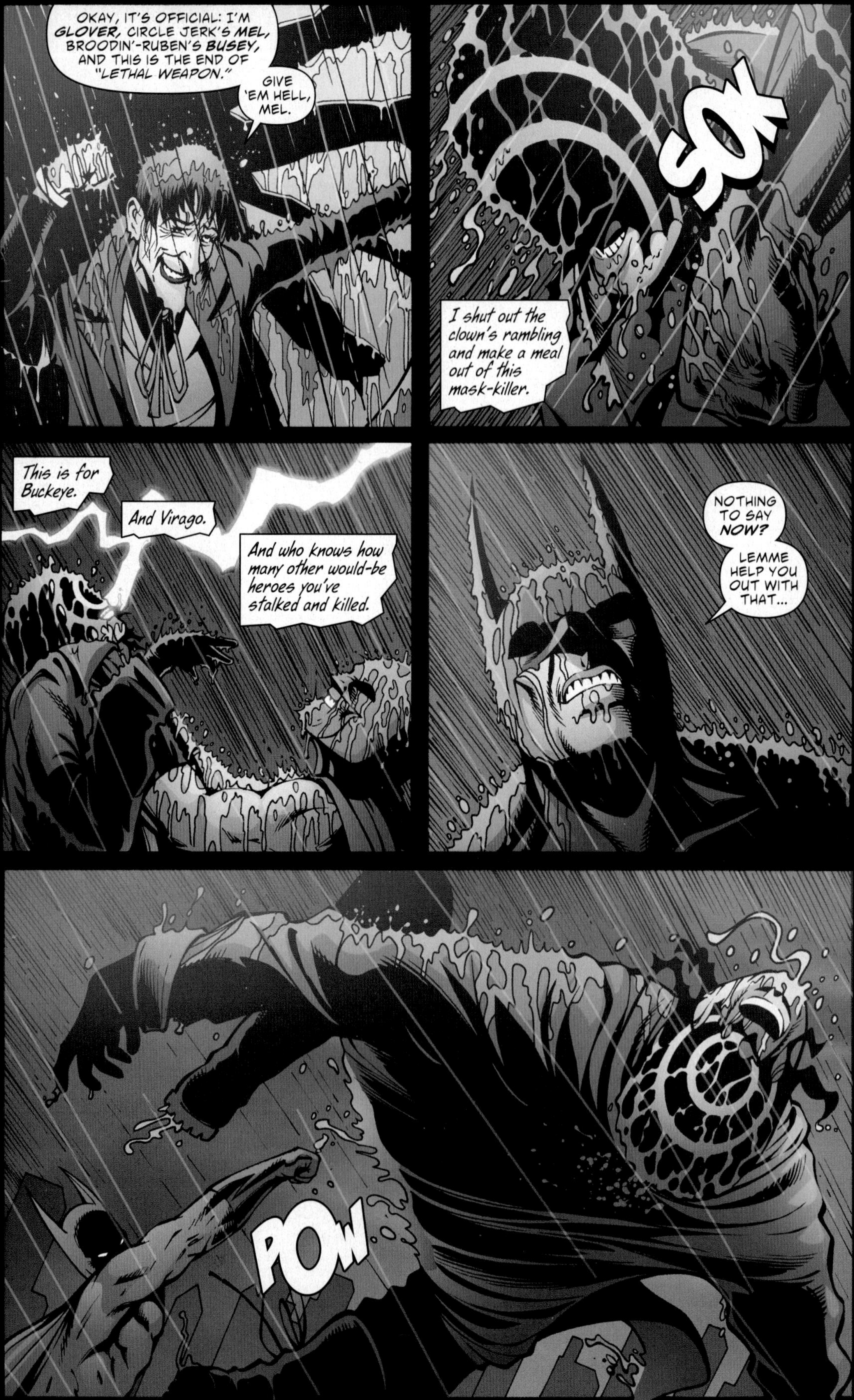
OKAY, IT'S OFFICIAL: I'M GLOVER, CIRCLE JERK'S MEL, BROODIN'-RUBEN'S BUSEY, AND THIS IS THE END OF "LETHAL WEAPON."
GIVE 'EM HELL, MEL.
SOK
I shut out the clown's rambling and make a meal out of this mask-killer.
This is for Buckeye.
And Virago.
And who knows how many other would-be heroes you've stalked and killed.
NOTHING TO SAY NOW?
LEMME HELP YOU OUT WITH THAT...
POW

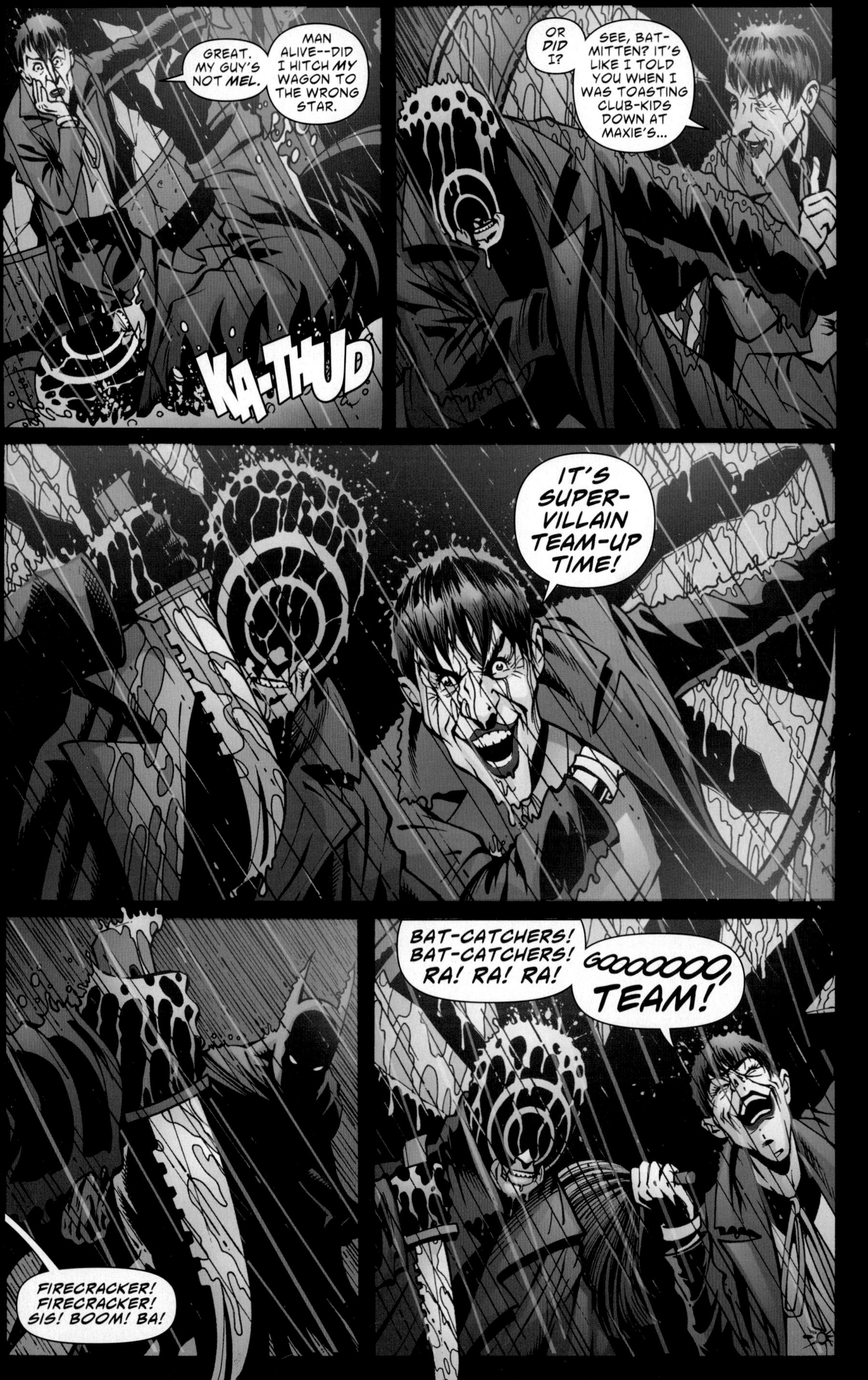
GREAT. MY GUY'S NOT MEL.
MAN ALIVE--DID I HITCH MY WAGON TO THE WRONG STAR.
KA-THUD
OR DID I?
SEE, BAT-MITTEN? IT'S LIKE I TOLD YOU WHEN I WAS TOASTING CLUB-KIDS DOWN AT MAXIE'S...
IT'S SUPER-VILLAIN TEAM-UP TIME!
FIRECRACKER! FIRECRACKER! SIS! BOOM! BA!
BAT-CATCHERS! BAT-CATCHERS! RA! RA! RA!
GOOOOOOO, TEAM!

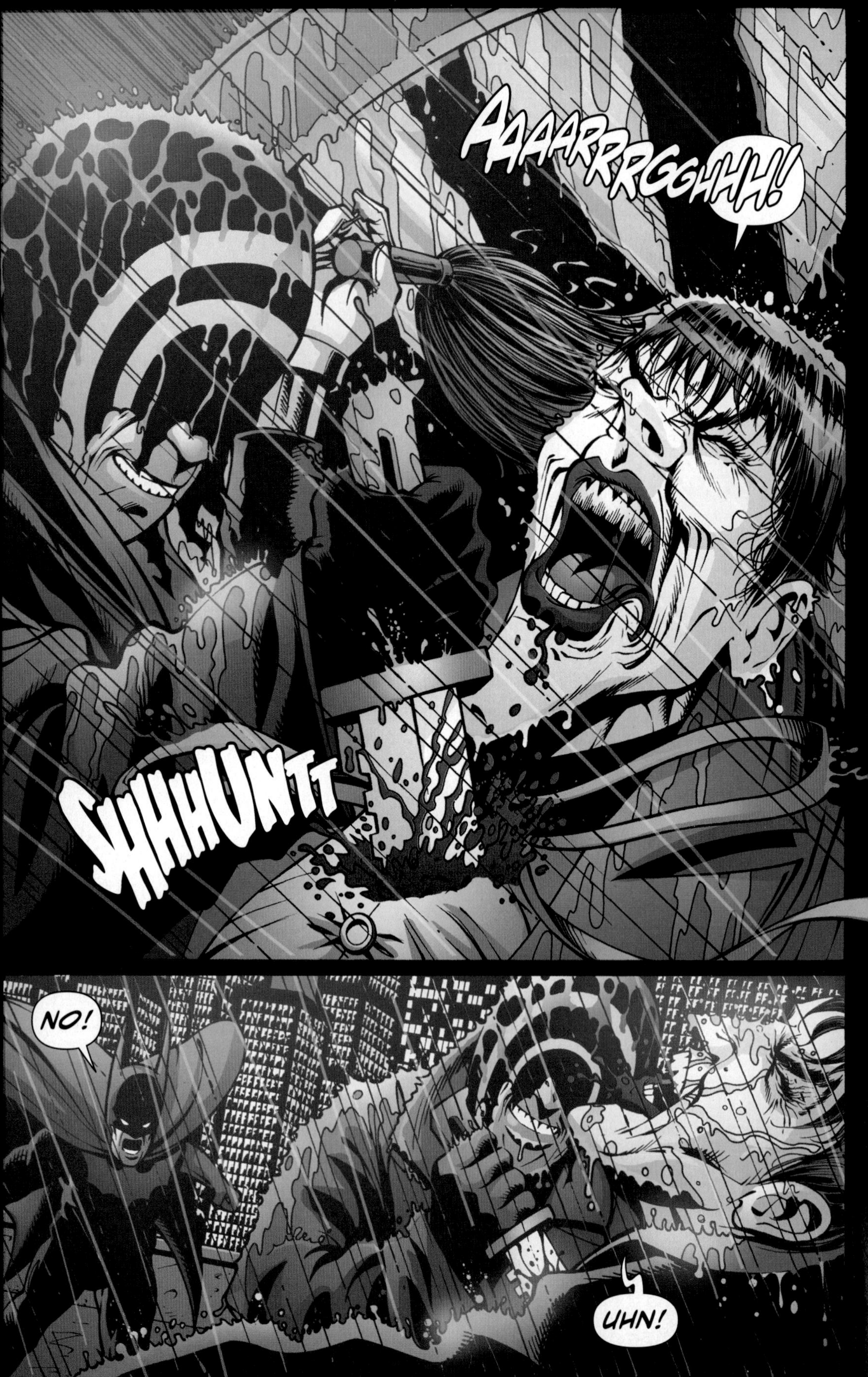
AAAARRRGGHHHH!
SHHHUNTT
NO!
UHN!

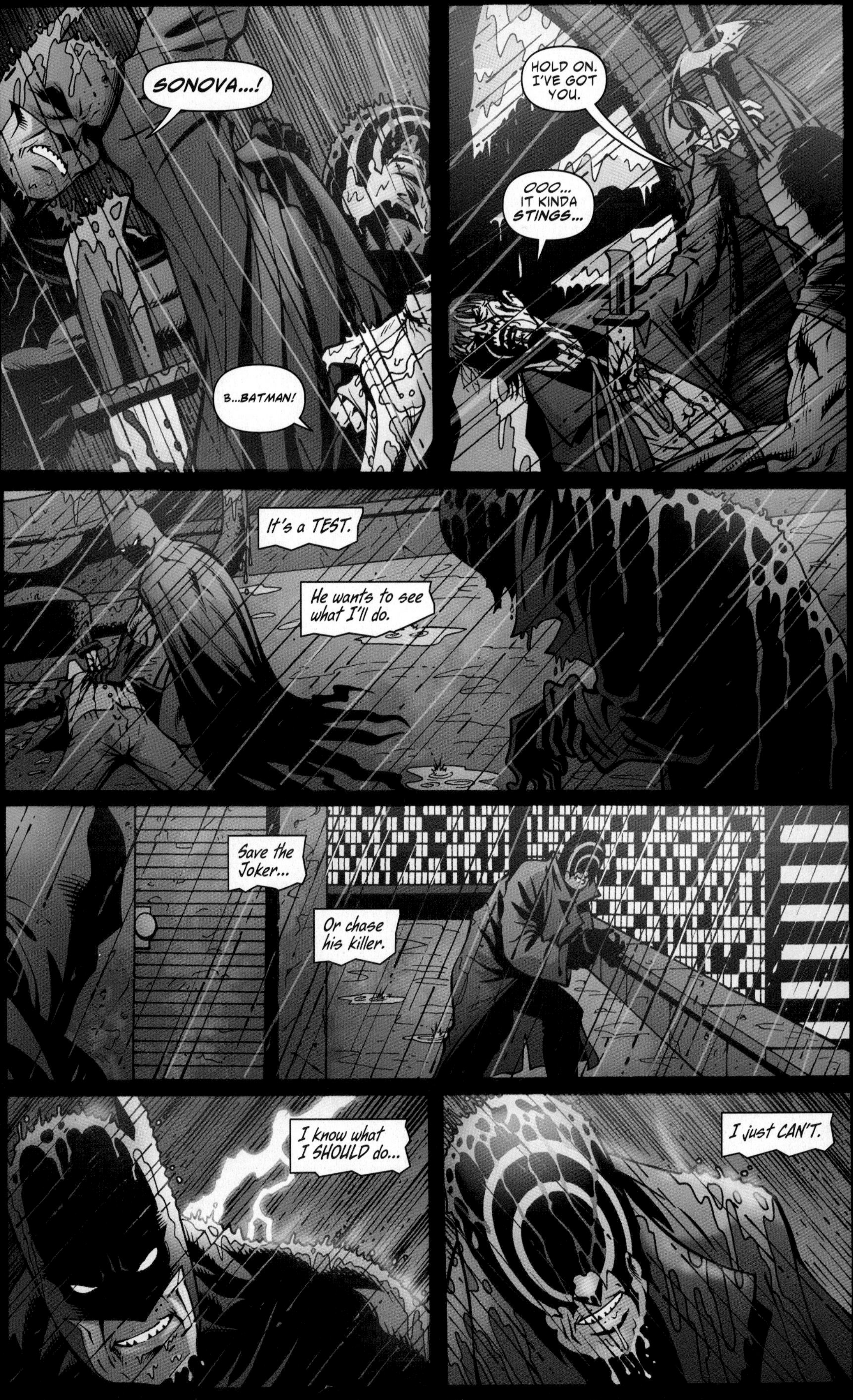
SONOVA...!
B...BATMAN!
HOLD ON. I'VE GOT YOU.
OOO... IT KINDA STINGS...
It's a TEST.
He wants to see what I'll do.
Save the Joker...
Or chase his killer.
I know what I SHOULD do...
I just CAN'T.

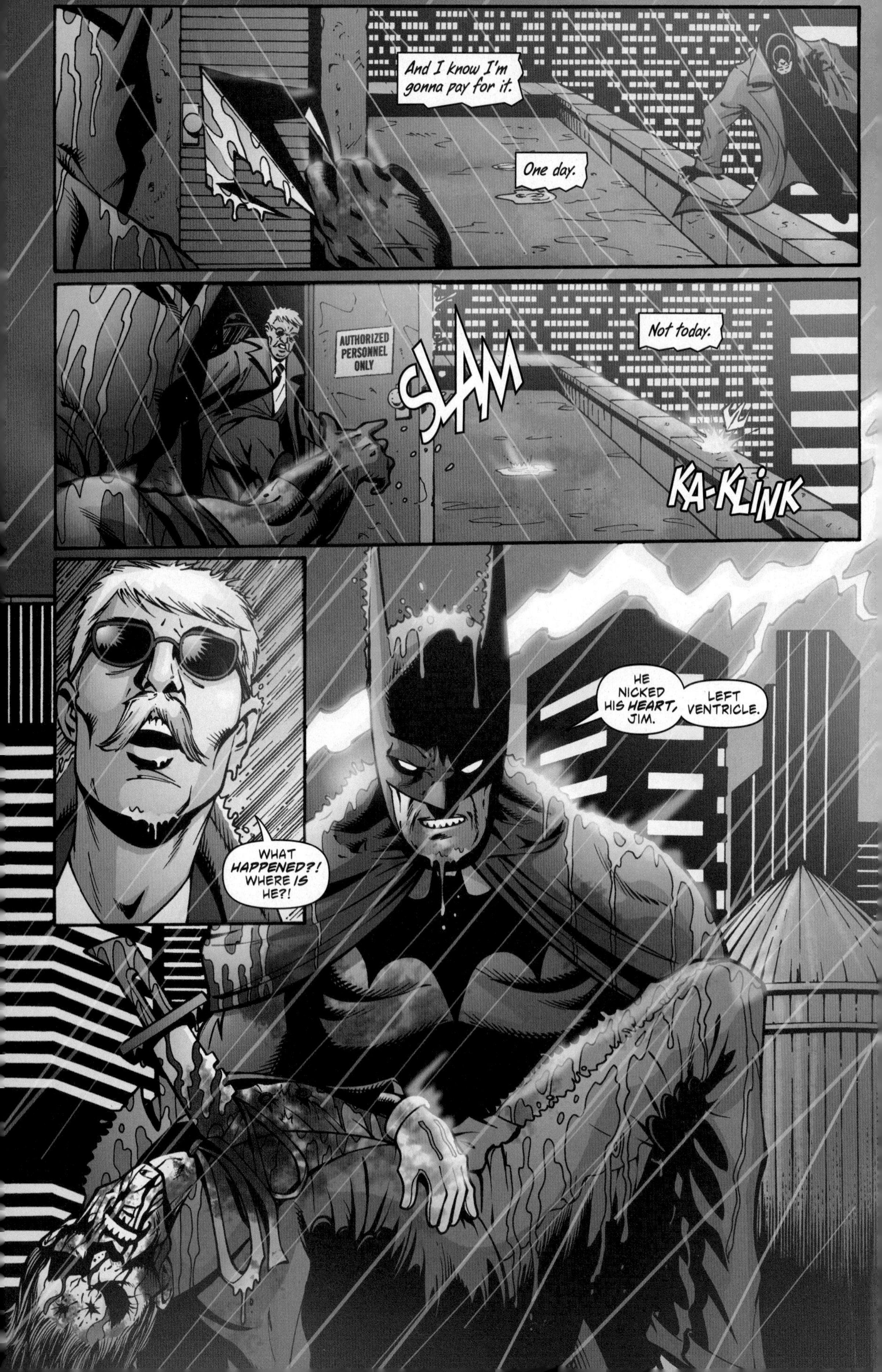

And I know I'm gonna pay for it.
One day.
AUTHORIZED PERSONNEL ONLY
SLAM
Not today.
KA-KLINK
WHAT HAPPENED?! WHERE IS HE?!
HE NICKED HIS HEART, JIM.
LEFT VENTRICLE.

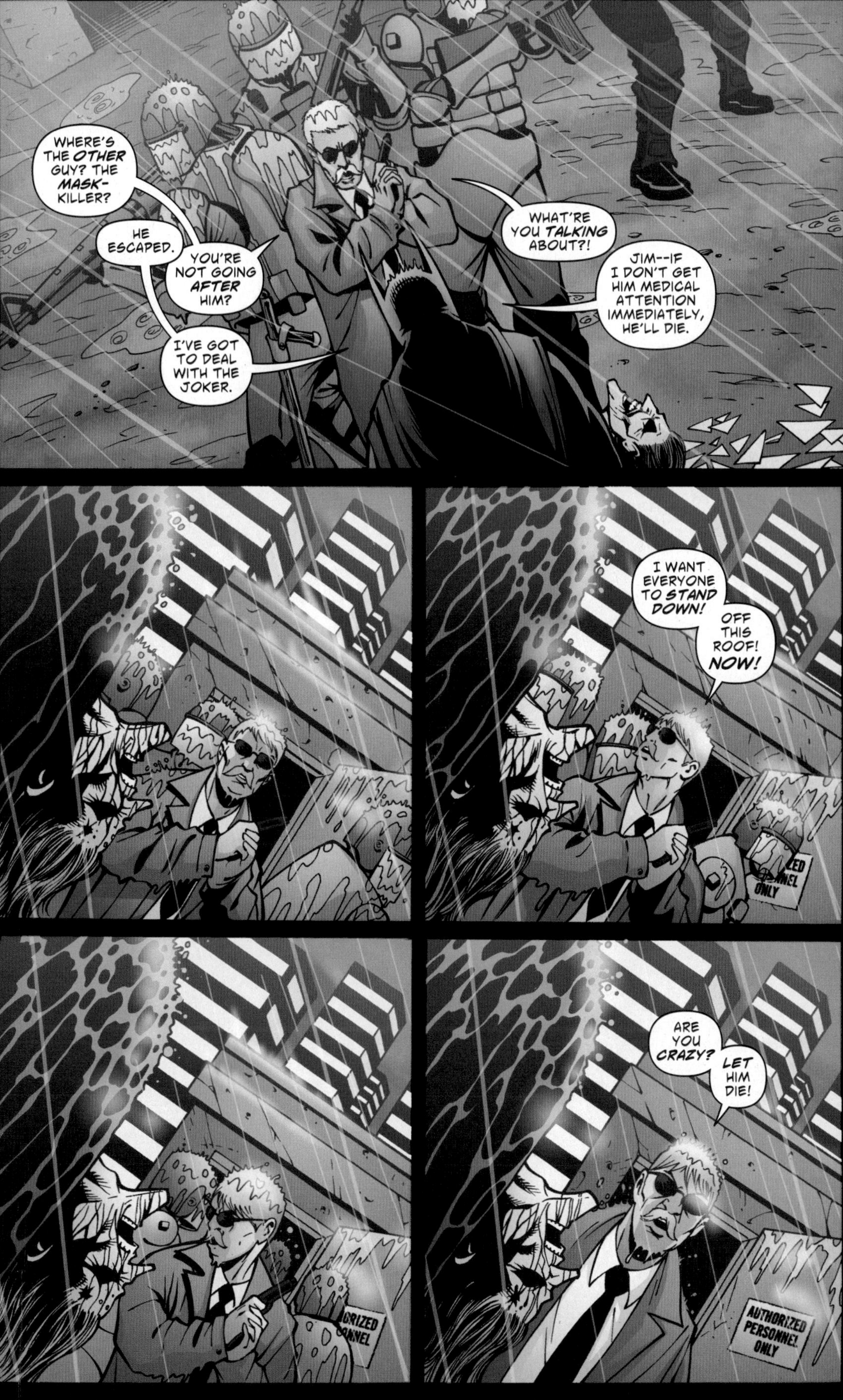

WHERE'S THE OTHER GUY? THE MASK-KILLER?
HE ESCAPED.
YOU'RE NOT GOING AFTER HIM?
I'VE GOT TO DEAL WITH THE JOKER.
WHAT'RE YOU TALKING ABOUT?!
JIM--IF I DON'T GET HIM MEDICAL ATTENTION IMMEDIATELY, HE'LL DIE.
I WANT EVERYONE TO STAND DOWN!
OFF THIS ROOF! NOW!
ARE YOU CRAZY?
LET HIM DIE!
AUTHORIZED PERSONNEL ONLY

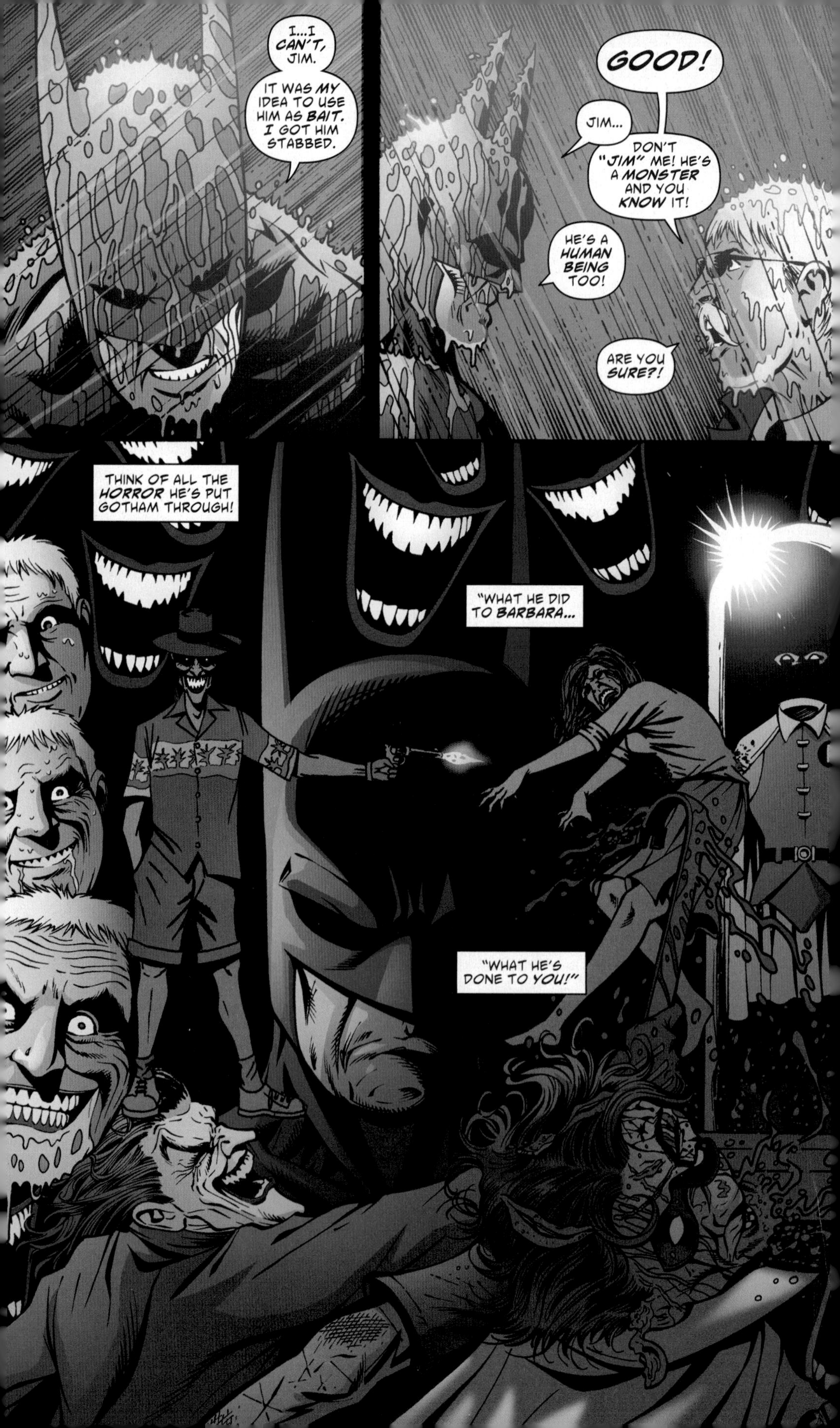

I...I CAN'T, JIM.
IT WAS MY IDEA TO USE HIM AS BAIT. I GOT HIM STABBED.
GOOD!
JIM...
DON'T "JIM" ME! HE'S A MONSTER AND YOU KNOW IT!
HE'S A HUMAN BEING TOO!
ARE YOU SURE?!
THINK OF ALL THE HORROR HE'S PUT GOTHAM THROUGH!
"WHAT HE DID TO BARBARA...
"WHAT HE'S DONE TO YOU!"

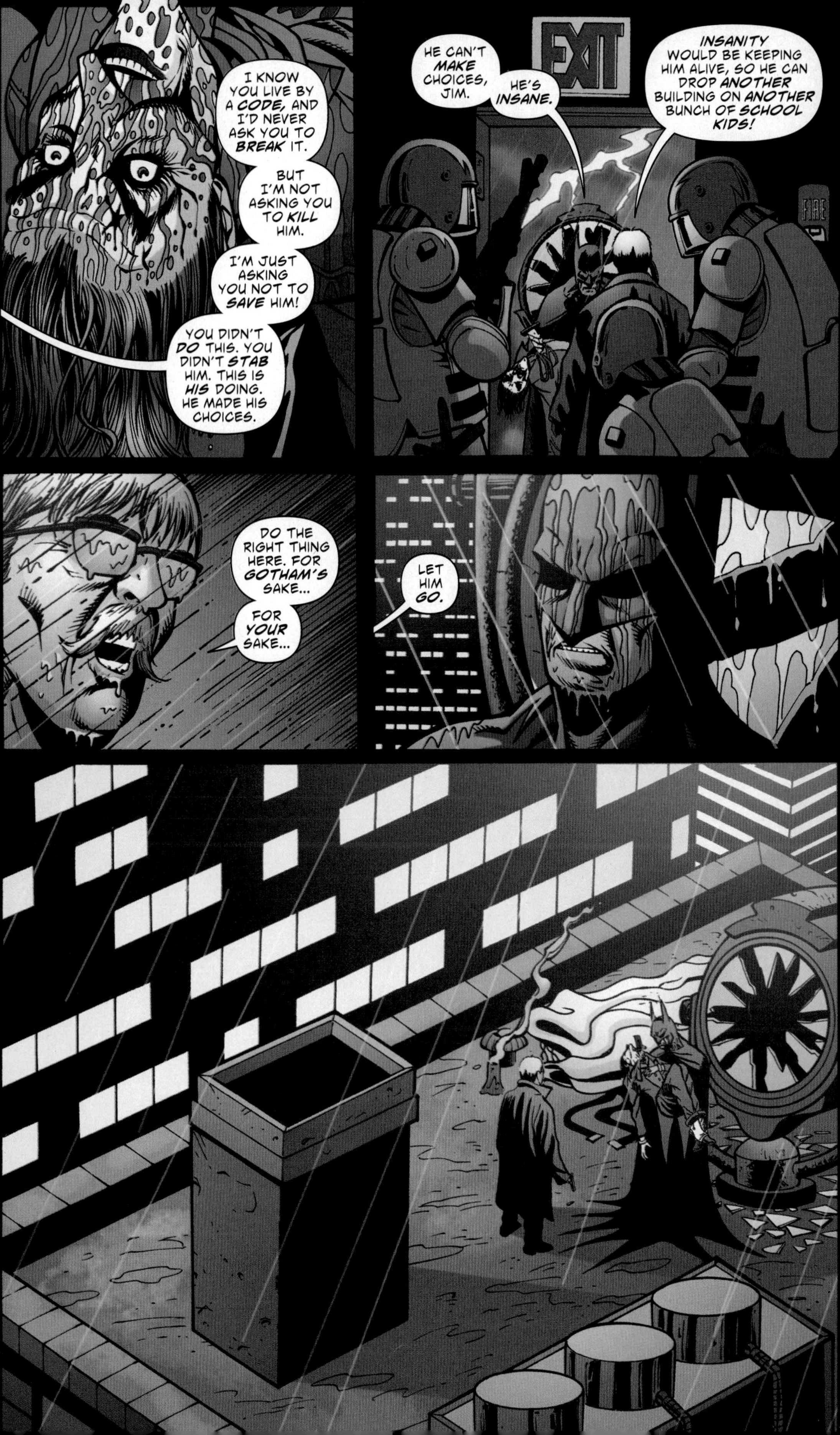
I KNOW YOU LIVE BY A CODE, AND I'D NEVER ASK YOU TO BREAK IT.
BUT I'M NOT ASKING YOU TO KILL HIM.
I'M JUST ASKING YOU NOT TO SAVE HIM!
YOU DIDN'T DO THIS. YOU DIDN'T STAB HIM. THIS IS HIS DOING. HE MADE HIS CHOICES.
EXIT
HE CAN'T MAKE CHOICES, JIM.
HE'S INSANE.
INSANITY WOULD BE KEEPING HIM ALIVE, SO HE CAN DROP ANOTHER BUILDING ON ANOTHER BUNCH OF SCHOOL KIDS!
DO THE RIGHT THING HERE. FOR GOTHAM'S SAKE...
FOR YOUR SAKE...
LET HIM GO.

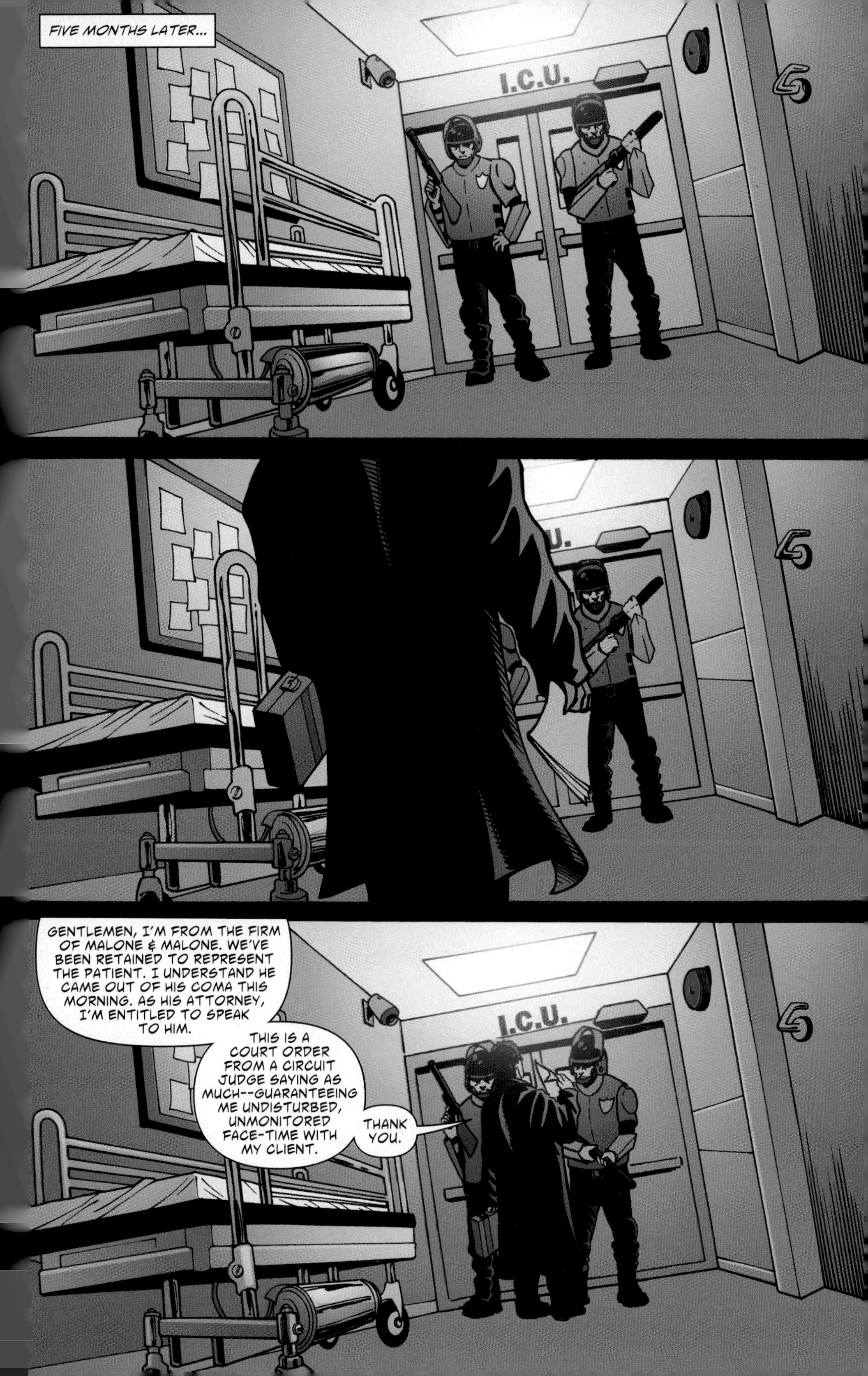
FIVE MONTHS LATER...
I.C.U.
GENTLEMEN, I'M FROM THE FIRM OF MALONE & MALONE. WE'VE BEEN RETAINED TO REPRESENT THE PATIENT. I UNDERSTAND HE CAME OUT OF HIS COMA THIS MORNING. AS HIS ATTORNEY, I'M ENTITLED TO SPEAK TO HIM.
THIS IS A COURT ORDER FROM A CIRCUIT JUDGE SAYING AS MUCH--GUARANTEEING ME UNDISTURBED, UNMONITORED FACE-TIME WITH MY CLIENT.
THANK YOU.

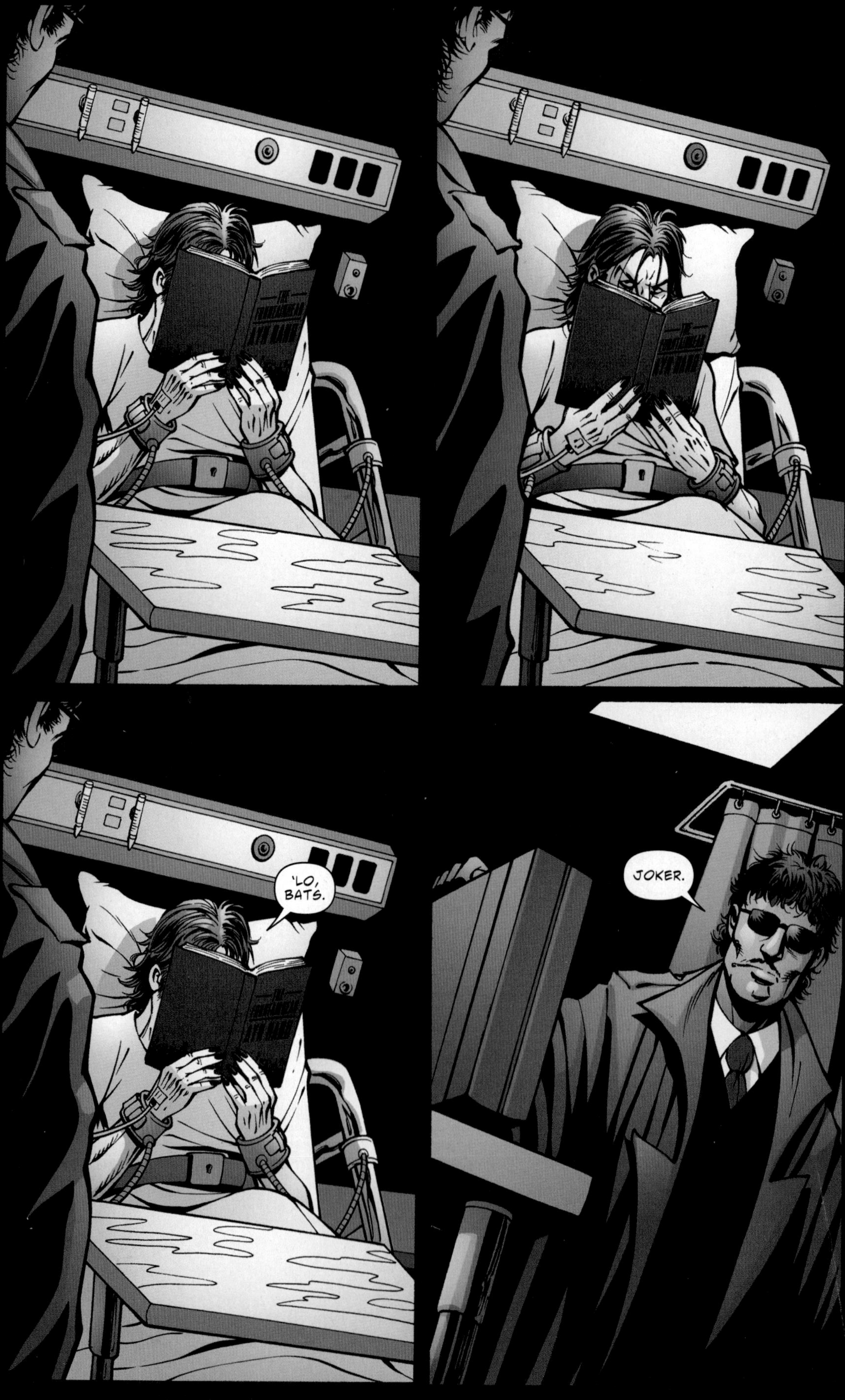
'LO, BATS.
JOKER.

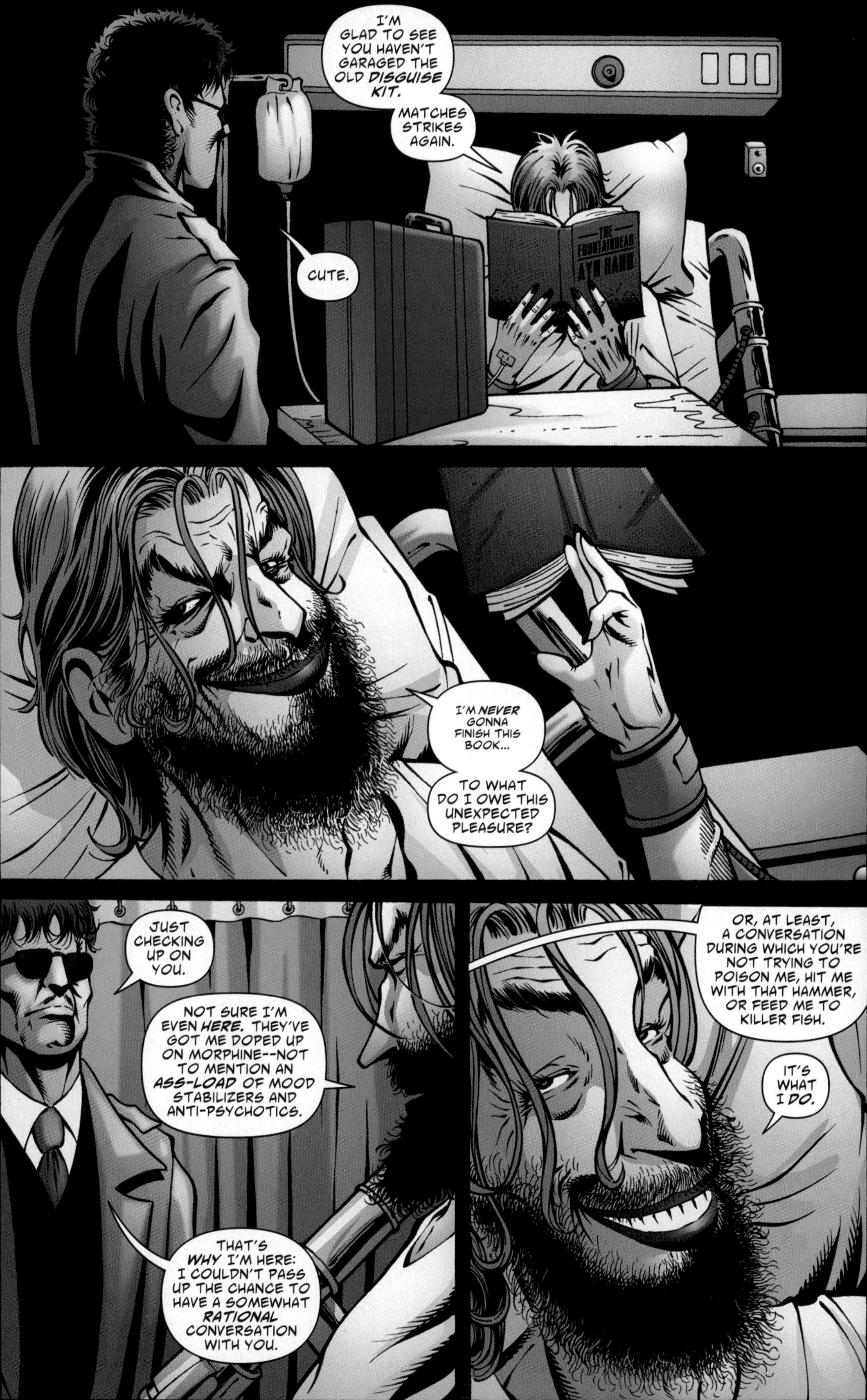

I'M GLAD TO SEE YOU HAVEN'T GARAGED THE OLD DISGUISE KIT.
MATCHES STRIKES AGAIN.
CUTE.
THE FOUNTAINHEAD AYN RAND
I'M NEVER GONNA FINISH THIS BOOK...
TO WHAT DO I OWE THIS UNEXPECTED PLEASURE?
JUST CHECKING UP ON YOU.
NOT SURE I'M EVEN HERE. THEY'VE GOT ME DOPED UP ON MORPHINE--NOT TO MENTION AN ASS-LOAD OF MOOD STABILIZERS AND ANTI-PSYCHOTICS.
THAT'S WHY I'M HERE: I COULDN'T PASS UP THE CHANCE TO HAVE A SOMEWHAT RATIONAL CONVERSATION WITH YOU.
OR, AT LEAST, A CONVERSATION DURING WHICH YOU'RE NOT TRYING TO POISON ME, HIT ME WITH THAT HAMMER, OR FEED ME TO KILLER FISH.
IT'S WHAT I DO.

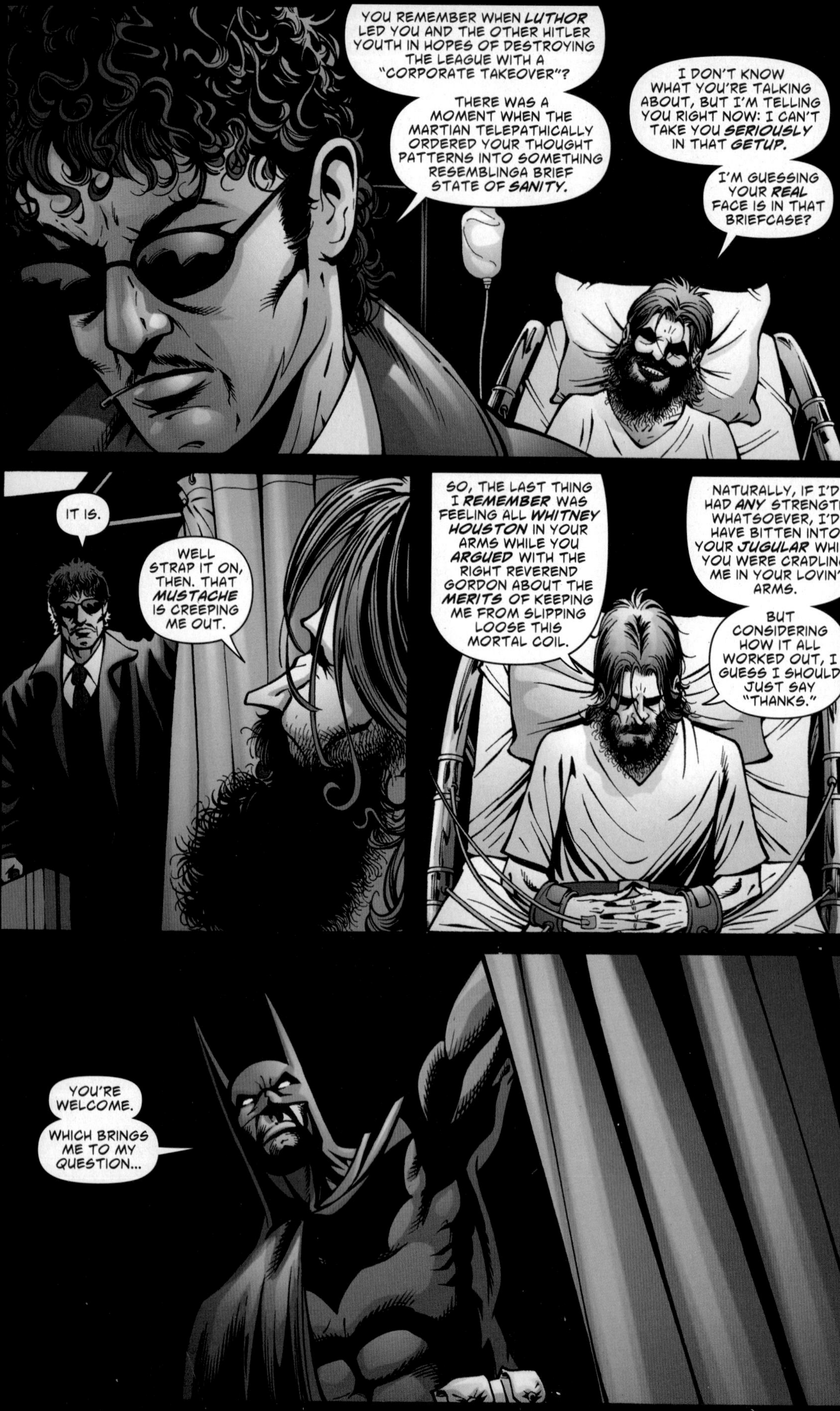
YOU REMEMBER WHEN LUTHOR LED YOU AND THE OTHER HITLER YOUTH IN HOPES OF DESTROYING THE LEAGUE WITH A "CORPORATE TAKEOVER"?
THERE WAS A MOMENT WHEN THE MARTIAN TELEPATHICALLY ORDERED YOUR THOUGHT PATTERNS INTO SOMETHING RESEMBLINGA BRIEF STATE OF SANITY.
I DON'T KNOW WHAT YOU'RE TALKING ABOUT, BUT I'M TELLING YOU RIGHT NOW: I CAN'T TAKE YOU SERIOUSLY IN THAT GETUP.
I'M GUESSING YOUR REAL FACE IS IN THAT BRIEFCASE?
IT IS.
WELL STRAP IT ON, THEN. THAT MUSTACHE IS CREEPING ME OUT.
SO, THE LAST THING I REMEMBER WAS FEELING ALL WHITNEY HOUSTON IN YOUR ARMS WHILE YOU ARGUED WITH THE RIGHT REVEREND GORDON ABOUT THE MERITS OF KEEPING ME FROM SLIPPING LOOSE THIS MORTAL COIL.
NATURALLY, IF I'D HAD ANY STRENGTH WHATSOEVER, I'D HAVE BITTEN INTO YOUR JUGULAR WHILE YOU WERE CRADLING ME IN YOUR LOVIN' ARMS.
BUT CONSIDERING HOW IT ALL WORKED OUT, I GUESS I SHOULD JUST SAY "THANKS."
YOU'RE WELCOME.
WHICH BRINGS ME TO MY QUESTION...

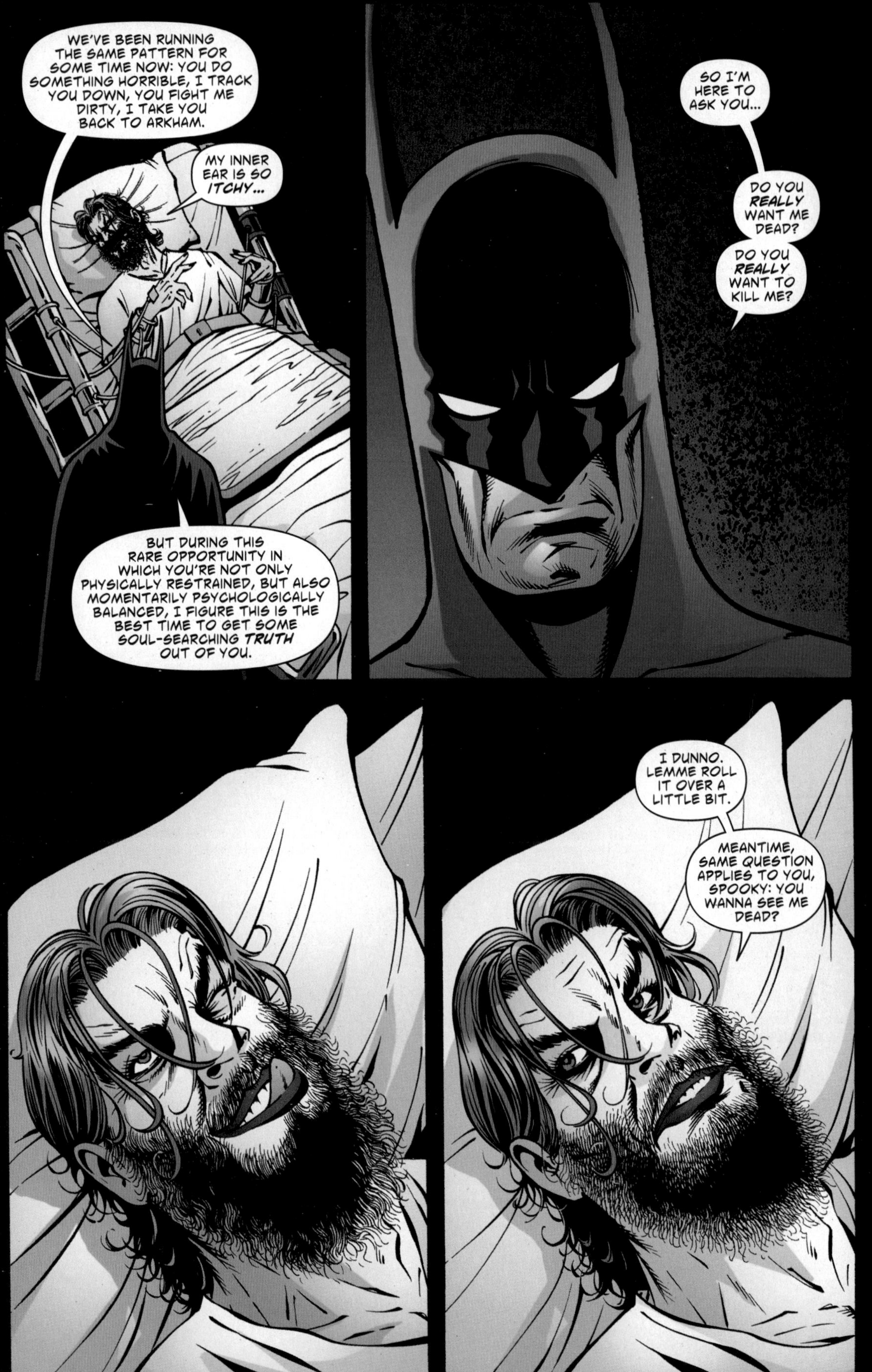
WE'VE BEEN RUNNING THE SAME PATTERN FOR SOME TIME NOW: YOU DO SOMETHING HORRIBLE, I TRACK YOU DOWN, YOU FIGHT ME DIRTY, I TAKE YOU BACK TO ARKHAM.
MY INNER EAR IS SO ITCHY...
BUT DURING THIS RARE OPPORTUNITY IN WHICH YOU'RE NOT ONLY PHYSICALLY RESTRAINED, BUT ALSO MOMENTARILY PSYCHOLOGICALLY BALANCED, I FIGURE THIS IS THE BEST TIME TO GET SOME SOUL-SEARCHING TRUTH OUT OF YOU.
SO I'M HERE TO ASK YOU...
DO YOU REALLY WANT ME DEAD?
DO YOU REALLY WANT TO KILL ME?
I DUNNO. LEMME ROLL IT OVER A LITTLE BIT.
MEANTIME, SAME QUESTION APPLIES TO YOU, SPOOKY: YOU WANNA SEE ME DEAD?

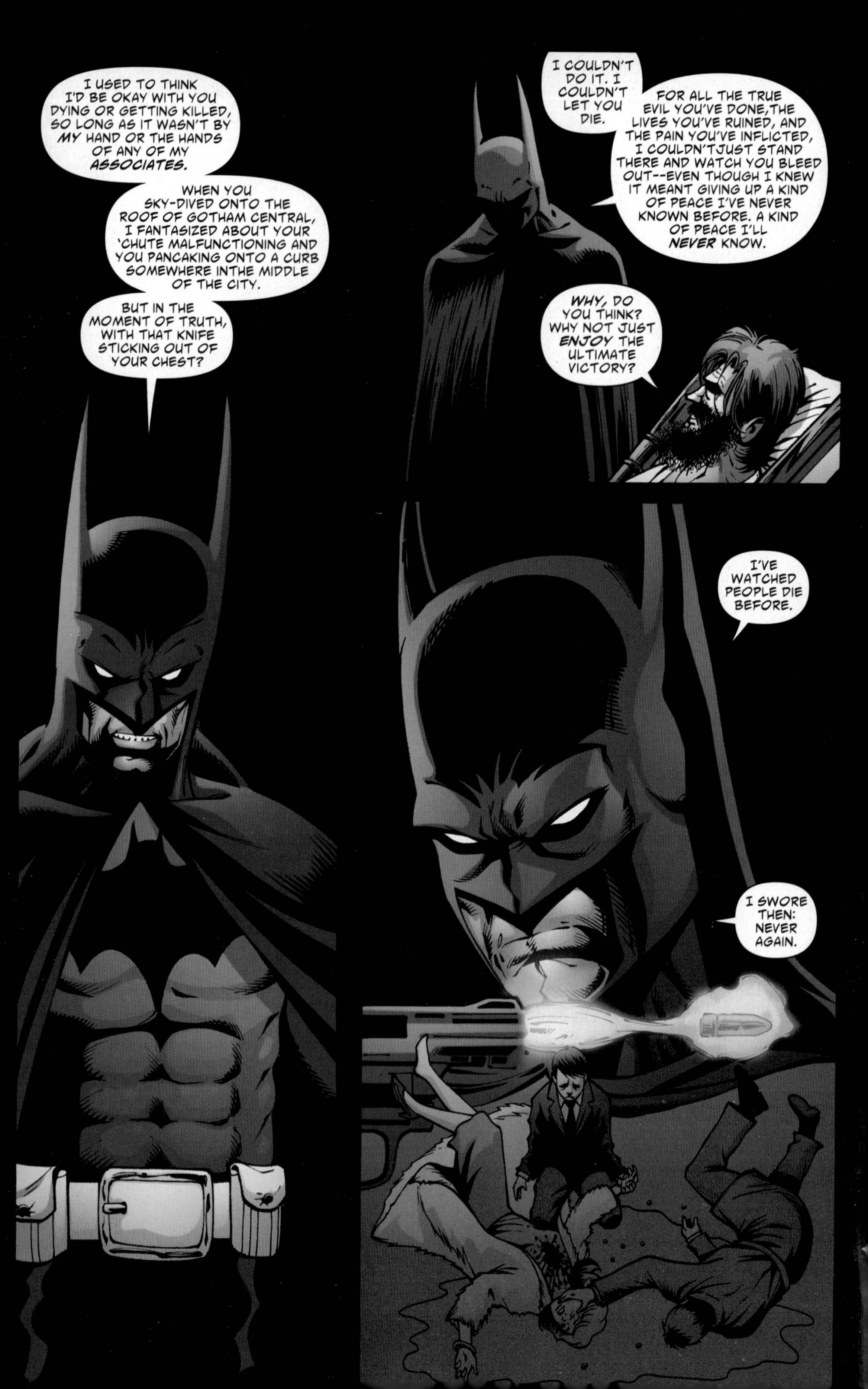
I USED TO THINK I'D BE OKAY WITH YOU DYING OR GETTING KILLED, SO LONG AS IT WASN'T BY MY HAND OR THE HANDS OF ANY OF MY ASSOCIATES.
WHEN YOU SKY-DIVED ONTO THE ROOF OF GOTHAM CENTRAL, I FANTASIZED ABOUT YOUR 'CHUTE MALFUNCTIONING AND YOU PANCAKING ONTO A CURB SOMEWHERE IN THE MIDDLE OF THE CITY.
BUT IN THE MOMENT OF TRUTH, WITH THAT KNIFE STICKING OUT OF YOUR CHEST?
I COULDN'T DO IT. I COULDN'T LET YOU DIE.
FOR ALL THE TRUE EVIL YOU'VE DONE, THE LIVES YOU'VE RUINED, AND THE PAIN YOU'VE INFLICTED, I COULDN'T JUST STAND THERE AND WATCH YOU BLEED OUT--EVEN THOUGH I KNEW IT MEANT GIVING UP A KIND OF PEACE I'VE NEVER KNOWN BEFORE. A KIND OF PEACE I'LL NEVER KNOW.
WHY, DO YOU THINK? WHY NOT JUST ENJOY THE ULTIMATE VICTORY?
I'VE WATCHED PEOPLE DIE BEFORE.
I SWORE THEN: NEVER AGAIN.

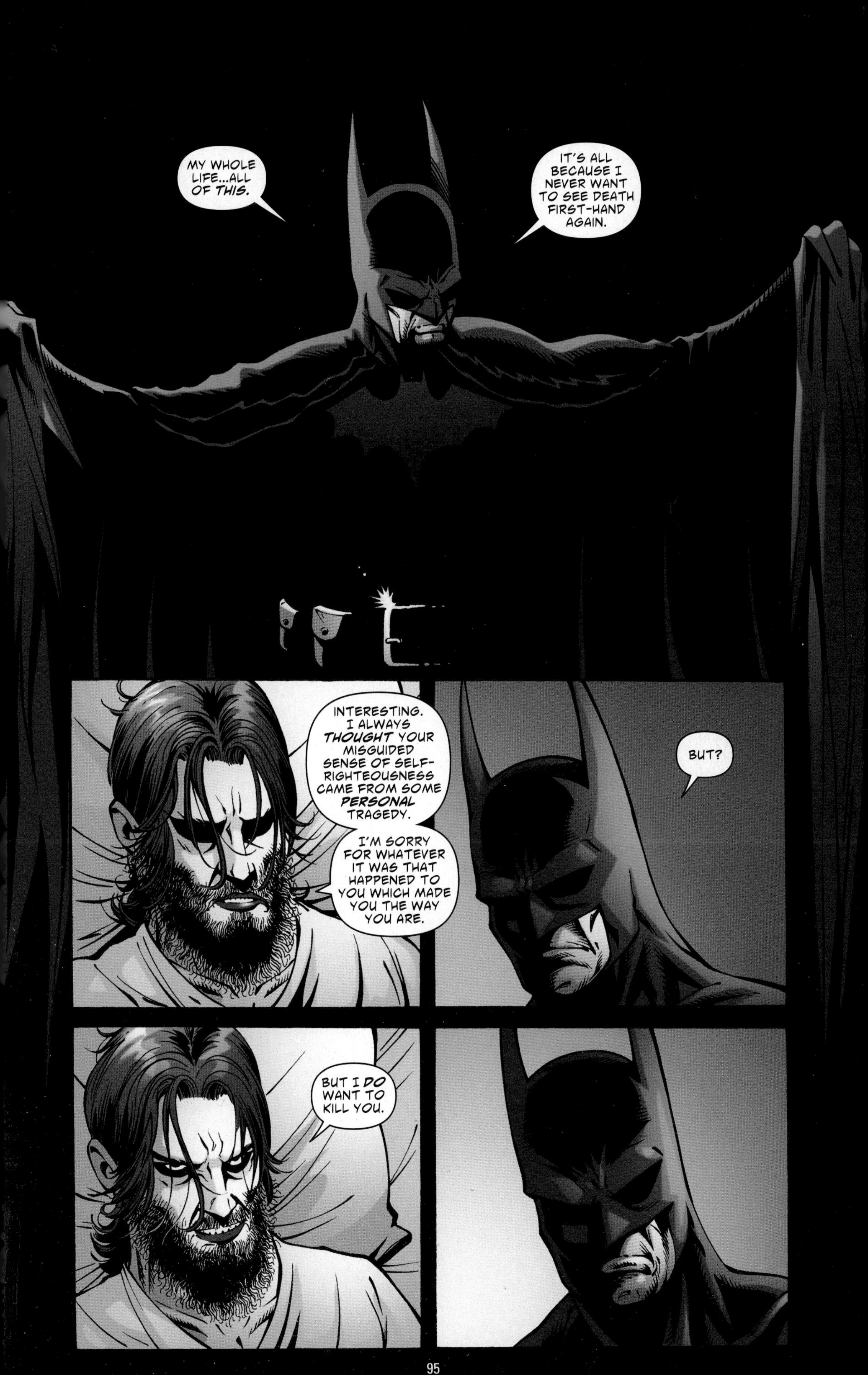
MY WHOLE LIFE...ALL OF THIS.
IT'S ALL BECAUSE I NEVER WANT TO SEE DEATH FIRST-HAND AGAIN.
INTERESTING. I ALWAYS THOUGHT YOUR MISGUIDED SENSE OF SELF-RIGHTEOUSNESS CAME FROM SOME PERSONAL TRAGEDY.
I'M SORRY FOR WHATEVER IT WAS THAT HAPPENED TO YOU WHICH MADE YOU THE WAY YOU ARE.
BUT?
BUT I DO WANT TO KILL YOU.

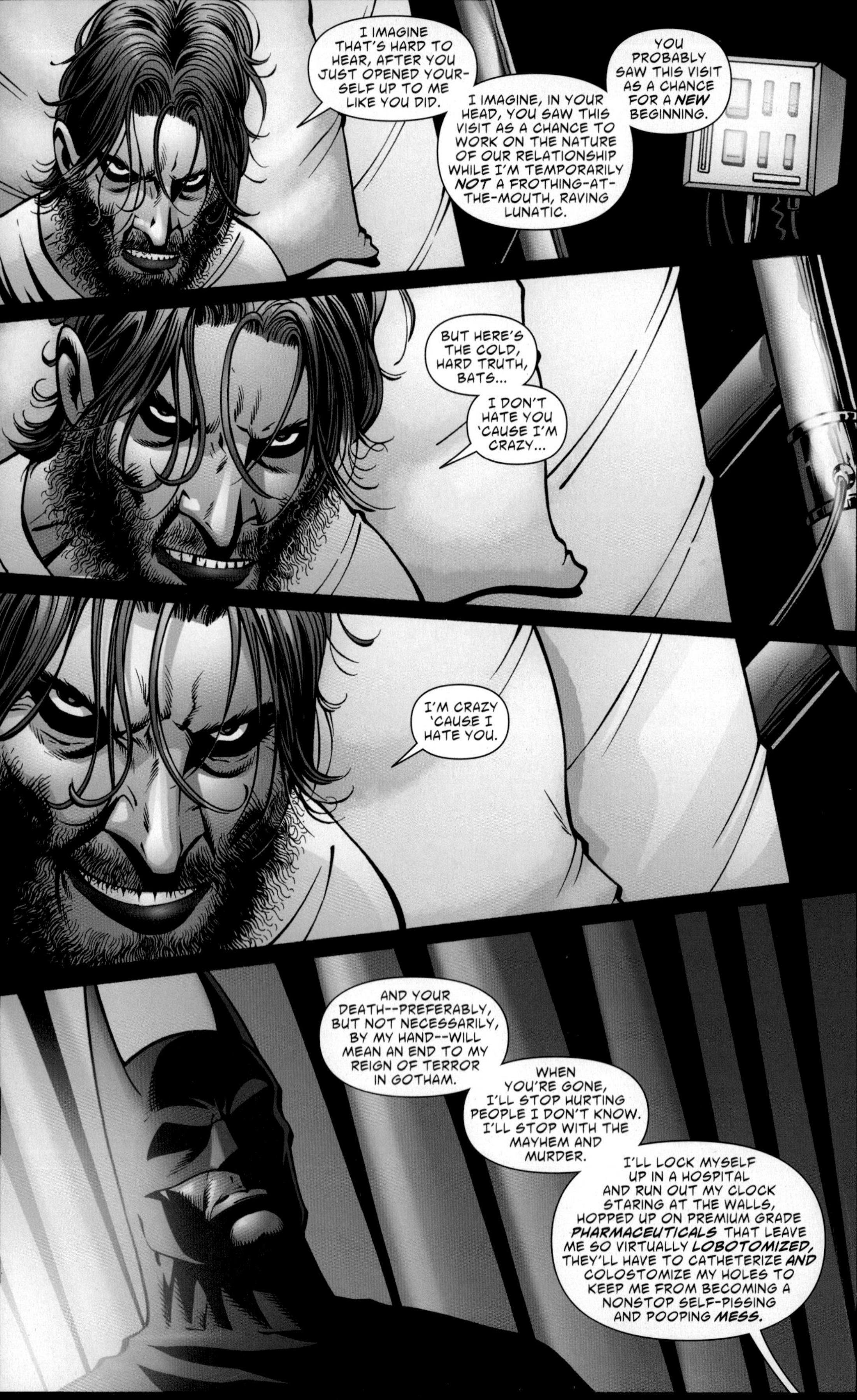
I IMAGINE THAT'S HARD TO HEAR, AFTER YOU JUST OPENED YOURSELF UP TO ME LIKE YOU DID.
I IMAGINE, IN YOUR HEAD, YOU SAW THIS VISIT AS A CHANCE TO WORK ON THE NATURE OF OUR RELATIONSHIP WHILE I'M TEMPORARILY NOT A FROTHING-AT-THE-MOUTH, RAVING LUNATIC.
YOU PROBABLY SAW THIS VISIT AS A CHANCE FOR A NEW BEGINNING.
BUT HERE'S THE COLD, HARD TRUTH, BATS...
I DON'T HATE YOU 'CAUSE I'M CRAZY...
I'M CRAZY 'CAUSE I HATE YOU.
AND YOUR DEATH--PREFERABLY, BUT NOT NECESSARILY, BY MY HAND--WILL MEAN AN END TO MY REIGN OF TERROR IN GOTHAM.
WHEN YOU'RE GONE, I'LL STOP HURTING PEOPLE I DON'T KNOW. I'LL STOP WITH THE MAYHEM AND MURDER.
I'LL LOCK MYSELF UP IN A HOSPITAL AND RUN OUT MY CLOCK STARING AT THE WALLS, HOPPED UP ON PREMIUM GRADE PHARMACEUTICALS THAT LEAVE ME SO VIRTUALLY LOBOTOMIZED, THEY'LL HAVE TO CATHETERIZE AND COLOSTOMIZE MY HOLES TO KEEP ME FROM BECOMING A NONSTOP SELF-PISSING AND POOPING MESS.

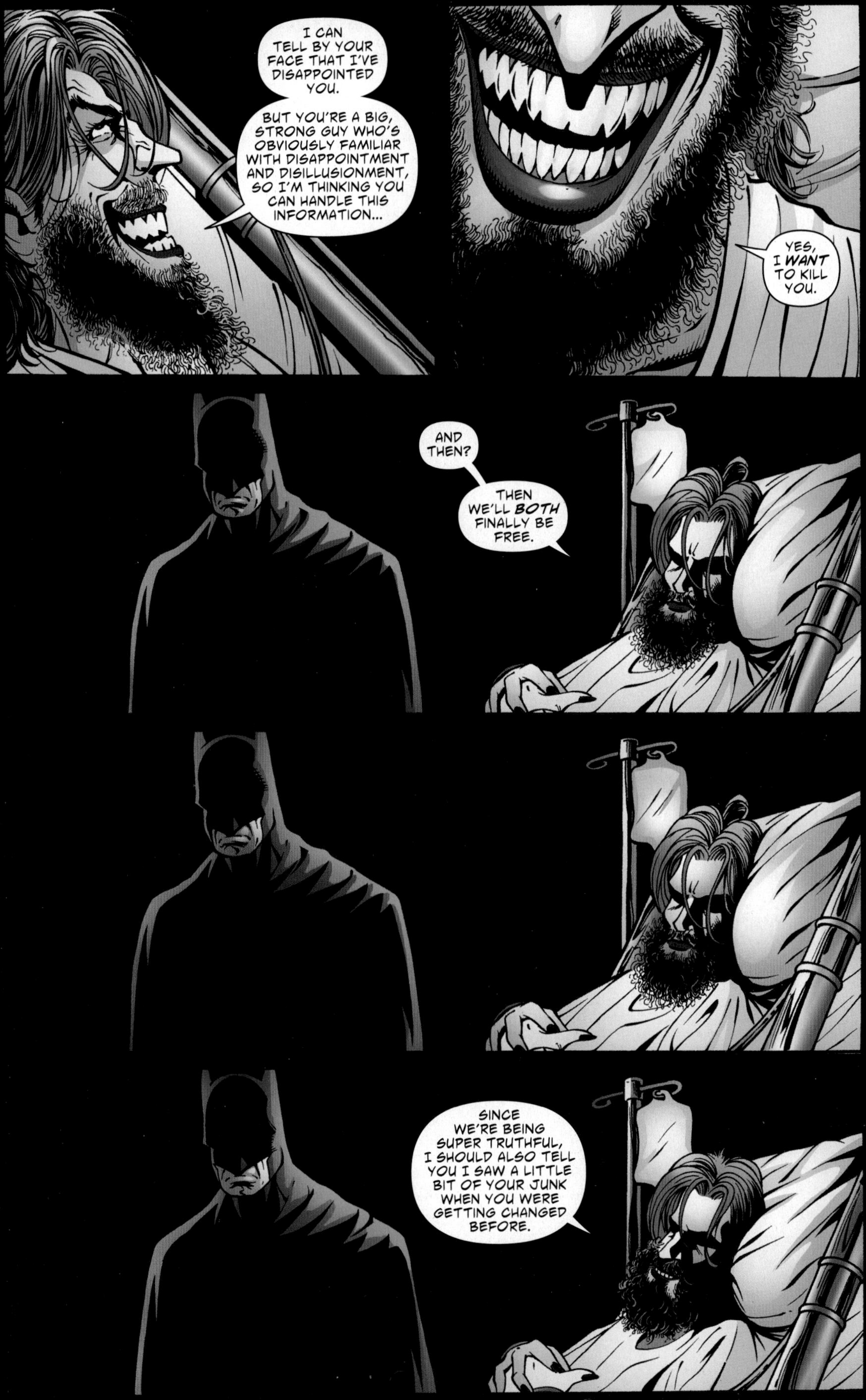
I CAN TELL BY YOUR FACE THAT I'VE DISAPPOINTED YOU.
BUT YOU'RE A BIG, STRONG GUY WHO'S OBVIOUSLY FAMILIAR WITH DISAPPOINTMENT AND DISILLUSIONMENT, SO I'M THINKING YOU CAN HANDLE THIS INFORMATION...
YES, I *WANT* TO KILL YOU.
AND THEN?
THEN WE'LL *BOTH* FINALLY BE FREE.
SINCE WE'RE BEING SUPER TRUTHFUL, I SHOULD ALSO TELL YOU I SAW A LITTLE BIT OF YOUR JUNK WHEN YOU WERE GETTING CHANGED BEFORE.

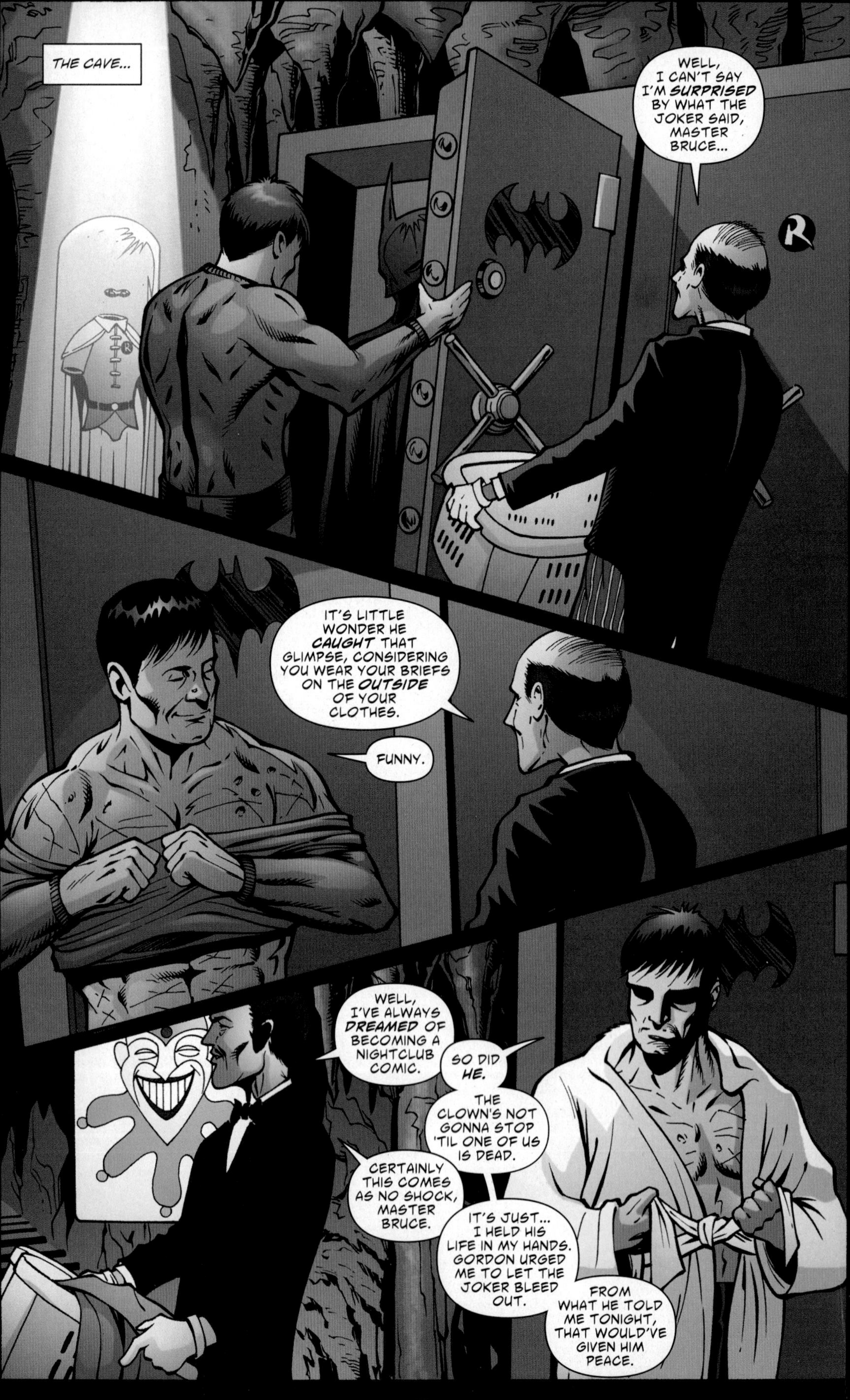
THE CAVE...
WELL, I CAN'T SAY I'M SURPRISED BY WHAT THE JOKER SAID, MASTER BRUCE...
IT'S LITTLE WONDER HE CAUGHT THAT GLIMPSE, CONSIDERING YOU WEAR YOUR BRIEFS ON THE OUTSIDE OF YOUR CLOTHES.
FUNNY.
WELL, I'VE ALWAYS DREAMED OF BECOMING A NIGHTCLUB COMIC.
SO DID HE.
THE CLOWN'S NOT GONNA STOP 'TIL ONE OF US IS DEAD.
CERTAINLY THIS COMES AS NO SHOCK, MASTER BRUCE.
IT'S JUST... I HELD HIS LIFE IN MY HANDS. GORDON URGED ME TO LET THE JOKER BLEED OUT.
FROM WHAT HE TOLD ME TONIGHT, THAT WOULD'VE GIVEN HIM PEACE.

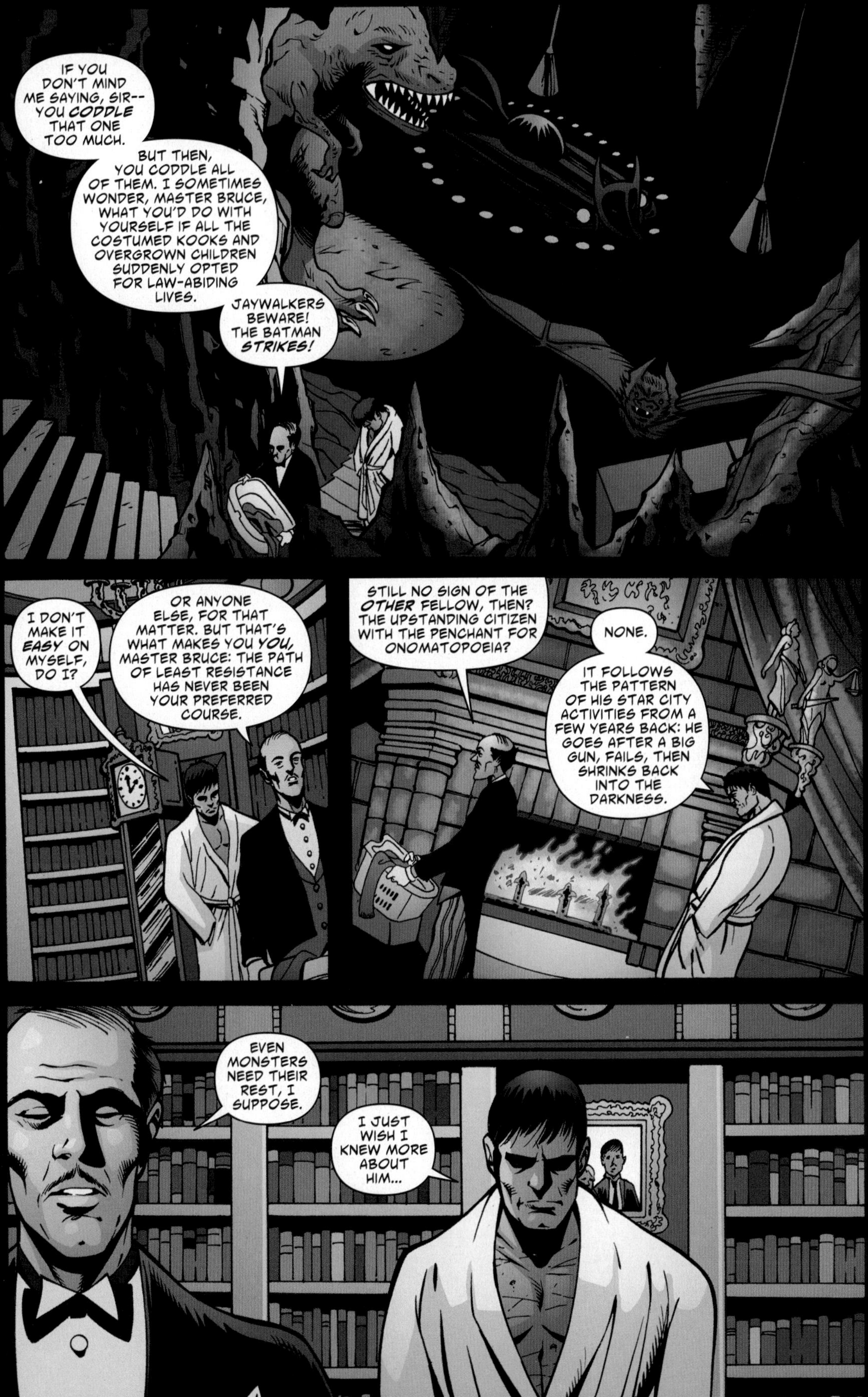
IF YOU DON'T MIND ME SAYING, SIR-- YOU CODDLE THAT ONE TOO MUCH.
BUT THEN, YOU CODDLE ALL OF THEM. I SOMETIMES WONDER, MASTER BRUCE, WHAT YOU'D DO WITH YOURSELF IF ALL THE COSTUMED KOOKS AND OVERGROWN CHILDREN SUDDENLY OPTED FOR LAW-ABIDING LIVES.
JAYWALKERS BEWARE! THE BATMAN STRIKES!
I DON'T MAKE IT EASY ON MYSELF, DO I?
OR ANYONE ELSE, FOR THAT MATTER. BUT THAT'S WHAT MAKES YOU YOU, MASTER BRUCE: THE PATH OF LEAST RESISTANCE HAS NEVER BEEN YOUR PREFERRED COURSE.
STILL NO SIGN OF THE OTHER FELLOW, THEN? THE UPSTANDING CITIZEN WITH THE PENCHANT FOR ONOMATOPOEIA?
NONE.
IT FOLLOWS THE PATTERN OF HIS STAR CITY ACTIVITIES FROM A FEW YEARS BACK: HE GOES AFTER A BIG GUN, FAILS, THEN SHRINKS BACK INTO THE DARKNESS.
EVEN MONSTERS NEED THEIR REST, I SUPPOSE.
I JUST WISH I KNEW MORE ABOUT HIM...

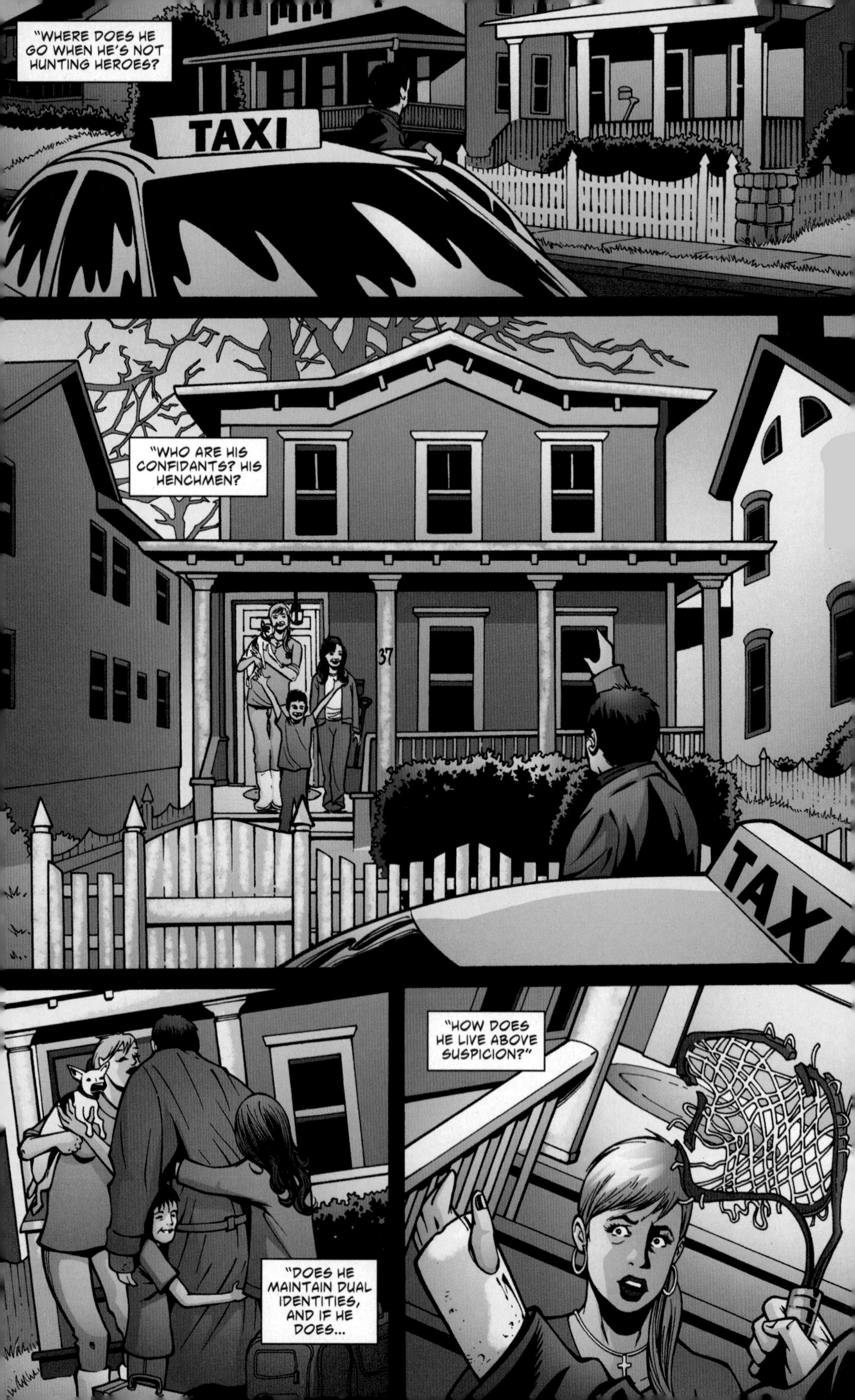
"WHERE DOES HE GO WHEN HE'S NOT HUNTING HEROES?
TAXI
"WHO ARE HIS CONFIDANTS? HIS HENCHMEN?
37
TAXI
"HOW DOES HE LIVE ABOVE SUSPICION?"
"DOES HE MAINTAIN DUAL IDENTITIES, AND IF HE DOES...

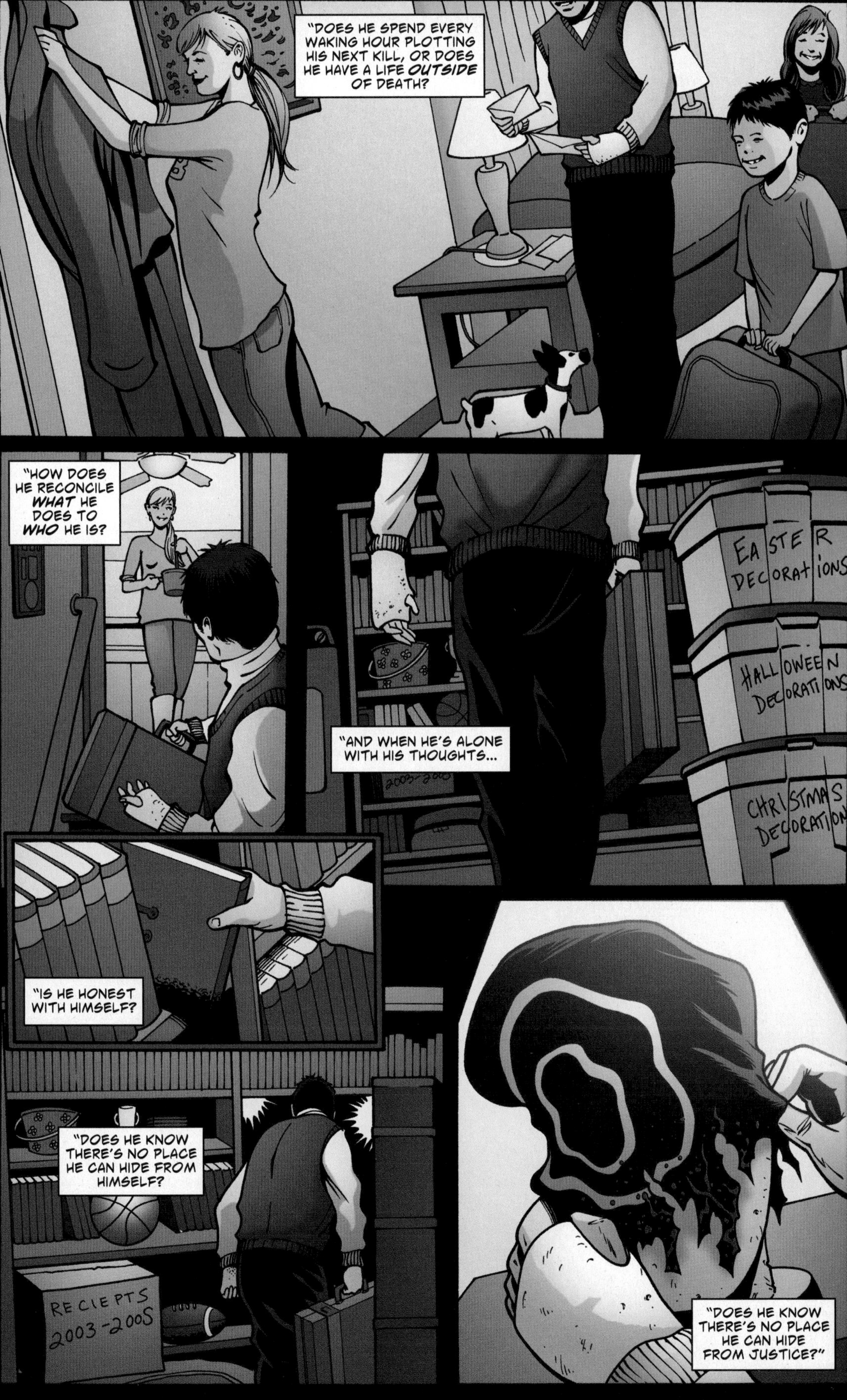
"DOES HE SPEND EVERY WAKING HOUR PLOTTING HIS NEXT KILL, OR DOES HE HAVE A LIFE *OUTSIDE* OF DEATH?
"HOW DOES HE RECONCILE *WHAT* HE DOES TO *WHO* HE IS?
EASTER DECORATIONS
HALLOWEEN DECORATIONS
CHRISTMAS DECORATIONS
"AND WHEN HE'S ALONE WITH HIS THOUGHTS...
"IS HE HONEST WITH HIMSELF?
"DOES HE KNOW THERE'S NO PLACE HE CAN HIDE FROM HIMSELF?
RECIEPTS 2003-2005
"DOES HE KNOW THERE'S NO PLACE HE CAN HIDE FROM JUSTICE?"

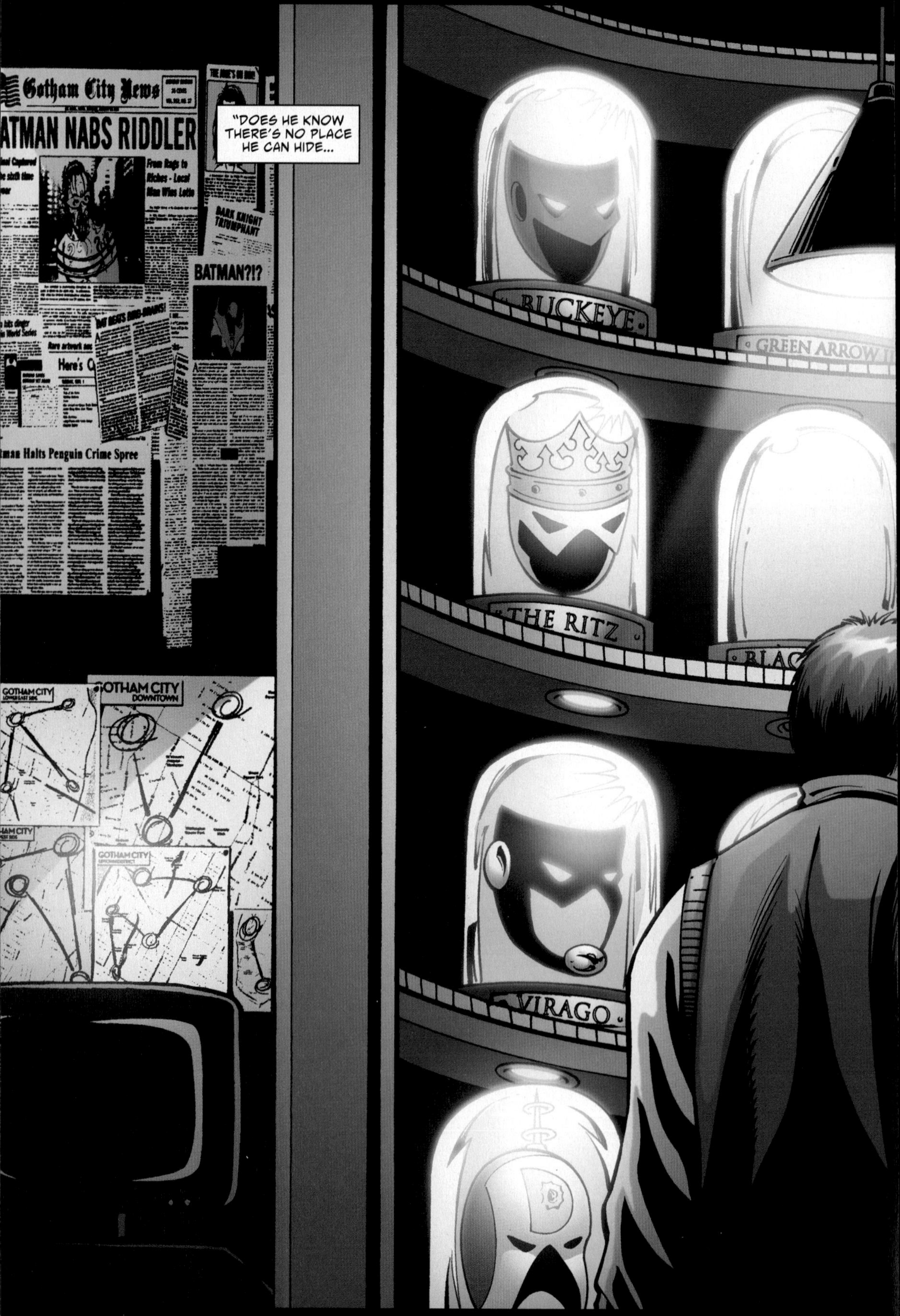
"DOES HE KNOW THERE'S NO PLACE HE CAN HIDE...
Gotham City News
ATMAN NABS RIDDLER
From Rags to Riches - Local Man Wins Lotto
DARK KNIGHT TRIUMPHANT
BATMAN?!?
Here's
tman Halts Penguin Crime Spree
GOTHAM CITY
DOWNTOWN
GOTHAM CITY
BUCKEYE
GREEN ARROW
THE RITZ
VIRAGO

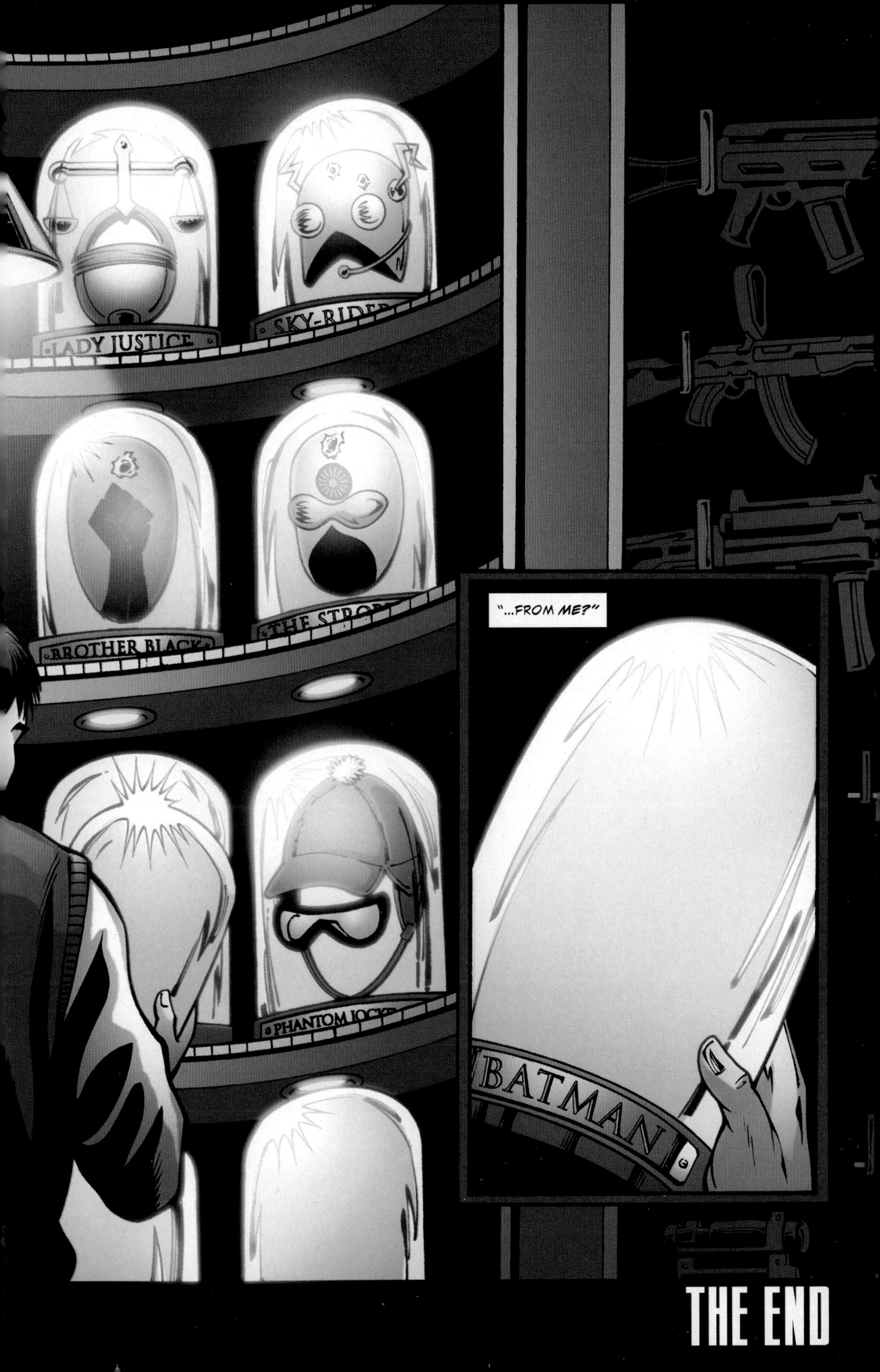
LADY JUSTICE
SKY-RIDER
BROTHER BLACK
"...FROM ME?"
BATMAN
THE END

Here's the script for the first draft of issue three. Compare it against the final comic and you'll see I was able to redeem myself for some eyebrow-raising dialogue ("Nothing to say now, murderer?" is the one that makes ME cringe). Thank God for last-minute dialogue polishes (and editors who'll make it happen, even though the book's about to print). However, page five was so offensive in a completely different way (over-the-top Joker dialogue) that we opted to remove it entirely from the printed issue. You'll notice its absence from the script that follows, as well: that's how off-color that bit was. Best we never speak of it again.

Anyway, peep the first draft. See what a difference the right dialogue and narration makes?

Batman: Cacophony

Part Three:

Baffles

By

Kevin Smith

EXT GOTHAM CENTRAL ROOFTOP - NIGHT

Panel One

A reverse of the last panel of issue two. Foreground: we're
over Onomatopoeia, waist-down, guns at his sides as they were
at end of last ish. In the mid/background, it's Batman
standing defensively, Joker happy, still cuffed to
the Bat signal, shattered glass from the Bat signal
in evidence on ground around him.

Panel Two

Close on Batman, chest-up.

                    BATMAN INTERNAL 1
          You've got him, Bruce.

                    BATMAN INTERNAL 2
          He's no match for your years of
          training.

Panel Three

A corresponding close on Ono, chest-up.

                    BATMAN INTERNAL
          Those guns are his only edge.

Panel Four

Insert panel: tight on Joker's hand grabbing a particularly
nasty, large shard of broken Bat signal glass; big enough to
be used as a weapon.

                    BATMAN INTERNAL (CONT'D)
          Even from this distance, you've got
          him...

Panel Five

The Joker madly swinging glass piece through the air, in
overhead arch.

                    BATMAN INTERNAL (CONT'D)
          Barring any *unseen* variables.

Panel Six

The Joker maniacally plunging the glass shard into Batman's
calf, with Batman reacting.

> JOKER
> SHOOT HIM NOW! SHOOT HIM NOW!

Panel Seven

Ono immediately throws up right gun-hand and fires.

> SFX
> BLAM!

PAGES TWO AND THREE

Splash Page:

Ono in the background, smoking gun pointed at Batman, who's
in the foreground, back sort of to us; but Bats' upper torso
is twisted toward us from the impact of the shot: right into
his cowl's forehead. Blood spraying everywhere. The Joker
is delighted. It would appear that Batman's been shot dead
through his skull. The air is filled with the Joker's
HAHAHAHAHAHAHA.

> BATMAN
> UHN!

> CREDITS
> Batman: Cacophony
> Part 3: Baffles
> Writer: Kevin Smith
> Artist: Walt Flanagan
> Inker: Sandra Hope
> Colorist: Guy Major
> Lettering:
> Editor: Dan DiDio
> Covers: Kubert
> Batman created by Bob Kane

PAGE FOUR

Panel One

Batman falling onto his back on the rooftop, apparently dead,
blood pouring from his head-shot.

> SFX
> (body hitting ground)
> THUD!

Panel Two

Onomatopoeia leaps into the air from his doorway perch.

Panel Three

Close on Ono's feet hitting the deck in the foreground,
some dust rising from the impact. In the back and mid ground,
the Batman is laying dead on the rooftop, out of the Joker's
reach. The Joker is beyond delighted.

                    SFX (CONT'D)
          FLOMMMP!

Panel Four

Ono, standing now, as if he'd landed with buckled knees.

                    ONOMATOPOEIA
          Flommmp.

Panel Five

The Joker's desperately trying to reach the out-of-reach
Batman, but he's still cuffed to Bat signal.

                    JOKER
          Uhn! Can't... reach...
               (balloon two)
          Listen here, Chatty-Kathy: can
          you... uhn... get me out of these
          cuffs...

PAGE SIX

Panel One

Chest-up on Ono, who now brings his bloody gun up, pointing
it at the off-panel Joker. Batman's unseen, below the bottom
of the frame.

Panel Two

The Joker reacting to the gun pointing at him. Ono's not in the
frame; just his pointing gun coming in from the right side of
the panel.

                    JOKER (CONT'D)
          Um... no sweat, Buddy.

Panel Three

Same set-up, but now Batman's hand has thrust up into the
frame, violently grabbing Ono's gun hand and snapping the
wrist. The Joker's gone wide-eyed.

                    SFX
          KRR-SNAP!

Panel Four

Ono reeling back, in pain, with snapped wrist, bringing other
gun hand around to shoot.

                ONOMATOPOEIA
          AAAHHHHHHH!

Panel Five

Close on Bats' foot coming up (from where it was laying on
the roof) kicking Ono's other gun from his other hand. It's
firing as it's kicked, but the shot hits nothing, thanks to
the kick-block.

                    SFX
          KICK!

                SFX (CONT'D)
          BLAM!

Panel Six

Close on Ono getting punched in the face by Batman's fist.

                SFX (CONT'D)
          KEE-RUNCH!

                ONOMATOPOEIA
          UHNFF!

PAGE SEVEN

Panel One

Ono on his butt, holding his snapped wrist to his chest, his
eye-line following the off-panel Batman, who's presumably
standing up. There's some rain starting to hit the roof.

              ONOMATOPOEIA (CONT'D)
          Uhn... Uhn...

                BATMAN INTERNAL
          Head still ringing, but it'll pass.

Panel Two

The Joker, looking scared, his eye-line following the off-panel
Batman, who's presumably standing up. More rain now; it's
getting heavier.

> BATMAN INTERNAL 1
> All I had to do was stand within
> striking distance of the clown and
> count on the Joker to *be* the Joker.

> BATMAN INTERNAL 2
> But I owe a bigger thanks to Floyd
> Lawton.

Panel Three

Biggest panel on the page: Batman standing over the grounded
Onomatopoeia (his back sort of to us). Lightning strikes
behind him far off in the distance. It's now raining full
out, from here on in.

> BATMAN INTERNAL 1
> I "borrowed" Deadshot's helmet
> technology: the secondary armor
> beneath the Kevlar headpiece, the
> blood pack liner for that Grand
> Guignol effect.

> BATMAN INTERNAL 2
> Normally, I prefer any innovations
> I incorporate to be my own, but
> hell...

> BATMAN INTERNAL 3
> A good idea's a good idea.

PAGE EIGHT

Panel One

Close on Batman's hand violently grabbing Onomatopoeia by his
snapped wrist.

> BATMAN INTERNAL
> And I just had *another* one...

> ONOMATOPOEIA
> AAAHHHHH!!!

Panel Two

Batman yanks Ono to his feet with one hand, and pulls back
with the other.

Panel Three

Batman punching Ono something fierce in the face, throwing
him backwards.

                        SFX
            KRAK!

Panel Four

Ono on the ground, throws a sweep kick across the ground
at Batman's feet, but Batman leaps into the air in place,
causing Ono to miss.

                    SFX (CONT'D)
                (missed leg sweep)
            WIFFFF!

Panel Five

Ono's kinda facing us in an upward-dog position. Batman comes
down from his hop-up, landing on Ono's calf hard, with a...

                    SFX (CONT'D)
            SNAP!

                    ONOMATOPOEIA
            UHNNN!

PAGE NINE

Panel One

The Joker, seeing all this happening off-panel, reacts with
a "I was with you the whole time"-kinda caught expression,
desperately trying to get his hand out of the Bat cuff at
the same time.

                    JOKER
            Uh... yeah. Get him, Bats.
                (balloon two)
            I knew you were going for that...
            uh... *playing possum* thing - which
            is the reason... the *ONLY* reason I
            pretended to stab you in the leg,
            see?
                (balloon three)
            For reals.

Panel Two

Tight on Ono's face being punched hard by a downward blow
from Batman's fist.

                         SFX
            SOK!

                         BATMAN INTERNAL
            I shut out the clown's rambling and
            make a meal out of this mask-
            killer.

Panel Three

Batman picking up Ono by his collar, lifting him off the
ground so he's over Bats.

                         BATMAN INTERNAL 1
            This is for Buckeye.

                         BATMAN INTERNAL 2
            And Virago.

                         BATMAN INTERNAL 3
            And who knows how many other would-
            be heroes you've stalked and
            killed.

Panel Four

Close on Batman, teeth gritted, looking up at Ono's face.

                         BATMAN
            Nothing to say *now*, murderer?
                  (balloon two)
            Lemme help you out with that...

Panel Five

Batman, post-punch (in body language); Ono flying at us.

                         SFX
            POW!

Panel One

The beaten Ono, landing beside the still-cuffed Joker, who
reacts terrified.

                    SFX (CONT'D)
        KA-THUD!

                    JOKER
        Man alive - did I hitch *my* wagon to
        the wrong star.

Panel Two

With the close Joker looking on, Ono struggles to roll over,
reaching into his coat.

                    JOKER (CONT'D)
        Or maybe not...
                (balloon two; smaller;
                whispering)
        Get it, buddy! Let's book a trip
        to that Last Resort!

Panel Three

Ono has pulled his massive hunting knife from his coat,
brandishing it weakly, as the Joker excitedly looks on,
cheering. The Joker is reaching into his own coat with
his free hand now.

                    JOKER (CONT'D)
        Now we're talking! Yes!

Panel Four

Over the raised knife-holding hand in the foreground, onto
Bats reacting in the mid-to-background.

                    OFF-PANEL JOKER
        Eat it, Bats! We're gonna put *real*
        holes in your dumb ass now!

Panel Five

Ono, sitting up sorta now, beside the yelling Joker, who
waves a small cheerleader pom-pom with his free hand.

                    JOKER
        Gut that *pig*! *Bury* that sweet
        steel into his *sanctimonious*...

PAGE ELEVEN

Panel One

Biggest panel on the page: Ono plunges the knife into the
Joker's heart. The Joker reacts wide-eyed. Blood shoots out
everywhere. (Guy: can you do that motion effect on Ono's
knife-hand that you did for ish one, when Bats punched
through the wall to get to Zsasz? Thanks.)

> SFX
> SHHHUNTTTTT!!!

> JOKER
> (weakly; small)
> Heart?

Panel Two

Close on Batman reacting.

> BATMAN INTERNAL
> No!

Panel Three

Ono hurls himself atop the knife, pushing it deeper. The
Joker's in agony, spitting up blood. Batman's racing toward
them.

> SFX
> SQUISH-UNT!

> JOKER
> AAAAAAARRRRRGGGGHHHHHH!!!

Panel Four

Batman pulls Ono off the Joker, throwing him backwards. The
knife is buried to the hilt in the Joker's chest.

> BATMAN INTERNAL 1
> Not *tonight*!

> BATMAN INTERNAL 2
> Not on *my* watch!

Panel Five

Batman is pressing down around the wound, trying to stop the
bleeding. Joker's losing consciousness.

> BATMAN INTERNAL 1
> He buried the knife so deeply, I
> can't risk extracting it, 'lest the
> Clown bleed out.

> BATMAN INTERNAL 2
> Applying pressure around the wound
> to stop the bleeding, but he's a
> geyser at this point.

> BATMAN INTERNAL 3
> On top of this, I have to worry
> about second attack from...

PAGE TWELVE

Panel One

Over Ono's arm and mangled wrist/hand that he's holding with
his free hand (but we're over his back). Batman's kneeling
at the Joker's side in profile, applying pressure to the
knife-wound, looking at us/Ono.

> BATMAN INTERNAL 1
> Oh.

> BATMAN INTERNAL 2
> I get it.

Panel Two

Corresponding over: Over Bat's (in profile), his head facing
Ono - who stands at the roof's edge, beside the roof exit,
"looking" at us, beaten, battered, clothes and mask torn
and bloody.

> BATMAN INTERNAL
> Stabbing the Joker wasn't a
> *diversion*.

> BATMAN INTERNAL 2
> It's a *test*.

Panel Three

Close on Batman. Still raining, don't forget.

> BATMAN INTERNAL
> It's a test of my *code*.

> BATMAN INTERNAL 2
> Save the life of someone whose very
> existence jeopardizes the lives of
> others...

Panel Four

Close on the beaten, slightly-hunched Ono - waiting.

> BATMAN INTERNAL
> Or stop someone whose very
> existence jeopardizes the lives of
> others...

> BATMAN INTERNAL 2
> As well as my own.

Panel Five

Over (meaning overhead, in this instance), Batman, looking
down on the bleeding-out, dying Joker. We should be looking
straight down. Rain pouring all around them; puddles.

> BATMAN INTERNAL
> I know what I *should* do...

> BATMAN INTERNAL 2
> I just *can't*.

PAGE THIRTEEN

Panel One

This panel is a mirror of panel two on the last page, only
now, Ono's not where he was standing in that panel; he's
completely vanished.

> BATMAN INTERNAL
> God help me, I just *can't*...

Panel Two

Same set-up as the previous panel, but in the foreground,
Batman's scooping up the Joker. In the background, the
stairwell door is being kicked open by Gordon and some
armed/armored Cops.

                    SFX
          SLAM!

                    GORDON
          What *happened*?! Where *is* he?!

Panel Three

Biggest panel on the page: Batman, standing in the rain,
holding the dying, unconscious Joker in his arms. Blood
and water run down his body, puddling on the rooftop.

                    BATMAN
          He stabbed the Joker, Jim.
          Through the *heart*.
                    (balloon two)
          He's *dying*.

PAGE FOURTEEN

Panel One

High overhead of the Cops fanning out, guns and rifles raised
defensively, looking for anyone else on the roof. Gordon
approaches the Joker-holding Batman.

                    GORDON
          Where's the *other* guy? The *Mask—*
          killer?

                    BATMAN
          He escaped.

                    GORDON
          You're not going *after* him?

                    BATMAN
          I've got to deal with the Joker.

                    GORDON
          What're you *talking* about?!

                    BATMAN
          Jim - if I don't get him medical
          attention immediately, he'll die.

Panel Two

Over Bats' shoulder, onto Gordon. Gordon's glaring at the
off-panel Batman. In the background, the Cops, looking
around. The stairwell is in evidence in the background.

Panel Three

Same set-up, but now the Cops in the background are reacting
to Gordon - who's calling back over his shoulder a bit, still
holding his look to Batman (whose face we still can't see).

                    GORDON
          I want everyone to *stand down*!
                (balloon two)
          Off this roof! *NOW*!

Panel Four

Same set-up, but the Cops in the background are heading
toward the stairwell exit. Gordon's looking back over his
shoulder slightly, to make sure the other Cops are leaving.

Panel Five

Same set-up, but now the Cops are all gone. Gordon's looking
at Batman again; glaring, really.

                    GORDON (CONT'D)
          Are you *crazy*?
                (balloon two)
          Let him die!

PAGE FIFTEEN

Panel One

Close on Batman, chest-up; surprised.

                    BATMAN
          I... I *can't*, Jim.
                (balloon two)
          It was *my* idea to use him as *bait*.
          I got him stabbed.

Panel Two

An angry Gordon gives Batman an earful.

> GORDON
> *No!*
>   (balloon two)
> What got him *stabbed* was his
> fundamental inability to ever be
> anything but *evil incarnate*!

> BATMAN
> Jim...

> GORDON
> Don't *"Jim"* me! He's a *monster* and
> you *know* it!

> BATMAN
> We can't let ourselves forget that
> he's a *human being* too!

> GORDON
> Oh yes we can! Think about all the
> *horror* he's wreaked in this city -
> for longer than I can *remember*!

Panel Three

Biggest panel on the page. A flashback of the Joker's
greatest hits, so to speak: random people clutching at their
own throats, their faces constricting in rictus grins; the
shooting of Barbara Gordon; the torturing of Jim Gordon
(Killing Joke); the beating of Jason Todd; anything else
you can think of, include. Maybe throw in Batman's head
into the middle or something, as if all these images are
swirling around in it. Your call.

> GORDON VOICEOVER
> Think about what he's done to the
> *people* in this city...

> GORDON VOICEOVER 2
> Think about what he did to *me*...

> GORDON VOICEOVER 3
> What he did to *Barbara*...

> GORDON VOICEOVER 4
> What he's done to *you*!

Panel One

Close on the face of the Joker in Batman's arms, hanging
back and lolling down. The water running down his rain soaked
face is mixed with blood; his hair, now soaked, is long, the
water pulling it toward the ground. Leave enough space for
all the off-panel Gordon's word balloons.

> GORDON
> I understood why you never killed
> him *yourself*: you've got a moral
> code I've respected for *years*.
> (balloon two)
> But I'm not asking you to *kill* him
> here...
> (balloon three)
> I'm just asking you not to *save* his
> worthless, *corrosive* life!
> (balloon four)
> You didn't *do* this. You didn't
> *stab* him. This is *his* doing.
> (balloon five)
> He made his choices.

Panel Two

INT STAIRWELL - SAME

We're in the stairwell, over the armored cops (who'd been on
the roof), hiding in the shadows at the top of the stairwell,
watching this scene play out in the distance.

> BATMAN
> He can't *make* choices, Jim.
> (balloon two)
> He's *insane*.

> GORDON
> *Insanity* would be keeping him
> *alive*, so he can drop *another*
> building on *another* bunch of *school
> kids*!

Panel Three

Close on Gordon.

>   GORDON (CONT'D)
>   Do the right thing here. For
>   *Gotham's* sake.
>   (balloon two)
>   For *your* sake.
>   (balloon three)
>   Let him *go*.

Panel Four

A profile of Batman holding the dying Joker in his arms, as Jim Gordon looks at him pleadingly. The rain falls.

Panel Five

Same shot, but pulled away more (so the figures are about 40% smaller, and we're seeing more of the roof/ surrounding buildings.

Panel Six

Same shot, but now pulled back even further, so Batman (holding dying Joker) and Gordon are very tiny figures.

PAGE SEVENTEEN

Panel One

INT HOSPITAL HALLWAY - NIGHT

We're at one end of a long corridor, at the other end of which stand two armed (with rifles) and armored Police. They guard a pair of what look like supermarket entry doors marked with the huge letters I.C.U. There's no bustle in the hallway as with most hospitals; the whole floor's empty, except for the armored guards, who're tiny in the distance. Throw a few pieces of hospital equipment into the hallway, though - just to nail our location home for the reader.

Panel Two

Same exact shot, but now a LAWYER is walking down the hallway (back to us), carrying a briefcase, heading for the I.C.U. Give him curly, fro-ish hair.

Panel Three

Same exact shot, but now the LAWYER is in front of the
armored guards, holding up a few pieces of paper that're
stapled together. The guards look at the paper.

> LAWYER
> Gentlemen, I'm from the firm of
> Malone & Malone. We've been
> retained to represent the patient.
> I understand he came out of his
> coma this morning. As his
> attorney, I'm entitled to speak to
> him.
> > (balloon two)
> This is a court order from a
> circuit judge saying as much -
> guaranteeing me undisturbed, un-
> monitored face-time with my client.

PAGE EIGHTEEN

Panel One

Close on the Joker, in a hospital bed, his face buried in Ayn
Rand's "The Fountainhead." His hair is visibly longer now.
He's hooked up to an I.V. unit. There are restraints around
his arms, wrists, chest - everywhere, really. He's got just
enough slack to read his book. In the foreground, we see a
shoulder of the Lawyer.

Panel Two

Same image, but now the Joker has lowered the book slightly,
to take in his guest. He looks like utter crap: like he's
been out for months. Maybe give him a green, straggly beard.

Panel Three

The Joker goes back to reading his book.

> JOKER
> 'lo, Bats.

Panel Four

The first time we're seeing the face of MATCHES MALONE
(aka, Bruce Wayne in disguise, a matchstick jutting out of
the corner of his mouth). He stands at the Joker's bedside.
His briefcase is placed on one of those wheeled hospital
tables that patients use.

> MATCHES
> Joker.

Panel One

The Joker continues reading his book. Matches looks on.

> JOKER
> I'm glad to see you haven't garaged
> the old *disguise kit*.
> > (balloon two)
> Matches strikes again.

> MATCHES
> Cute.

Panel Two

Joker tosses his book to the side.

> JOKER
> > (smaller; as if a sotto aside)
> I'm *never* gonna finish this book...
> > (balloon two; regular size)
> To what do I owe this unexpected
> pleasure?

Panel Three

Matches looking down at the Joker in bed.

> MATCHES
> Just checking up on you.
> > (balloon two)
> I'm sure they already let you know
> you've been in a coma for five
> months now.

> JOKER
> Ayup. Now they've got me *doped up*
> on *morphine* - not to mention an *ass-
> load* of mood stabilizers and anti-
> psychotics.

> MATCHES
> That's why I'm here. I couldn't
> pass up the opportunity to have a
> somewhat *rational* conversation with
> you.

Panel Four

The Joker offering a sheepish grin.

>   OFF-PANEL MATCHES
>   Or, at least, a conversation during
>   which you're not trying to poison
>   me, hit me with that hammer, or
>   feed me to killer fish.

>   JOKER
>   It's what I *do*.

PAGE TWENTY

Panel One

Matches turns his back to the Joker and looks out
the curtained window. The Joker is rolling his eyes.

>   MATCHES
>   We've only ever had one other
>   chance to do this: after *Luthor* put
>   together that bid to destroy the
>   League with a "corporate takeover."
>   (balloon two)
>   The Martian telepathically ordered
>   your thought patterns into
>   something resembling a brief state
>   of *sanity*.

>   JOKER
>   I don't know what you're talking
>   about, but I'm telling you right
>   now: I can't take you *seriously* in
>   that *get-up*.
>   (balloon two)
>   I'm guessing your *real* face is in
>   that briefcase?

Panel Two

Matches holds his briefcase in one hand, and closes a curtain
(the kind hung from the ceiling around a patient's bed in the
hospital; a privacy curtain) with his other hand - as if he's
gonna get dressed.

                    MATCHES
          It is.

                    JOKER
          Well strap it on, then. That
          mustache is creeping me out.

Panel Three

On the Joker, strapped into bed.

                    JOKER (CONT'D)
          So, the last thing I *remember* was
          you Costner-ing me in your arms
          like I was *Whitney Houston*, while
          you *argued* with the right reverend
          Gordon about the *merits* of keeping me
          from slipping loose this mortal coil.
               (balloon two)
          Naturally, if I'd had *any* strength
          whatsoever, I'd have bitten into
          your *jugular* while you were
          cradling *me* in your lovin' arms.
               (balloon three)
          But considering how it all worked
          out, I guess I should just say
          "thanks."

Panel Four

Batman, now fully dressed in his gear, slides the curtain
open.

                    BATMAN
          You're welcome.
               (balloon two)
          Which brings me to my question...

Panel One

On the Joker, trying to scratch his ear by rubbing his head
on the pillow (since his hands are restrained).

> OFF-PANEL BATMAN
> We've been doing this for some time
> now: you do something horrible, I
> track you down, you fight me
> viciously, I take you back to Arkham.

> JOKER
> My inner ear is so *itchy*...

> OFF-PANEL BATMAN
> But during this rare opportunity in
> which you're not only physically
> restrained, but also momentarily
> psychologically balanced, I figure
> this is the best time to get some
> soul-searching *truth* out of you.

Panel Two

Close on Batman.

> BATMAN
> So I'm here to ask you...
>> (balloon two; it should be
>> more distant from balloon
>> one - as if he's giving a
>> pregnant pause)
> Do you *really* want me dead?
>> (balloon three)
> Do you *really* want to kill me?

Panel Three

Close on the Joker, mulling that thought over. Remember,
he's drugged-up, so his expression can't be too crazy. He
should look like a six year old trying to solve a math
equation.

Panel Four

Same set-up, but now the Joker opens his mouth to speak.

> JOKER
> I dunno. Lemme roll it over a little bit.
> > (balloon two)
> Meantime, same question applies to
> you, Spooky: you wanna see me dead?

PAGE TWENTY TWO

Panel One

Long panel going down the left side. All Batman.

> BATMAN
> I used to think I was okay with you
> dying or getting killed, so long as
> it wasn't by *my* hand or the hands
> of any of my *associates*.
> > (balloon two)
> When you sky-dived onto the roof of
> Gotham Central, I fantasized about
> your 'chute malfunctioning and you
> pancaking onto a curb somewhere in
> the middle of the city.
> > (balloon three)
> But in the moment of truth, with
> that knife sticking out of your chest?

Panel Two

Batman looking down, ashamed sort of. The Joker takes this in.

> BATMAN (CONT'D)
> I couldn't do it. I couldn't let
> you die.
> > (balloon two)
> For all the true evil you've done,
> the lives you've ruined, and the
> pain you've inflicted, I couldn't
> just stand there and watch you
> bleed out - even though I knew it
> meant giving up a kind of peace
> I've never known before. A kind of
> peace I'll never know.

> JOKER
> *Why*, do you think? Why not just
> *enjoy* the ultimate victory?

Panel Three

Close on Batman, looking momentarily forlorn. Over his shoulder (or around him) we see ghostly images of the gun muzzle, the pearl necklace breaking, and the young Bruce kneeling on the ground between his dead parents.

                    BATMAN
          I've watched people die before.
               (balloon two)
          I swore then: never again.

PAGE TWENTY THREE

Panel One

Wider on Batman now. He holds his cape out a bit, examining himself - as if he's saying, "Look at all this..."

                    BATMAN (CONT'D)
          My whole life... all of *this*.
               (balloon two)
          It's all because I never want to
          see death first-hand again.

Panel Two

Joker, in bed, restrained.

                    JOKER
          Interesting. I always *thought*
          your misguided sense of self-
          righteousness came from some
          personal tragedy.
               (balloon two)
          I'm sorry for whatever it was that
          happened to you which made you the
          way you are.

Panel Three

Close on Batman.

                    BATMAN
          Thank you.

Panel Four

Close on Joker.

                    JOKER
          But I *do* want to kill you.

Panel Five

On Batman, who barely reacts.

PAGE TWENTY FOUR

Panel One

The Joker.

> JOKER (CONT'D)
> I imagine that's hard to hear,
> after you just opened yourself
> up to me like you did.
> (balloon two)
> I imagine, in your head, you saw
> this visit as a chance to work on
> the nature of our relationship
> while I'm temporarily *not* a
> frothing-at-the-mouth, raving
> lunatic.
> (balloon three)
> You probably saw this visit as a
> chance for a *new* beginning.

Panel Two

Closer on the Joker.

> JOKER (CONT'D)
> But here's the cold, hard truth, Bats...
> (balloon two)
> I don't hate you 'cause I'm crazy...

Panel Three

Even closer on the Joker.

> JOKER (CONT'D)
> I'm crazy 'cause I hate you.

Panel Four

On Batman.

> OFF-PANEL JOKER
> And your death - preferably, but
> not necessarily, by my hand - will
> represent the end of my reign of
> terror in this city. In this world.
>> (balloon two)
> When you're gone, I'll stop hurting
> people I don't know. I'll stop
> with the mayhem and murder.
>> (balloon three)
> I'll lock myself up in a hospital
> and run out my clock staring at the
> walls, hopped up on premium grade
> *pharmaceuticals* that leave me so
> virtually *lobotomized*, they'll have
> to catheterize and colostomize my
> holes to keep me from becoming a
> non-stop self-pissing and pooping
> *mess*.

PAGE TWENTY FIVE

Panel One

On the Joker again.

> JOKER
> I can tell by your face that I've
> disappointed you.
>> (balloon two)
> But you're a big, strong guy who's
> obviously familiar with
> disappointment and disillusionment,
> so I'm thinking you can handle this
> information...

Panel Two

Closer on the Joker, smiling.

> JOKER (CONT'D)
> Yes, I *want* to kill you.
>> (balloon two)
> And one day, I'm *going* to kill you.
>> (balloon three)
> And then?
>> (balloon four)
> Then we'll *both* finally be free.

Panel Three

Batman standing near Joker's bedside. The pair don't really look at one another. They just dwell in the moment.

Panel Four

Same.

Panel Five

Same, but now the Joker speaks.

> JOKER (CONT'D)
> Since we're being super truthful,
> I should also tell you I saw a little
> bit of your junk when you were
> getting changed before.

PAGE TWENTY SIX

INT BAT CAVE

Panel One

Wide on a section of the cave we haven't seen previously in our book: Bruce hangs his cape and cowl in a vault-like single suit closet. Alfred is standing nearby with a laundry basket.

> CAPTION
> The Cave...

> ALFRED
> Well I can't say I'm *surprised* by
> what the Joker said, Master
> Bruce...

Panel Two

Closer now. Bruce pulls off his shirt. Alfred dutifully stands by, waiting for the laundry.

> ALFRED (CONT'D)
> It's little wonder he caught a
> glimpse, since you wear your briefs
> on the *outside* of your clothes.

> BRUCE
> Funny.

Panel Three

Wide again. The shirt's in the laundry basket, and Bruce is pulling on a robe. Some bats fly by in the foreground.

                    ALFRED
          Well, I've always *dreamed* of
          becoming a nightclub comic.

                    BRUCE
          I now know for sure: the Clown
          won't stop 'til I'm dead.

                    ALFRED
          Certainly this comes as no shock,
          Master Bruce.

                    BRUCE
          It's just... I held his life in my
          hands. Gordon urged me to let the
          Joker bleed out.
               (balloon two)
          From what he told me tonight, that
          would've given him peace.

PAGE TWENTY SEVEN

Panel One

Another wide shot from a different angle. Bruce now tosses his leggings and Bat-shorts into the laundry basket Alfred holds.

                    ALFRED
          Some men and women want to change
          the *world*, so they run for office.
          Some men and women want to change
          themselves, so they study
          and meditate.
               (balloon two)
          The only difference between you and
          those people is the fundamentals
          with which you and they enact that
          change.
               (balloon three)
          Those people take a more
          traditional route to implement the
          changes they want to see. *You?*
          You find it easier to put on these
          clothes and hurl yourself into the
          path of danger and death on a
          nightly basis to realize the
          changes you seek.

Panel Two

INT STUDY

Bruce and Alfred emerge from the secret passageway into the
Bat cave: a hidden door in a massive wall of bookshelves.

                         BRUCE
              I don't make it *easy* on myself, do I?

                         ALFRED
              Or anybody else, for that matter.
              But that's what makes you *you*,
              Master Bruce: the path of least
              resistance has never been your
              preferred course.

Panel Three

INT LIVING ROOM

Massive. Huge, man-sized fireplace, lit. Bruce and
Alfred very small, walking through it.

                         ALFRED (CONT'D)
              Still no sign of the *other* fellow,
              then? The upstanding citizen with
              the penchant for onomatopoetics?

                         BRUCE
              None.
                   (balloon two)
              It follows the pattern of his Star
              City activities from a few years
              back: he goes after a big gun,
              fails, then shrinks back into
              the darkness.

Panel Four

Alfred in the foreground, about to pass out of the panel.
Bruce behind him.

                         ALFRED
              Even monsters need their rest, I suppose.

                         BRUCE
              I just wish I knew more about him...

Panel One

EXT SUBURBAN STREET - DAY

Wide (across the street) on a taxi cab idling in front of
a modest two story house, complete with white picket fence.
A MAN is climbing out of the cab, carrying a briefcase. We
don't see both of his arms, though. There are other houses
on the block, in the yards of which normal things are
happening: lawn mowing, kids playing, joggers jogging.

> BRUCE VOICE-OVER
> Where does he go when he's not
> hunting heroes?

Panel Two

Over the roof of the cab, we're on the back of the Man
emerging from the cab in the foreground. In the background,
we see a FAMILY emerging from the house: Mother, seven and
eight year old daughter and son. Even a dog. They're all
wearing excited smiles.

> BRUCE VOICE-OVER (CONT'D)
> Who are his confidants? His
> henchmen?

Panel Three

The cab's pulling away. In the yard, the kids are hugging
the Dad's legs, as the Dad kisses the Mom (thus hiding his
face). There are two suitcases in evidence, sitting beside
them, as well as the Man's briefcase.

> BRUCE VOICE-OVER (CONT'D)
> Does he maintain dual identities,
> or is he this murderous creature
> all the time?

Panel Four

The Mom studies/holds what appears to be a cast on the Dad's
forearm and wrist. She wears a concerned expression. The
man holds up a broken tennis racket, indicating the source
of his wrist injury. We still don't see his face.

> BRUCE VOICE-OVER (CONT'D)
> How does he live above suspicion?

Panel One

INT HOUSE - DAY

The son and daughter carry the bags in the front door in the background, and the Man (cut off at the shoulders by the top of the panel) looks through some mail on a table. The Mom is hanging his top coat on a coat hanger by the door.

>   BRUCE VOICE-OVER (CONT'D)
>   Does he spend every waking hour
>   plotting his next kill, or does he
>   have a life *outside* of death?

Panel Two

INT BASEMENT STAIRWELL

The Man is descending the stairs, his back to us, looking up at his wife, who's in the doorway at the top of the stairs, stirring a pot she's holding. The man holds his briefcase up, indicating some work to be done downstairs.

>   BRUCE VOICE-OVER (CONT'D)
>   How does he reconcile *what* he does
>   to *who* he is?

Panel Three

INT BASEMENT

Pool table, boxes with Christmas decorations, etc. Our man passes them by, heading toward a bookshelf. We still don't see his face.

>   BRUCE VOICE-OVER (CONT'D)
>   And in the wee small hours of the
>   morning, when he's alone with his
>   thoughts...

Panel Four

Insert: close on man pulling back hinged book in book case.

>   BRUCE VOICE-OVER (CONT'D)
>   Is he honest with himself?

Panel Five

The book case clicks open, affording us a view of a hidden
room that the Man is entering.

                    BRUCE VOICE-OVER (CONT'D)
               Does he know there's no place he
               can hide from himself?

Panel Six

Close on the Onomatopoeia mask being pulled over a
dummy head. There's some evidence of the bloody battle
with Batman.

                    BRUCE VOICE-OVER (CONT'D)
               Does he know there's no place he
               can hide from justice?

PAGE THIRTY

SPLASH PAGE

Note: the page should be a horizontal splash, not a vertical
one.

It's Onomatopoeia's trophy room/lair. Along a wall are long
shelf-like beams upon which sit domed glass cases. Some have
nothing in them, but others sport domino masks and headpieces
of past kills, along with name-plates to identify them:
Buckeye, Virago (see Green Arrow issues for mask designs).
There are ten other masks for characters we didn't see Ono
kill in comics, but can assume he's been busy: The Strobe,
Phantom Jockey, The Ritz, Sky-Rider, Brawler, Washingtonian,
Lady Justice, Bible Belt, The Ringer, Brother Black. There
are empty jars marked "Blue Beetle", "Steel", "Green Arrow
I", "Green Arrow II", and "Black Canary". The masks in the
glass domes/jars should look like Robin's costume in the
Bat-Cave: seemingly hovering in mid air.

Put some computers in the room, too. Maps of Gotham
pinned to walls with lines indicating prey he's following.
Articles hang, ripped from newspapers, that detail Batman's
many recent busts and activities. There's also an arsenal
of serious firepower: guns of all sizes, as well as
hunting knives.

In the midst of all this, the Man, his back to us, studies a
glass dome for which we can't see the label.

                    BRUCE VOICE-OVER (CONT'D)
          Does he know there's no place he
          can hide...

INSERT PANEL: Close on the glass dome, in his hands, that's
labeled "The Batman."

                    BRUCE VOICE-OVER (CONT'D)
          ...from *me*?

                         THE END

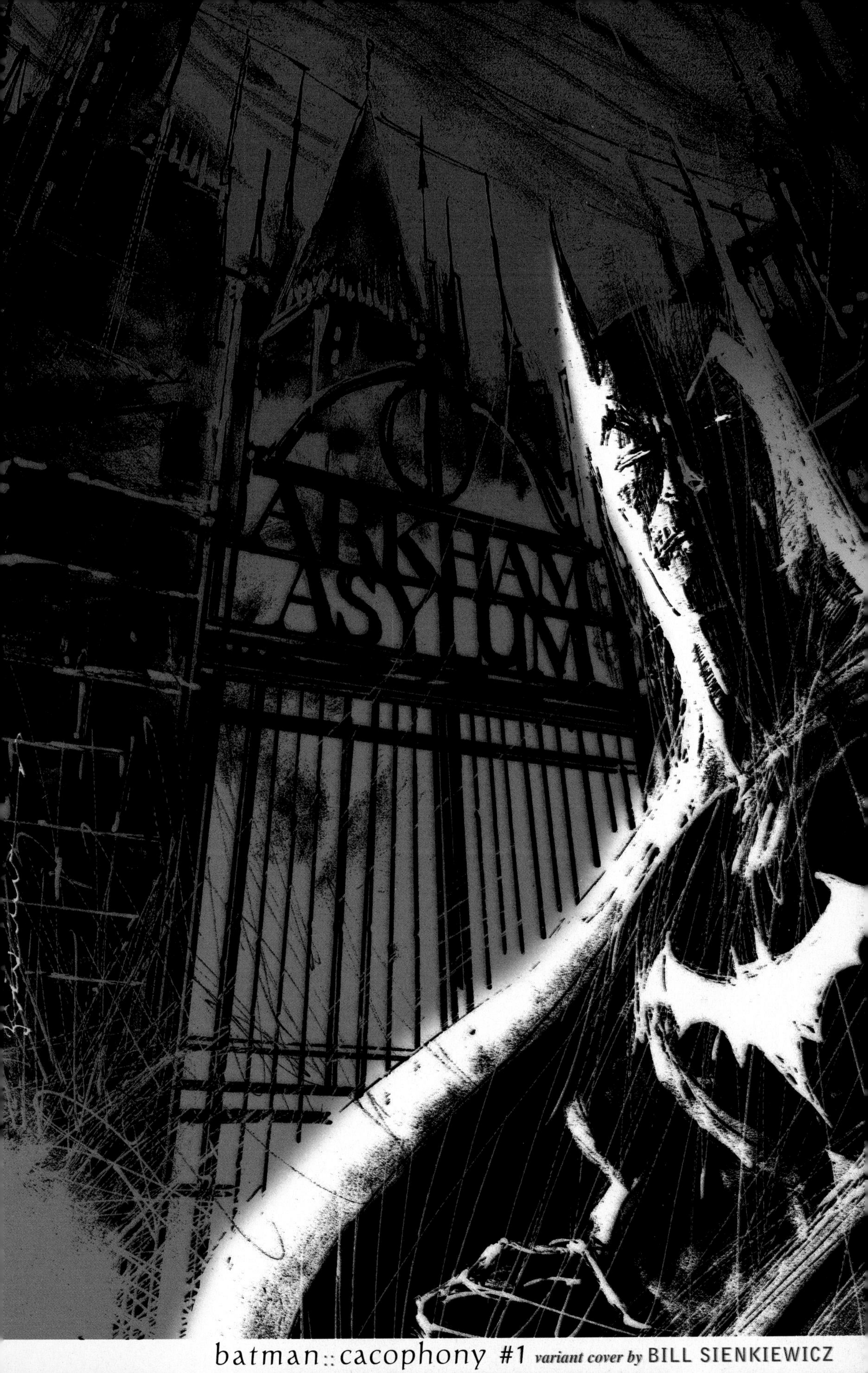
ARKHAM ASYLUM

batman :: cacophony #1 *variant cover by* BILL SIENKIEWICZ

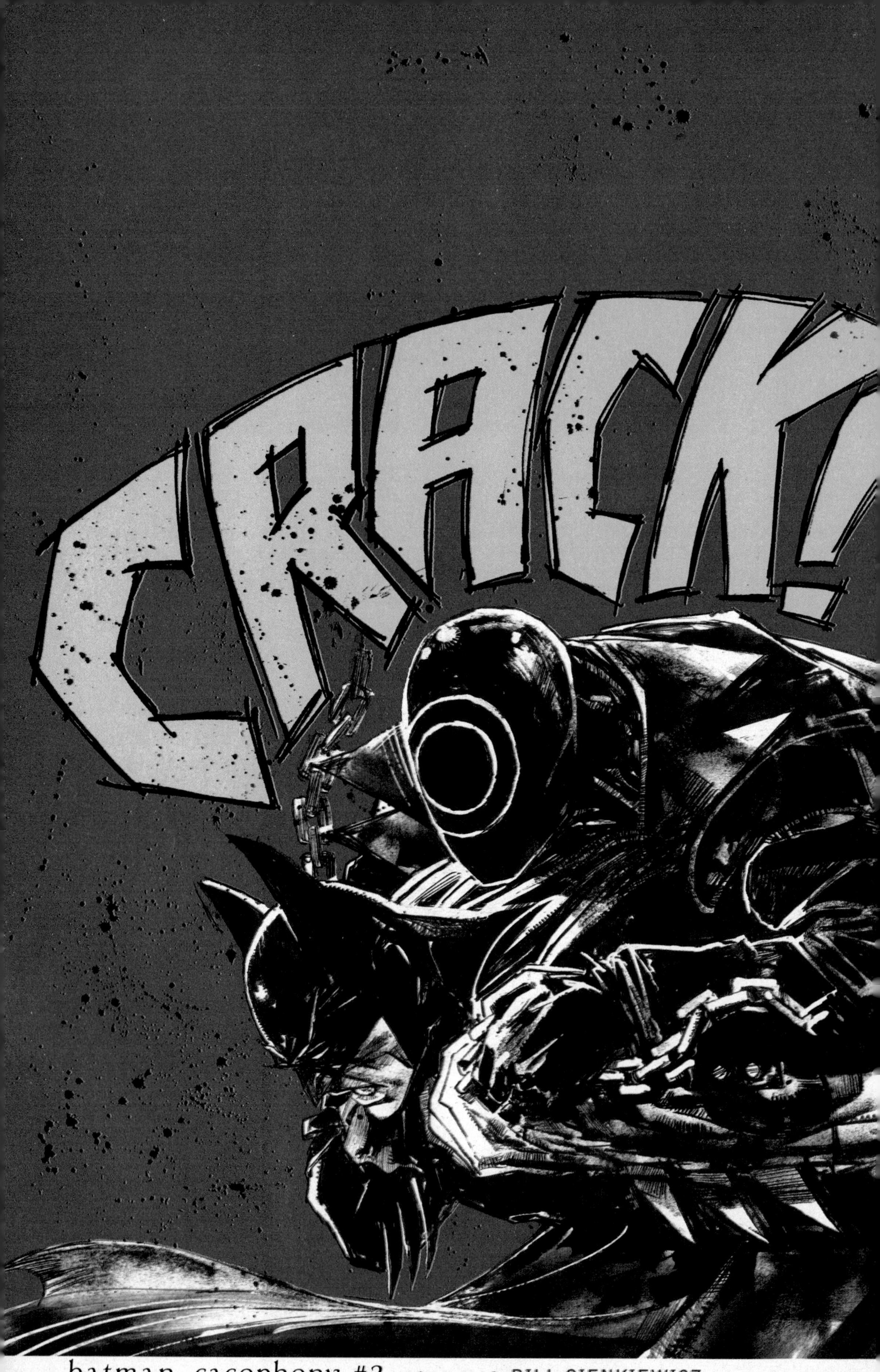
CRACK!

batman :: cacophony #2 *variant cover by* BILL SIENKIEWICZ

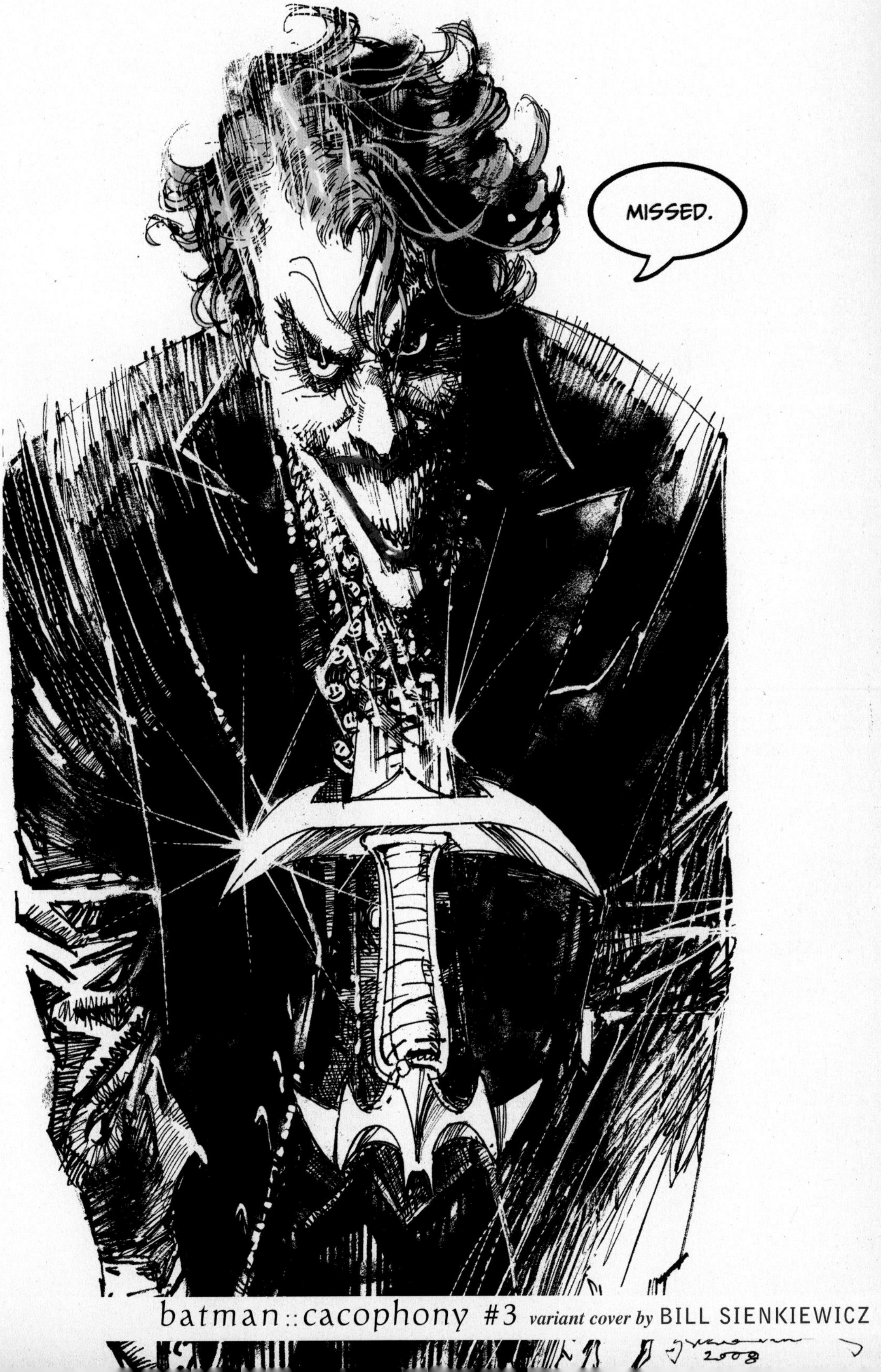
MISSED.

batman::cacophony #3 *variant cover by* BILL SIENKIEWICZ

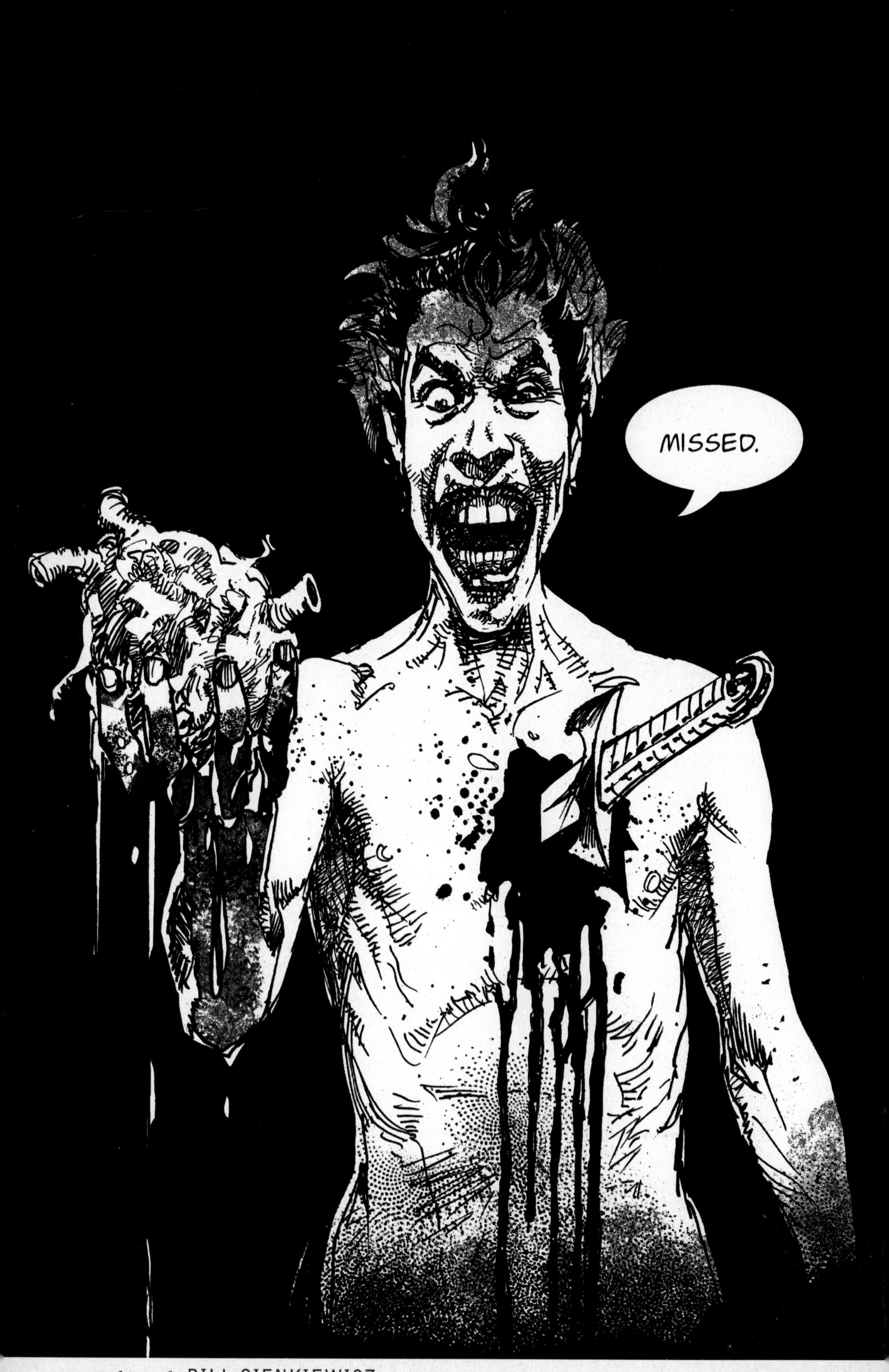
MISSED.

unused cover by BILL SIENKIEWICZ

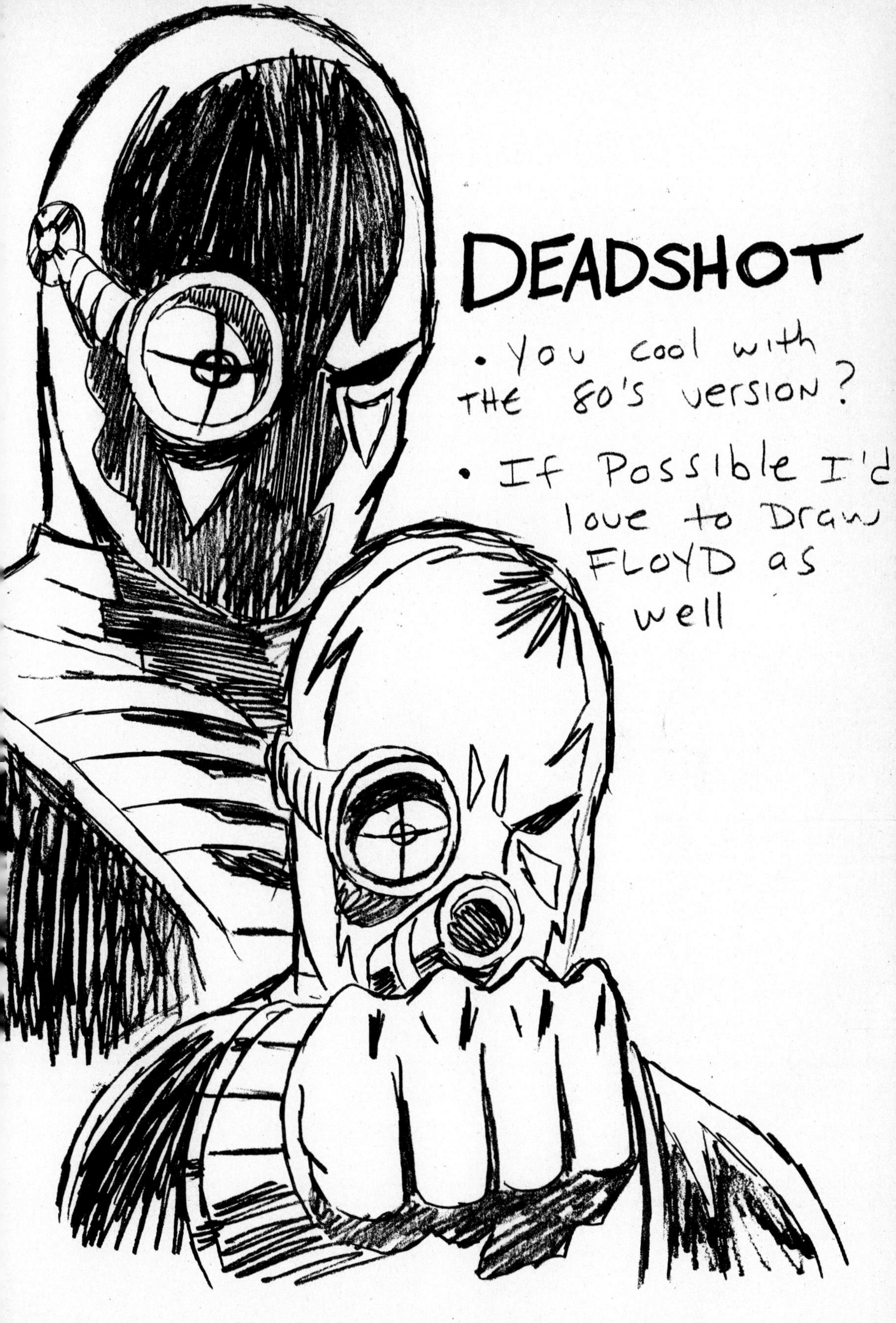
DEADSHOT
• You cool with THE 80's version?
• If Possible I'd love to Draw FLOYD as well

sketches by WALT FLANAGAN

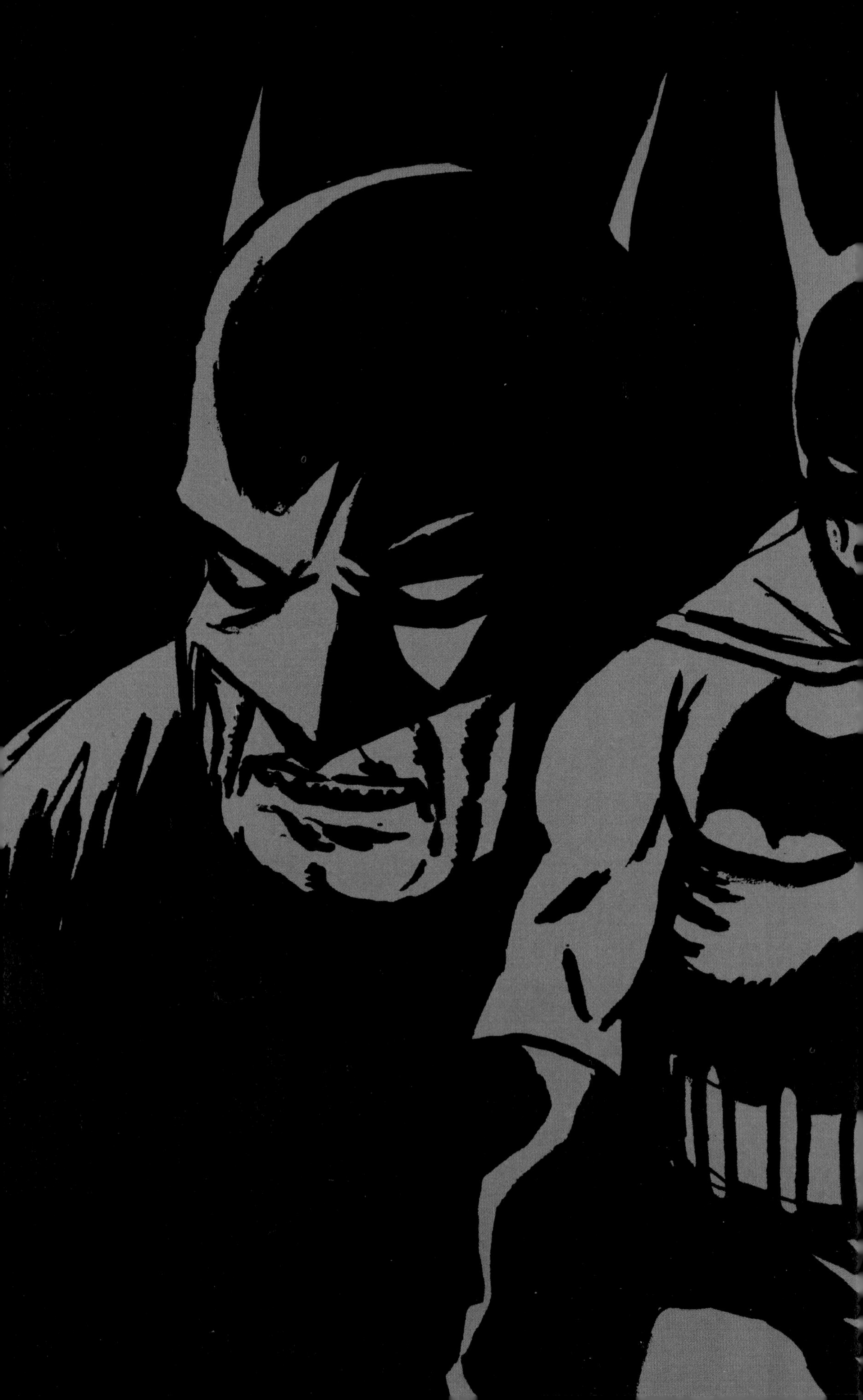

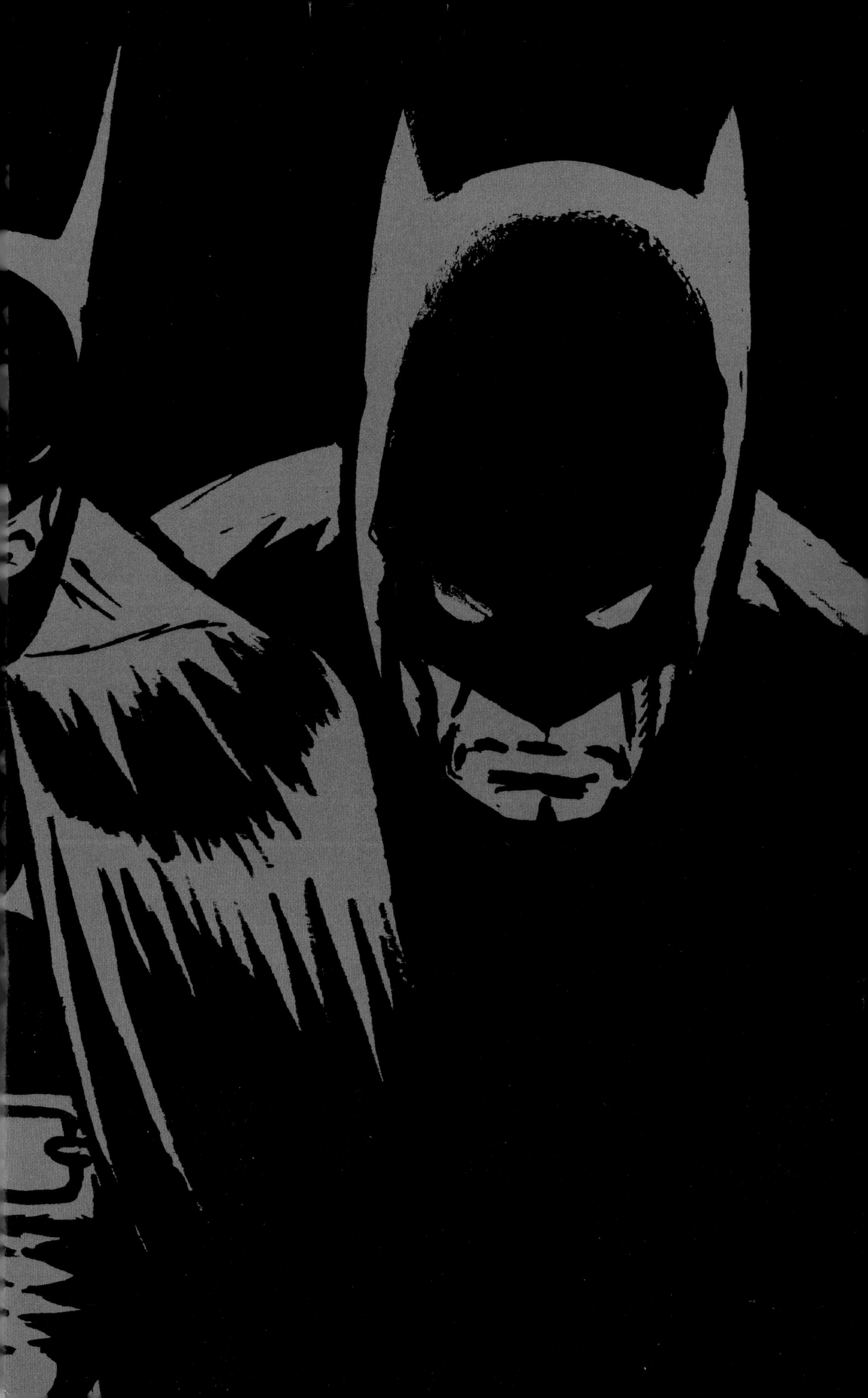

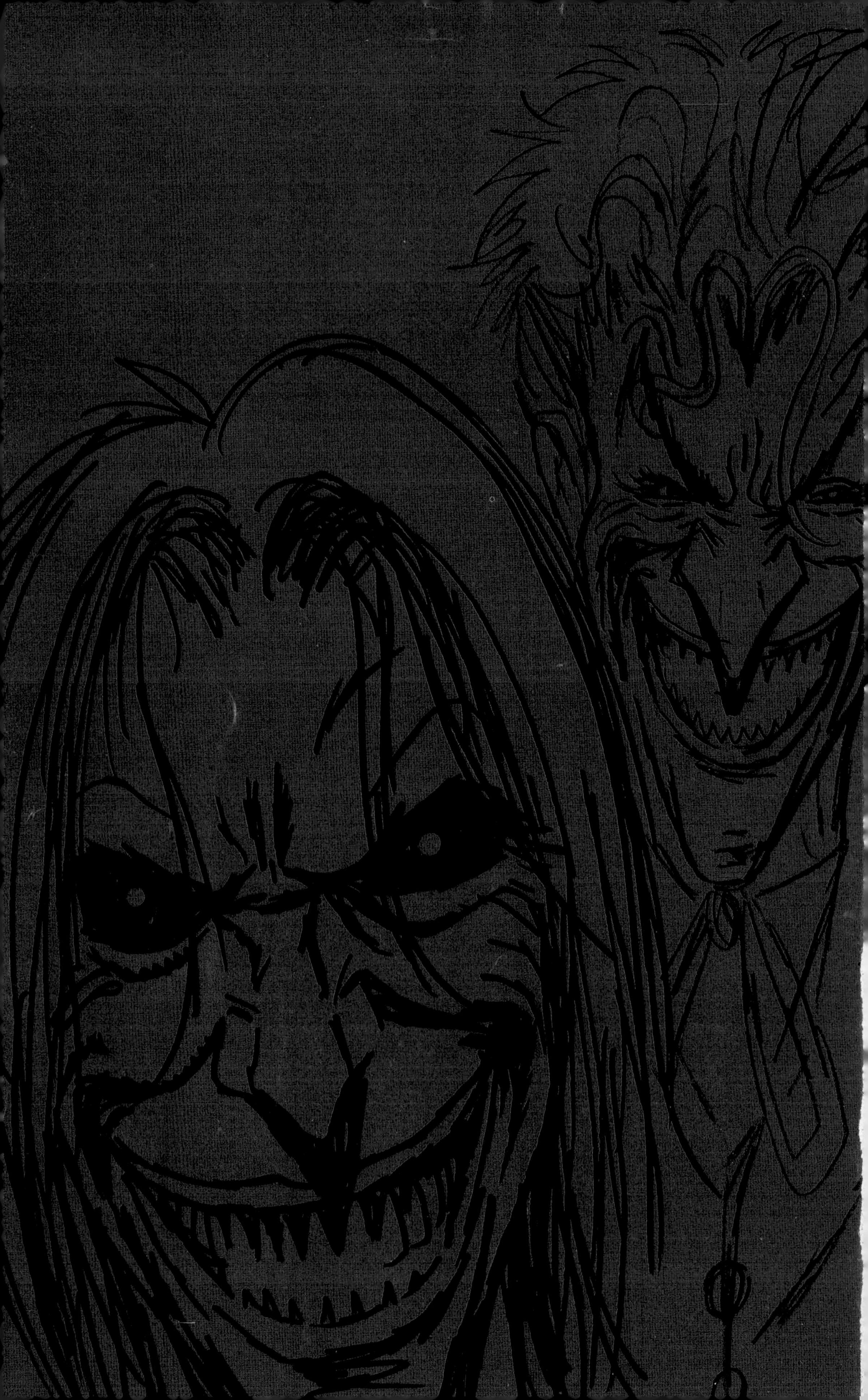